Henry George: Dreamer or Realist?
by Steven B. Cord

D1498040

ṭe name of Henry George, once relegated
historians and economists to the dim and
ṭant past, has been encountered with in-
ṭasing frequency in their recent writings.
Historians have come to realize that
ṭorge exerted an important influence on
ṭ development of American democratic
ṭught. Numerous reformers of the Pro-
ṭsive Era acknowledged that their think-
ṭ had been vitally affected by an early
ṭding of *Progress and Poverty.* Wrote
ṭwton D. Baker about Henry George: "I
ṭ inclined to believe that no writer of our
ṭes has had a more profound influence
ṭon the thinking of the world." George
ṭs one of the first to impress upon the
ṭerican people that poverty and depres-
ṭns were social evils demanding govern-
ṭnt action. He was a pioneer in arousing
ṭ fellow countrymen against the deprada-
ṭns of monopolists. Although his single
ṭproposal has been rejected, many urban
ṭormers see much merit in his proposal
ṭtax land values more heavily. His fol-
ṭ·ers abroad have successfully applied his
ṭproposal in scattered places. His ethical
ṭlysis has attracted much favorable at-
ṭtion.

ṭhis study reviews that treatment ac-
ṭded Henry George by American econ-
ṭists and historians from 1879 to the
ṭsent. Their statements have been care-
ṭy compared to Henry George's writings
ṭsee how accurately his ideas were
ṭluated.

ṭhe research points to the rather sur-
ṭing conclusion that, despite his newly
ṭognized importance as a seminal figure

in both history and economics, Henry
George's ideas have not been well understood by many writers in those fields. To
this day, their evaluations of George have
been weakened by vagueness and inaccuracy, leaving a distorted image of the
man and his ideas. For instance, despite
his consistent opposition to public ownership of land, George was commonly termed
a land nationalist. He was dubbed a socialist and an anarchist, although he vigorously
opposed their doctrines. He has been regarded by some as a radical revolutionary
while others see him as merely raising a
tempest in a teapot. Few are aware of the
applications of George's ideas throughout
the world. A misunderstanding of the mechanics of land value taxation has caused
most of the misconceptions. This study
should clarify George's proper place in
American history and economics.

Dr. Cord also shows that there was more
support for George and his idea of land
value taxation among economists than is
generally realized. *His ideas are viewed by
many authorities today as having practical
application to the problems of urban renewal as well as to land reform in underdeveloped nations.* The recent adoption of
George's tax reform idea in Hawaii lends
current interest and importance to what
he said. For all these reasons, it becomes
very necessary to clarify the historical record concerning Henry George, as this study
attempts to do. It should be of compelling
interest to both historians and economists.

HENRY GEORGE: DREAMER OR REALIST?

HENRY GEORGE:
Dreamer or Realist?

by STEVEN B. CORD

Philadelphia
University of Pennsylvania Press

7500

Printed in the United States of America

OCLC

ACKNOWLEDGMENTS

Many people have helped in the completion of this work. Special thanks must go to the Robert Schalkenbach Foundation, whose research grant came at a critical moment; to Professor Frederick D. Kershner, Jr. of Teachers College, Columbia University, who has given generously of his time and made many valuable suggestions; and to my wife for her competent help and support every step of the way.

PREFACE

THE NAME OF HENRY GEORGE, ONCE RELEGATED BY HISTORIANS and economists to the dim and distant past, has been encountered with increasing frequency in their recent writings.

Historians have come to realize that George exerted an important influence on the development of American democratic thought. George was one of the first to impress upon the American people that poverty and depressions could bring down the established social order, yet this need not be so if the government took the proper legislative steps. He was one of the first to arouse his fellow countrymen against the evils of monopoly. Numerous reformers of the Progressive Era acknowledged that their thinking had been vitally affected by an early reading of *Progress and Poverty*.

As for economists, many regard George's proposal of land value taxation as having special merit today in urban renewal and tax reform. Those who advocate this tax are not so much textbook writers as specialists in the fields of housing and city planning. For instance, *House & Home*, leading trade magazine for the housing construction in-

7

dustry, devoted its entire August 1960 issue to land value taxation and declared:

Most cities are generating new slums faster than they can salvage and rebuild their old slums. Urban decay and blight are spreading into new areas faster than all the billions we are spending for urban redevelopment and public housing can salvage existing slums. This is bound to happen as long as our urban tax system subsidizes slums by undertaxation and discourages improvements by overtaxation. . . . Said the *House & Home* Roundtable [a February 1960 conference of builders and city planners sponsored by H&H] on money and inflation: *"Heavier land taxes would make slumlords improve their property to get enough added income to pay their added taxes. . . .* a substantial part of the local tax burden now carried by improvements (like houses) should be shifted to the land itself. . . .

Taxing land more heavily would let homebuilders offer better homes for less money . . . would reduce the taxes on good homes by increasing the taxes on vacant and underused land . . . would cut the cost of highway extension by cutting the land costs for the right of way." (*H&H*, pp. 140-143.)

Another consistent advocate of land value taxation has been *The American City,* a leading trade magazine in the field of municipal government and finance. Its editor, Harold S. Buttenheim, was an effective advocate in the successful campaign for Pennsylvania's Graded Tax Law, which has already resulted in modified land value taxation in Pittsburgh and Scranton.

It is important, then, that a man who has been such a formative influence in American history should be well understood and carefully assessed by historians and economists, all the more since his tax proposal is looked upon by many authorities as being applicable to current problems. However, there are many who claim that Henry George and his ideas have been subject to serious distortion and misstatement in the past, and that recent scholarship has done little to alter the picture handed down by their predecessors.

If in fact the public image of Henry George has been

less than accurate, it is important that the record should be set straight. If land value taxation has any validity, then it should be well understood and given a fair trial in the court of history and economics. It will be the purpose of this study to review objectively the judgment of historians and economists on Henry George from his day down to the present time, and to evaluate the accuracy of these judgments.

At this point, the reader might find it useful to be presented with a brief preview of this study. The first section consists of background material: a survey of the American intellectual scene during George's active years, a presentation of his economic ideas and attitude toward *academia* plus relevant biographical details. There then follows the views about Henry George and his ideas as expressed by those historians and economists who have achieved eminence in their respective fields or who have written extensively on these special subjects. Their statements will be carefully set against Henry George's writings to see how accurately his ideas were understood. At appropriate places, résumés of the relevant intellectual milieu in America are given. The last chapter contains summary and conclusions. Throughout this account an effort has been made to remain true to the historian's moral obligation to separate fact from bias and to deal as objectively as possible with what has been a highly controversial subject.*

* The reader's attention might profitably be called to certain parts of the book. The sections on E.R.A. Seligman (Chap. 2), M. Slade Kendrick (Chap. 4), and Harold Groves (Chap. 4) are particularly recommended for a quick introduction to the views of public finance economists. The best defense of George's views appears in the sections on Eli Schwartz and James E. Wert (Chap. 4) and on *House & Home's* August 1960 issue (Chap. 4). Historians will be particularly interested in the section on Charles Albro Barker (Chap. 5). The section on how land rent taxation would affect landowners and land users (Chap. 1) would also seem to be of prime importance, as

The sources upon which the conclusions are based represent the widest possible selection. No top-ranking historian or economist who has published his views on George has been knowingly omitted. The historians of social thought have been canvassed with particular thoroughness. Every major biographer receives mention. Articles, magazines, pamphlets, reports and speeches have been used extensively. The sheer number of textbooks and their diversity in dealing with George present a special problem. Mass attack has proven to be the best approach. At least forty-five books have been perused in each of the fields of public finance and the history of economic thought. So have approximately thirty textbooks in land economics, sixty in history and eighty in economics. Obviously, for reasons of conciseness not all of these texts can be referred to in this study; rather, an attempt has been made to give a consensus of textbook opinion.

Has an accurate image of Henry George and his ideas emerged from the pages of American history and economics? Does a tax on land values have a place in urban renewal today? It is hoped that the study which follows will shed revealing light on these questions.

---

would Harry Gunnison Brown's survey of the actual application of land rent taxation in Australia and New Zealand (Chap. 5). The final chapter would seem to be indispensable, but a complete reading of the whole work is necessary in order to fully comprehend its conclusions and suggestions.

TABLE OF CONTENTS

HENRY GEORGE:
DREAMER OR REALIST?

I

THE JUDGMENT OF HIS
CONTEMPORARIES, 1879-1897

WHEN HENRY GEORGE FINISHED *Progress and Poverty* IN May 1879 and set out to find a publisher, he naturally realized that the book he had written ran counter to the prevailing economic and social ideas. But little could he know that these ideas were soon to change, in no small measure due to his efforts.

Just what were these prevailing ideas with which George chose to do battle? In 1879, American social thought was very much influenced by the evolutionary theories of Charles Darwin, especially as formulated by the English philosopher, Herbert Spencer. Darwin's ideas of the survival of the fittest and adaptation to nature were applied by Spencer to human society. Competition in all phases of social life, but especially the economic, were regarded as the method by which God or Nature, depending upon one's religious views, rewarded the most able. As the latter guided society in all its endeavors, society would evolve from lower to more advanced stages. If a man is rich, he is rich because he is able, and the degree of his wealth measures the degree of his ability. Poverty was regarded,

15

especially by those who succeeded, not as an indication that opportunity was lacking but that ability was lacking. More recently, these ideas of Spencer have become known as Social Darwinism.

Even more than Spencer, his advocates in America argued that nothing much can be done by man to alter the effects of competition, which they regarded as a law of nature. Nor should he try to alter these natural laws even if he could, because competition can only lead to steady social improvement approaching ultimate perfection. William Graham Sumner, the leading Social Darwinist on these shores, once declared, "The truth is that the social order is fixed by laws of nature precisely analogous to those of the physical order. The most that man can do . . . by his ignorance and conceit [is] to mar the operation of the social laws."[1] Frequent comparison was made with the law of gravity; no mere mortal could alter it, nor should he if he could. It would not be difficult to trace the roots of Social Darwinism back through American history to early Puritanism.

There was nothing, then, that could be done to alleviate social ills. Society was bound to improve, yes, but the workings of the evolutionary process of competition were slow, very slow. How long and gradual was the evolution of man through the milleniums, advocates of Social Darwinism pointed out; could society, composed of men, evolve much faster? Once Henry George heard E. L. Youmans, the famous professor and editor, denounce poverty and corruption in New York City. "What do you propose to do about it?" George asked. "Nothing!" replied Youmans with a sigh. "You and I can do nothing at all. . . . We can only wait for evolution. Perhaps in four or five thousand

[1] William Graham Sumner, "Reply to a Socialist," in *The Challenge of Facts and Other Essays*, pp. 55-62.

years evolution may have carried men beyond this state of things."[2]

In 1879, classical economics was enjoying its last period of unchallenged supremacy. Although it antedated Social Darwinism by a good many years, it managed to reach the same conclusion, namely that wealth rewarded the able and that poverty was the badge of inability. But whereas Social Darwinists couched their arguments in terms of the doctrine of natural evolution, the classical economists used technical arguments which applied more specifically to their own field. Presupposing a state of free competition, classical economists argued that the prices of the market place automatically directed the flow of land, labor, and capital into the most efficient and productive channels. Prices always reflected true value. Still another presupposition of the classical economists was the theory of the economic man. This theory held that all of us, in our capacities both as consumers and as producers, always acted rationally and with full economic knowledge to satisfy our desires with the least effort. The economic effect of man's irrational sentiments and cultural beliefs were completely overlooked. The classicists did not generally take conscious note of the economic man theory; they simply took it for granted.

To all of this Henry George took no exception, for he was undoubtedly a classical economist himself. In fact, he carried the doctrine of classical economics to its logical conclusion by advocating an end to land monopoly, and if some of the conclusions he reached seem unrealistic today, it is partly because the classical assumptions on which his theories rested were more than shaky.

This is not to say that George was in perfect agreement with his fellow economists. When they assumed that

[2] Henry George, *A Perplexed Philosopher*, pp. 163-4n.

monopolies could not long exist because they would inevitably attract competitors, George deduced otherwise
from personal experience. He was one of the first to agitate
for government regulation of utility monopolies, and to
him our land tenure system contained aspects of monopoly. Nor did he agree with his contemporaries when they
maintained that depressions were a temporary economic
phenomenon, because if they by chance should occur, the
price system would soon make the necessary adjustments
and the economy would then once more sail smoothly into
the future. George's extensive personal experience told
him that depressions were not necessarily short-lived or in-
frequent.

Because it advocated the doctrine of *laissez faire,* classical economics had no remedies to offer for the economic
maladjustments that were beginning to be so troublesome
in the newly industrialized United States. No wonder economics became known as the "dismal science." No wonder,
too, that George's advocacy of land reform excited the out-
spoken opposition of those classical economists who so
vociferously proclaimed that the government had no economic function at all.

While the twin doctrines of Social Darwinism and classical economics held sway, the reform movement was
dominated by men of high Victorian ideals, quite conscious of their upper class background, whose main goal
was no more than the purification of government. They
were patrician reformers, men like Tilden and Schurz,
more interested in political than economic changes, in
moral rather than social improvement. They were still reacting against feudalism and European aristocracy—the
spectre of Metternich constantly haunted their thinking
—and, consequently, to them government was the root of
all evil. Throughout history, had not governments always

opposed the great goddess Liberty? To these early reformers, the concept of "government" brought to mind
sinecures, privileges, graft, oppression, even ill-bred cigar-
smoking politicians of low degree. If the government would
leave business alone and limit itself only to the maintenance of public order, competition would guarantee
economic opportunity and equality. As a result, the greatest reform they could think of was the establishment of the
civil service to replace the spoils system.

Social Darwinism, classical economics, and the genteel
reformism of Mugwumpery were bound to be adversely
affected by the depression of the 1870's. This was to be the
most severe economic crisis of the nineteenth century.
For years idle workers and idle factories blighted the land.
Tramps swarmed the highways, crime became a pressing
national problem, and strikes burst forth with a violence
that forebode worse things to come. People wanted a solution for the problems that beset them, and they wanted
it desperately.

As the 1880's proceeded, the ideological center of reform
gradually moved leftward to favor the belief that government should interfere in economic activities in order to
protect free competition. To be sure, *laissez faire* was not
discarded, but a newer brand of reformers was gradually
impressing upon the country the idea that economic
forces unleashed by industrialization needed government
regulation. Competition, they asserted, must now be protected and regulated by the government.

Influences from abroad played an important part in this
shift in economic thinking. Many young economists were
returning from German universities imbued with the idea
that economics was an evolutionary science. This so-called
German historical school of economics denied the existence
of any immutable natural laws and emphasized the im-

portance of the government as an active economic agent, particularly in the distribution of wealth. They believed that since economic laws were not universal and might differ from society to society, economists should not arrive at conclusions through mere speculation but from empirical investigation.

The Austrian school of economic thought was also becoming quite popular. It shifted the emphasis in economic thinking from wealth, cost, and supply, to value, price, and demand. The Austrian approach made possible the use of mathematics for the expression of theory, and calculus became a valuable part of an economist's education.

An important sign of the times occurred in 1886 when the 9th edition of the *Encyclopedia Britannica* replaced its old article on the laws of political economy with a new one which surveyed the thinking of the new schools of economics.

The proponents of these new schools formed the American Economic Association in 1885, which gradually came to dominate American economic thought. This association attempted to raise the professional standards of economics teaching in colleges, and was soon influential enough to require postgraduate training for professors of economics. Less than ten years before the founding of the A.E.A., Henry George had been seriously considered for an academic post despite the fact that he had not even graduated from high school, and his case was by no means exceptional. After the founding of the A.E.A., George would come to be regarded as an amateur, an outsider.

The growing influence of the Austrian and German schools tended also to isolate George from the mainstream of economic thought, for he did believe in immutable natural laws and he did talk about wealth, cost, and supply rather than their correlates. He was, in many respects, the last of the old-time classical economists, and before *Progress and Poverty* was ten years old, it was outdated in the minds of his economist contemporaries.

Characteristically, George, of course, fought back. In his last work, *The Science of Political Economy* (1897), George criticized the Austrian and German schools for their lack of principles, incomprehensibility, voluminousness, and poorly defined terms. These schools of thought, he said, were "admirably calculated to serve the purpose of those powerful interests dominant in the college under our organization, that must fear a simple and understandable political economy, and who vaguely wish to have the poor boys who are subjected to it by their professors rendered incapable of thought on economic subjects."[3]

If classical economics was challenged in the turbulent 1880's, so too was its companion doctrine of Social Darwinism. Reformers like Ward, Ely, Rose, and Holmes made use of evolutionary theory as effectively as had the earlier conservatives. They argued that government could hurry evolutionary progress toward a better society by improving the social environment in which men live and work. No longer should social progress be left strictly to the slow workings of nature. In fact, they took the pragmatic view (then coming into style) that there were no immutable laws of nature, and so successful were these new Reform Darwinists that by the end of the century the term "natural law" had become anathema to most progressive thinkers. A new faith in the beneficence of government was sharply challenging the old faith in natural law.

When George argued that society can do something about the problem of poverty, and not in four or five

[3] Henry George, *Science of Political Economy*, p. 208.

thousand years either, he was paving the way for the Reform Darwinists who followed. However, the reform he advocated was based on the philosophy of natural law which the new reformers rejected in favor of evolutionary ideas. They also wanted an active and socially responsible government, as did George, but to them a welfare program *per se* completely overshadowed any theoretical and moral speculations concerning the source of revenue. The Reform Darwinists even regarded morals as subject to evolution. As might be expected, when they turned to the subject of taxation, they were attracted to the income tax because of its great potentialities as a source of revenue and as a means of correcting the inequitable distribution of wealth. In a way, when George helped bring about the rise of the new Reform Darwinism, he was diverting the intellectual mainstream in America even further away from his own beliefs.

It is interesting to note that in 1879, when *Progress and Poverty* first appeared, the transition from Social to Reform Darwinism, from classical to neo-classical economics, from Mugwump to Progressive, was just beginning to take place. The irresistible impetus of this change in the progress of American social thought was being provided by the new science and the new industrialism. Henry George, then, stood at the nexus of two different worlds of thought, and elements of both can be found in his writings.

George's Economic Analysis

It was in the midst of this philosophical maelstrom that George wrote his masterwork, *Progress and Poverty*. As will soon appear, there was great disagreement over what he actually said in this book. These were his main ideas:

1. The material progress initiated by industrialization has not mitigated the lot of the average person. In fact, it has actually worsened his position by making him less self-sufficient. Industrialization has put him at the mercy of forces beyond his control. As far as the average man is concerned, poverty has been the inevitable concomitant of industrial progress and it is this paradox that George seeks to resolve.

2. If workingmen are oppressed, it is not by the owners of capital; they, too, suffer from inadequate demand and recurring depressions. High profits tend merely to attract competition, which in turn lowers these profits into rough equilibrium with the return from an equal investment of ordinary labor. (While George excoriated the monopolists of capital, he did not regard them as the main cause of poverty and depression.) George accepted *in toto* the assumption of classical economics that industrial competition was near-perfect and that there was a high degree of interchangeability and mobility between capital and labor. To George capital was only another form of labor inasmuch as it represented savings, the accumulated labor of the past. He could see no reason why past labor should be worth more than present labor.

3. In the long run, land rent tends to absorb the gains produced by population expansion and material progress, thus keeping wages and interest near the subsistence level. George's reasoning is based on Ricardo's widely accepted Law of Rent, which held that rent is the difference between what can be produced on good land over marginal land with the same application of labor and capital. He maintained that overall production increases would bring poorer land into use and, at the same time, enhance the value of urban land (the disappearance of the frontier and the growth of cities have indeed been the concomitants

of an increase in production). Thus, the difference in productivity between good land and poor, between urban land and marginal, would grow, and it is this difference that determines rent. If rent grows too quickly, then there is little left for wages and interest.

4. In the short run, George conceded the possibility that wages and interest could expand faster than land rent. But it is during such periods of prosperity that the seeds of the coming depression are spread. In prosperous times, people begin to feel that land prices will steadily increase well into the foreseeable future; everyone knows that prosperity increases the demand for land and unlike other items of value, the supply of land is strictly limited. People are therefore willing to pay more for land than its present usefulness warrants, a phenomenon called land speculation and which, no doubt, has preceded every major depression. Eventually, the cost of land—expressed either as a selling price or annual rent—becomes a crushing burden on the active factors in production, labor and capital, who must eventually find further production unprofitable. They stop producing, and a depression sets in. The extension of credit may postpone the evil day, but the longer it does so the sharper will be the ensuing crisis. If the underlying economy is unsound, the credit superstructure can be no more than a temporary expedient.

5. Now comes the all-important question of ethics. Private ownership of land is unethical, said George, because labor is the sole justification of private property; in other words, only things produced by labor should be privately owned, thus excluding land. Also, if all men are created equal then they must have an equal right to the opportunities afforded by Nature, such as air, land, and sea.

Since ethics is the keynote of any reform, it is proper to quote George extensively on this issue:[4]

What constitutes the rightful basis of property? What is it that enables a man justly to say of a thing, "It is mine?" From what springs the sentiment which acknowledges his exclusive right as against all the world? Is it not, primarily, the right of a man to himself, to the use of his own powers, to the enjoyment of the fruits of his exertions? Is it not this individual right, which springs from and is testified to by the natural facts of individual organization—the fact that each particular pair of hands obey a particular brain and are related to a particular stomach; the fact that each man is a definite, coherent, independent whole—which alone justifies individual ownership? As a man belongs to himself, so his labor when put in concrete form belongs to him . . .

The equal right of all men to the use of land is as clear as their equal right to breathe the air—it is a right proclaimed by the fact of their existence. For we cannot suppose that some men have a right to be in this world and others no right.

If we are all here by the equal permission of the Creator, we are all here with an equal title to the enjoyment of his bounty—with an equal right to the use of all that nature so impartially offers. This is a right which is natural and inalienable; it is a right which vests in every human being as he enters the world, and which during his continuance in the world can be limited only by the equal rights of others. There is in nature no such thing as a fee simple in land. There is on earth no power which can rightfully make a grant of exclusive ownership in land. If all existing men were to unite to grant away their equal rights, they could not grant away the right of those who follow them. For what are we but tenants for a day? Have we made the earth, that we should determine the rights of those who after us shall tenant it in their turn?

However, George did *not* advocate the confiscation of land by the government, arguing that the same end could be more easily and practically accomplished by collecting all land-rent for government use through taxation. He wanted the government to collect land rent, not to con-

[4] Henry George, *Progress and Poverty*, pp. 334, 338.

fiscate land titles. This tax on land values, he felt, would be more than adequate to cover government needs; hence, the phrase "single tax."

6. George spoke glowingly of the wonderful benefits that the single tax would bestow upon society. With land speculation made unprofitable by land value taxation, depressions would no longer be possible. As land prices approached zero because the government was collecting land rent through taxation, labor would have freer access to land and therefore unemployment would disappear. With land speculation eliminated, then wages and interest would get a bigger share of the total production. With speculative rent and taxes abolished, the production of wealth would receive an immense stimulus—it would be "like removing an immense weight from a powerful spring."[5] Since land ownership was a prime source of great wealth and privilege, the public collection of land rent would end the gross inequality in the distribution of wealth. The government, with its tax collection machinery greatly simplified, could now undertake great welfare programs, spending the public money on public benefits (limited only, of course, by the total amount of revenue the single tax on land values could provide). As the fear of want vanishes, man's finer instincts would hold sway, making excessive coercion unnecessary. Although he expected great things from the single tax, he regarded it not as a cure-all, an end in itself, but as a means of removing the principal obstacle, the private collection of rent and all its evil consequences, from the pathway of the evolutionary progress of mankind.

George's Attitude Toward the Academic World

Such a utopian approach to economics was sure to bring George into conflict with academic economists, who were

[5] Henry George, *Progress and Poverty*, p. 434.

inclined by nature and position to view their subject more calmly and conservatively. In fact, this sharp antagonism between George and these economists pre-dated the publication of *Progress and Poverty*. In 1877, George had been invited to give a lecture to the students and faculty of the University of California at Berkeley, with the prospect that he might be appointed to fill a separate chair of political economy, soon to be established. He chose as his title "The Study of Political Economy" and proceeded to make remarks which were guaranteed to lose him any chance he might have had for the professorship. He pointed out that the development of political economy had been hindered because it dealt so directly with "sensitive pocket-nerve" and that any conclusions it might reach would be passionately opposed by men and institutions whose financial interests or very existence may be challenged. Other sciences have made great progress in the last hundred years, but political economy has not because "it is not ignorance alone that offers opposition, but ignorance backed by interest, and made fierce by passions."[6]

George criticized the most popular textbooks in political economy for defending the interests of land and capital, and for offering the distressed laborer no advice save that he should refrain from rearing children.[7]

For the study of political economy you need no special knowledge, no extensive library, no costly laboratory. You do not even need text-books nor teachers, if you will but think for yourselves. All that you need is care in reducing complex phenomena to their elements, in distinguishing the essential from the accidental, and in applying the simple laws of human action with which you are familiar. Take nobody's opinion for granted; "try all things; hold fast that which is good." In this way, the opinions of others will help you by their suggestions,

[6] Henry George, Jr., *Life of Henry George*. New York: Robert Schalkenbach Foundation, 1900, p. 276. This book devotes an interesting chapter to this speech.

[7] *Ibid.*, p. 278.

elucidations and corrections; otherwise they will be to you
but as words to a parrot. . . . All this array of professors, all
this paraphernalia of learning, cannot educate a man. They can
but help him to educate himself. Here you may obtain the
tools; but they will be useful only to him who can use them.
A monkey with a microscope, a mule packing a library, are fit
emblems of the men—and unfortunately, they are plenty—who
pass through the whole educational machinery, and come out
but learned fools, crammed with knowledge which they cannot
use—all the more pitiable, all the more contemptible, all the
more in the way of real progress, because they pass, with themselves and others, as educated men.

Although George was in agreement with the classical
economists in advocating observation as the principal tool
for the study of political economy, the underlying emotional tone of his speech was one to make the faculty
members in his audience shift uneasily in their seats. It
was not the kind of speech to make in applying for a job.
But there were other numerous instances in which George
welcomed rather than avoided controversy with the academic world, although avoidance might have been the
wiser strategy.

George never received the offer of a professorship, nor
was he invited to speak to the California faculty again,
although notations in his diary infer that he had begun
work on a second lecture. Perhaps it was felt that this
crusading editor who asked that all institutions, no matter
how time- or interest-honored, be open to question and
possible attack, would not be a welcome addition to a
faculty already wracked, as happened to be the case, by
strong cross-currents of controversy. Of course, it is possible to speculate that if George had received this professorship, history may have taken a different turn.

In a letter to a friend in 1879, soon after the publication
of *Progress and Poverty,* George discussed the reception
he expected for his book. He wrote that "the professors

will first ignore, then pooh-pooh, and then try to hold the shattered fragments of their theories together."[8] George indicated here a certain contempt for professors as the automatic defenders of the status quo that has character-ized the Georgist movement even to the present day.

The incident which most typified George's relations with the academic world occurred at the 1890 convention of the American Social Science Association in Saratoga. This convention was entirely devoted to a debate on the merits of the single tax. Henry George himself and Wil-liam Lloyd Garrison, the son of the famous abolitionist, were among the five debaters who spoke in favor of the idea; the other advocates were an editor, a lawyer, and an assessor. None were professional economists. Five pro-fessors opposed the idea, and two men, President Andrews of Brown and Professor Edmund James of the University of Pennsylvania, took a middle position.

The high point of the proceedings was a sharp emotion-ally-charged dispute between George and Professor Edwin R. A. Seligman. Seligman was at this time just twenty-nine years old, only recently returned from study in Germany and already of professorial rank at Columbia University. His future as the leading American tax economist still lay before him.

Early in the prolonged debate, Seligman delivered an extended speech in which he said:[9]

There are to-day economists, worthy of the name, who are protectionists; there are economists, justly so called, who are socialists; but throughout the wide world to-day there is not a single man with a thorough training in the history of eco-nomics, or an acquaintance with the science of finance, who is an advocate of the single tax on land values. In biology, in

[8] Henry George, Jr., *Life of Henry George*, p. 323.
[9] E. R. A. Seligman, "The Single Tax Discussion," *American Social Science Association*, Sept. 5, 1890, p. 85.

astronomy, in metaphysics, we bow down before the specialist; but every man whose knowledge of economics or of the science of finance is derived from the daily papers, or one or two books with lopsided ideas, thinks that he is a full-fledged scientist, able to instruct the closest student of the markets or of the political and social organisms . . . neither the American people nor the scientific student of finance will ever accept a scheme which is palpably unjust . . . and which seeks to put the burdens of the many on the shoulders of the few.

To George, this was the red flag. His reply bristled with acerbity. He agreed that the college professors were against the single tax, but for the reason that they owed their jobs to the privileged class:[10]

And just as Macaulay has said—if there were any large pecuniary interests concerned in denying the law of gravitation, that law would not be acknowledged to this day. It certainly would not be in the universities and colleges.

George then went on to castigate Seligman for implying that the layman must passively accept the word of the professional economist:[11]

But if we cannot all study political economy—the science whose phenomena lie about us in our daily lives, and enter into our most important relations, and whose laws lie at the bottom of questions we are called on to settle with our votes—then democratic republican government is doomed to failure; and the quicker we surrender ourselves to the government of the rich and learned, the better.

George concluded with these remarks:[12]

Let me say a direct word to you professors of political economy, you men of light and leading, who are fighting the single tax with evasions and quibbles and hair-splitting. We single tax men propose something that we believe will make the life of the masses easier, that will end the strife between capital and labor, and solve the darkening social problems of our time.

[10] Henry George, "The Single Tax Discussion," *American Social Science Association*, Sept. 5, 1890, p. 98.
[11] *Ibid.*
[12] *Ibid.*

If our remedy will not do, what is your remedy? It will not do to propose little goody-goody palliatives, that hurt no one, help no one, and go nowhere. You must choose between the single tax, with its recognition of the rights of the individual, with its recognition of the province of government, with its recognition of the rights of property, on the one hand, and socialism on the other.

Gentlemen, don't quibble and split hairs about this matter. It is too solemn, too important. It involves the happiness, the health, the lives, the very souls, of human beings. It involves the progress of society, the fate of civilization. *If you have had superior education, if you have had what to so many of us has been denied, the leisure for study,* the opportunity to cultivate what is highest and best in your powers, the more is it incumbent on you to meet the question frankly and fairly. If you will not accept our remedy, what is your remedy? There must be some deep wrong underlying our organization to-day. If it is not the wrong we point to, the wrong that disinherits men of their birth-right, what is it? . . .

What is proposed on [the professors'] side? More restrictions, more interference, more extensions of government into the individual field, more organization of class against class, more bars to the liberty of the citizen. In turning from us, even though it be to milk-and-water socialism, you are turning to the road that leads to revolution and chaos, you are using your influence to intensify the fight in the dark that, as it goes on, must evolve the forces that destroy civilization. [italics mine]

This is the spirit of Jacksonian democracy talking, the spirit which regarded suspiciously government by the rich and learned, which felt that the world could be rejuvenated by a simple yet sovereign remedy. To George, poverty was the world's punishment for inequitable social conditions.

Seligman replied that while college professors may have been hired and fired in former days on the basis of their opinions, this was no longer true in the universities of 1890. ". . . . The professors are selected [today], not because of any preconceived opinions, but because of

their ability to pursue the truth, the pure naked truth."[13]
Many social reforms, he said, had been initiated by college
professors.

While Seligman may have been right in claiming that
American professors enjoyed a high degree of academic
freedom, many were the professors of his day who were
discomfited or actually dismissed because they were pur-
suing the "naked truth" as they saw it. For instance, Joseph
Dorfman writes that in 1898 John R. Commons addressed
a convention of the American Economic Association and
stated that George and Marx represented the thought of
the soon-to-be dominant working class. Shortly afterward,
Commons was notified by the Rev. James Roscoe Day,
the Chancellor of Syracuse University, where he was employed, that his chair of sociology was abolished. Other
examples would include E. B. Andrews, who was ousted
from Brown for his pro-Bryan views, H. C. Adams (from
Cornell), Bemis (Chicago), Ross (Stanford), Davenport
and Veblen (from many places).[14]

The young Columbia professor concluded his remarks
with a statement which probably expressed the attitude
of most of his fellow economists:[15]

Mr. George, you ask us, if the single tax is not the remedy,
what is the remedy? Ay, that is the question. . . . If we thought
that you had solved the problem we would enthrone you high
on our council seats, we would reverently bend the knee and
acknowledge in you a master, a prophet. But when you come to
us with a tale that is as old as the hills, when you set forth in

[13] E. R. A. Seligman, "The Single Tax Discussion," *American Social
Science Association,* Sept. 5, 1890, p. 87.
[14] See Joseph Dorfman, *The Economic Mind in American Civilization,* v. 3 (New York: Viking, 1959 [first edition 1946]), pp. 240, 268,
and Dorfman, *Thorstein Veblen and His America* (New York:
Longmans Greeen, 1955), p. 61, for the academic troubles of the
1880's and 1890's.
[15] E. R. A. Seligman, "The Single Tax Discussion," *American Social
Science Association,* Sept. 5, 1890, p. 98.

your writings doctrines that have been long exploded, when you in the innocence of your enthusiasm seek to impose upon us a remedy which appears to us as unjust as it is one-sided, as illogical as it is inequitable, we have a right to protest. All careful students beware of the man with the *ism*. This is not the first time that the enthusiast has supposed that he has discovered a world-saving panacea. The remedy lies not in any such lop-sided idea: the remedy is the slow and gradual evolution in a hundred ways of the moral conscience of mankind.

The acrimony which marked this George-Seligman debate at Saratoga in 1890 was to characterize the relations of single taxers with academic economists right down to our own time. This was unfortunate from the single taxers' point of view, because the professional economists, especially those in the universities, were the guardians of their science, the propagators and filterers of new ideas for the oncoming generation. Cordial relations with the academic economists could have helped the single tax cause greatly.

In *The Science of Political Economy*, his last book left unfinished at his death in 1897, George continued his case against the professors. He felt that the universities were under the control of the privileged interests and "whoever accepts from them a chair of political economy must do so under the implied stipulation that he shall not really find what it is his professional business to look for."[16]

The Progress of the Single Tax Movement During George's Lifetime

Despite George's anti-academic attitude, the professors could hardly ignore the book he had written, so extremely popular did it become within a year of its date of publication. At first *Progress and Poverty* sold slowly, as might be expected of so long a work on so difficult a subject, but

[16] Henry George, *The Science of Political Economy*, xxxv.

early in 1881 orders for the book suddenly began to pour into his publisher's office (Appleton). Not long afterwards, *Popular Science Monthly* ran four articles on the book, two by George, and soon notice was taken by numerous other periodicals. *Progress and Poverty* was on its way to become the publishing sensation of the 1880's, the largest selling work in political economy ever published in America.

What can account for the phenomenal success of this book? One reason was George's mastery of literary style; he seemed to write with a pen of fire. This may not be apparent to the cursory modern reader because much of *Progress and Poverty* deals with economic theory, which even George could not make thrilling. But when he wrote descriptively or when he dwelt on the benefits that would arise from the single tax and liberty unfettered, his words sang of a new day a-borning in a way that left few of his Victorian contemporaries unmoved. He dealt directly with such deeply felt problems of his time as poverty and depressions. His approach seemed logical and appealing and much of what he said was both new and true. Although history may have disproven a large part of his economic analysis, few nineteenth-century thinkers were yet equipped to see his errors. These errors were in the classical economic assumptions that he made, and his assumptions were those of his critics as well. Not the smallest reason for the success of George's masterwork was the headline-making "land for the people" agitation that had just begun in Ireland. It served to make *Progress and Poverty* appear very timely indeed.

In the first two years following publication, while George was being widely discussed, the converts he made were not organized into any single grand crusade. Yet, according to one of his critics, George had "arrayed on his side not a few of our ablest literary men, magazine writers,

Presidents and Professors in colleges and universities, statesmen and jurists of recognized ability and integrity, together with some leading merchants and manufacturers."[17]

For a time George became a leading literary lion. *Frank Leslie's Illustrated Newspaper* of March 3, 1883, reported that "only a few nights ago in the parlors of a wealthy but thoughtful New York citizen, on Gramercy Park, Mr. George was listened to for hours by an audience of fashionable ladies and gentlemen in full dress, and several wealthy men arose and announced their concurrence in his views! Nothing more strange and anomalous has recently taken place in our society. When millionaires become agrarians, the fact is not to be ignored."[18] The writer foresaw, however, that the author of *Progress and Poverty* might not be thus lionized if conditions should arise in which his theories became a real issue.

In 1882, after returning from a well-publicized trip to Ireland, many of New York's political, legal, religious, and commercial leaders gave George a rousing testimonial dinner at Delmonico's. Few of those who attended were thoroughly conversant with George's ideas, however. A few years later, when George had become sufficiently important to make his theories an issue, many of those who had feted him at Delmonico's took front rank among the "Society Savers" arrayed against him. He was able to see the humor in this situation and with a light touch he remarked, "Those gentlemen gave me a complimentary dinner once."[19] How right the reporter for *Leslie's* had been!

Though he tried hard to organize a workingman's

[17] A. N. Young, *The Single Tax Movement.* Princeton: Princeton University Press, 1915, p. 87, quoting James Taylor, *American Political Philosophy,* p. 23.

[18] *Ibid.,* p. 80.

[19] Henry George, Jr., *Life of Henry George,* p. 401.

crusade for the single tax, George never quite succeeded. He came closest to this goal in 1886, when, yielding to the petition of 34,000 labor union members, he ran for mayor of New York City on a third labor party ticket. He lost the election but did surprisingly well, getting even more votes than the Republican candidate, a young man by the name of Theodore Roosevelt. Some well known historians, such as John R. Commons, felt that the corrupt Tammany machine then in power used bribery and their control of the election machinery to deny him an election he actually won.

This campaign garnered much publicity for George, which was really what he was after in the first place, and encouraged him to run for the Secretary of State position in the statewide election of the following year. However, his showing on this occasion was disappointing; the socialists diverted much of his union support and economic conditions had improved after 1886, thus reducing the economic discontent that had been so helpful in the mayoralty campaign. After the failure of this labor party, George drew most of his supporters from the middle class.

It was in these political campaigns that the term "single tax" was born, and that a change of emphasis in George's thinking took place. Whereas in the earlier years he emphasized the evils of poverty, after 1887 he gave considerable attention to the practical effects of the single tax, and his critics changed focus with him. George spent the rest of the 1890's as an editor, lecturer, and author of magazine articles and books. In 1897, while running once more for mayor of New York City, he died.

Although the single tax was nowhere adopted directly into the tax system of the United States, George was very instrumental in changing the direction of American social thought. Literally dozens of Progressive leaders of the following generation attested that they owed their initial interest in reform to the reading of Henry George's books. Yet it is equally true that while numbers of Progressives endorsed the land value tax, lip service was as far as many of them would go in aiding the new idea.

It is against this background that one should set the reception of George's idea by the historians and economists.

Criticisms of Sumner, Field, and Francis A. Walker

The attack from the professional ranks was started, appropriately enough, by that arch-defender of the status quo, William Graham Sumner. His article in *Scribner's Monthly* for June 1881 minced no words. It was a scathing and rather arrogant attack devoid of analytic criticisms. Sumner wrote that to refute all the misstatements in *Progress and Poverty* would require the writing of "a correct treatise on sociology from the first principles up to some of the most refined applications." He made allusions to Henry George's lack of formal education by stating that unfortunately sociology was "yet the free arena for all the people with hobbies, crude notions, world philosophies, and schemes," and declared that George had not fitted himself for his task "by any correct study of sociology." He lamented the fact that "as respectful attention is given to a book like this as to the most careful work of a highly trained and scientific observer." To him "the unkindest cut of all was that Professor Cliffe Leslie [a well-known British economist] should take notice of this book as a special and representative product of American Political Economy."[20] Henry George quite

[20] William Graham Sumner, "Henry George," *Scribner's Monthly*, June 1881, pp. 312-313. Actually, this article appeared in the editorial columns and is unsigned, but both A. N. Young and Charles Albro Barker ascribe its authorship to Sumner. It is certainly written

rightly rejoiced upon reading this article, for it only added fuel to his fire and did his cause more good than harm.

Summer's views gained support from the Rev. A. L. Chapin, who wrote in his widely distributed economics textbook early in the decade that the single tax was "a wild scheme of iniquity and folly."[21] We will never know exactly what was said about Henry George in the political economy classrooms of the 1880's, but Edwin A. Ross, the famous sociologist, gives us a good idea. In his auto-biography Ross recalled that in his small-town midwestern college in 1883, "the tight little intellectual world we were led into was bound by Presbyterianism, Republican-ism, protectionism, and capitalism. Many were the 'sacred cows' we were taught not to worry about. Our text in political economy was beneath all contempt, but Henry George's *Progress and Poverty* was bootlegged among us and swept me off my feet. I, who was later to set such store by Malthus, was for three years anti-Malthus owing to the influence of that book."[22]

One reason why conservatives of the 1880's approached the single tax with such near-hysteria was that they be-lieved that its adoption would mean the confiscation of land by the government. Also, they thought it would pro-vide excessive governmental revenue, and tyranny and corruption would be the result. Justice David Dudley Field, a prominent lawyer, jurist, and publicist, in a debate with Henry George, which was published in *The*

---

in Sumner's distinctive style. A May 12, 1881 letter by Henry George to Edward Taylor reads in part: " 'Scribner's' will have an article pitching into me, which I hear privately is by Professor Sumner." See George, Jr., *Life*, p. 349.

[21] Joseph Dorfman, *The Economic Mind in American Civilization*, v. 3, p. 23.

[22] Edwin A. Ross, *Seventy Years of It*, p. 15.

North American Review of July 1885, estimated that the single tax might produce a revenue four times greater than the government expenditures of his time.[23]

But it is the criticisms of Francis A. Walker which deserve the most detailed attention. Walker was regarded as the leading American economist of his time. He had been an adjutant general in the Civil War, and was the earliest professional economist to attack the old wage-fund theory of John Stuart Mill, preceding Henry George in this by a few years. He established the Census Bureau on an efficient basis and made it useful for the collection of economic statistics. Although an acknowledged conservative, he accepted the first presidency of the reformist American Economic Association when it was founded in 1885, and in 1890 he became the president of the Massachusetts Institute of Technology, modernizing and enlarging that institution until his death in 1897.

Walker attacked George in magazine articles in 1881 and 1882, and his widely used textbook, *Political Economy*, published in 1883, dismissed George's proposal with the statement, "I will not insult my readers by discussing a project so steeped in infamy."[24] However, later in 1883 Walker found it necessary to do just that by publishing a book entitled *Land and Its Rent*. This book was based on a series of lectures Walker delivered at Harvard University and was in the main directed against Henry George. This little book contains the most incisive and detailed criticism of the economic analysis of *Progress and Poverty* that has ever been published.

The argument against George begins inauspiciously with a misrepresentation of George's proposal. According to Walker, George argued for "the natural and inalienable

[23] David Dudley Field vs. Henry George, "Land and Taxation," *North American Review,* July 1885, p. 8-9.
[24] Charles Barker, *Henry George,* pp. 428-9.

right of all individual members of the human race in-
discriminately to enter and enjoy at will each and every
lot and parcel of land upon the globe, and every building
which may have been or may hereafter be erected thereupon." (p. 141). In fact, George argued otherwise; he
asserted that each man's equal right to land could be
achieved if the government would collect the land rent
by taxation, and he vigorously opposed the government
seizure of land titles. He constantly defended private
property in buildings, even maintaining that they sould
not be subject to taxation.

But Walker did not really warm up to his argument
until a later part of his book when he plunged into a
lengthy attack upon George's economic system. "How
much is there in the view," he wrote, "that commercial
disturbance and industrial depression are due chiefly to
the speculative holding of land? . . . Mr. George makes
no point against private property in land . . . unless he can
show that it is, of all species of property, peculiarly the
subject of speculative impulses." (p. 162). He supported
this statement by citing random examples, all of which
related to agricultural land only.

Walker then proceeded to attack another of George's
central theses, namely that "irrespective of the increase
of population, the effect of improvements in methods of
production and exchange is to increase rent," this effect
being carried so far that "all the advantages gained by the
march of progress go to the owners of land, and wages do
not increase." (p. 167). Walker cited empirical evidence
to show that the condition of the wage worker actually
had improved. In order to show that capitalists also had
bettered their position he quoted Professor Emile de
Laverleye: "Immense fortunes amassed so rapidly in the
United States, like those of Mr. Gould and Mr. Vander-

bilt, were the results of railway speculation, and not of the greater value of land." (p. 169). Exception might be taken to these examples, as Gould and Vanderbilt were notoriously unfair competitors, stock-waterers and monopolists whom George had criticized on these very grounds. George never said that the only economic crime was the private collection of land rent.

Walker attacked George on theoretical as well as on empirical grounds. He maintained that there was one type of increase in production which would enhance the demand for labor without enhancing the demand for land, thereby raising wages but not rent. Production increases due to improvements in quality rather than quantity are of this type. He gives examples: "Here is the rude furniture of a laborer's cottage, worth perhaps $30. The same amount of wood may be made into furniture worth $200 for the home of the clerk, or into furniture worth $2,000 for the home of the banker. . . . The actual material derived from the soil which would go into a picture by a master, worth thousands, makes a smaller draught upon the productive essences of the soil than a chromo of the Prodigal's Return, sold from a cart for $2, frame included." (p. 172).

Walker offered another argument in criticism of George's thesis that rent absorbs the benefits of material progress. He stated that improvements and inventions in transportation "actually operate powerfully, directly, and exclusively in reducing the demand for land. . . . Whatever quickens and cheapens transport, acts directly in the reduction of rents, and cannot act in any other way, since it throws out of cultivation the poorer lands previously in use for the supply of the market, enabling the better soils at a distance to take their place, thus raising the lower limit, or, as it is called, the 'margin' of cultivation,

and thus reducing rents." (p. 175). Walker was true to
Ricardo's Law of Rent here, for he assumed that rent is
the difference between what can be produced on good
land over what can be produced on the most inferior
land. Walker maintained that this difference would be
reduced by improvements in transportation because outlying lands (previously of little use) would now become
more productive, thus reducing total land rent.

What are we to say of Walker's criticisms as stated in
Land and Its Rent? When he points out that the statistical
facts prove that poverty has not increased with progress,
that wages have not fallen over the years, and that rent
has not increased faster than total production, he would
find complete agreement among practically all present-
day economic observers. Because the factual evidence is so
overpowering, Walker would find very little disagreement
even among many present-day Georgists. Facts speak
louder than theories.

Yet, quite rightly, Walker did not overlook George's
theoretical arguments. After all, it is quite possible that
these arguments were correct except that factors which
George overlooked might tend to limit land rent; if such
is the case, then George's economic analysis, as far as it
goes, would still be of use to us.

However, Walker seems justified in his theoretical
criticism that production increases which come from improvements in quality rather than quantity tend to increase wages and interest rather than rent. Certainly, a
new textile machine might produce a finer weave without
requiring the use of more cloth, in which case the value
of the final product would go up but there would be no
increase in the demand for land, hence rent. An even more
important consideration was that the use of this new
machine would not bring into production land hitherto un-

used, and thus even according to George's own theories neither wages nor interest would be kept at the subsistence level. These were vital criticisms of an important part of *Progress and Poverty*.

Walker assumed too extreme a position when he stated that George, in explaining depressions, had no case unless he could show that only land is subject to speculation, although the objection contained much truth. Speculation on the stock market was no small contributory cause to the 1929 debacle. Not only that, it seems likely that all prices were rising too fast in the twenties, and the resulting sudden price adjustment in 1929 brought on the depression. It is well known that prices react faster than changes in supply, thus causing depressions and inflation. Walker certainly proved that speculation in land was not the only form of speculation and that land speculation was not the only cause of depression. Yet it certainly is one cause, perhaps an important cause, and keeping land out of use or charging a monopoly price for it is an unmitigated social and economic evil.

It is possible to question Walker's argument that improvements in transportation narrow the difference in productivity between good land and marginal, thereby reducing rent according to Ricardo's Law. After all, do not improvements in transportation greatly increase the value of urban lands? Are not wharves and land surrounding wharves made more valuable by improvements in shipping? Do not better highways make city land more valuable? Improvements in transportation may have the effect of reducing rent, as Walker states, but Walker cannot prove this with the Law of Rent.

It is of some interest to note that in *Land and Its Rent*, Walker did not concern himself with the merits or demerits of George's land value tax proposal, but only with

George's economic analysis of poverty and depressions. The question to which Walker addressed himself was: "Is land speculation and private landownership the sole cause of these two economic evils?" In the 1880's, most people were interested in learning whether George had really solved these grand economic problems. Only later did they become interested in land value taxation as a solution to more limited economic problems, such as tax reform, urban overcrowding, slums, and the like.

It may be interesting to follow Walker's thinking for a few years beyond the 1883 publication of *Land and Its Rent,* since his attitude toward George altered in a way that mirrored the general academic change of view. In 1890, Walker delivered an address before the annual meeting of the American Economic Association entitled "The Tide of Economic Thought." By this time, he was able to treat Henry George in a cooler and calmer tone. What had caused him to make the "steeped in infamy" remark previously referred to was George's intention not to compensate landowners for the land rents they would lose under the single tax proposal. In 1890 Walker was able to say that "conceding compensation to existing owners, the proposition is one which an honest man can entertain."[25] He personally still had objections to the scheme, but it seemed to him that economists at large "have rather been inclining to the view that somewhat more of economic rent than is now taken by the State might be brought into the treasury."[26] Walker doubted that practical politicians could get the votes from small farmers and small village lot-owners for such a scheme.

His position was spelled out more clearly in the 1893

[25] Francis A. Walker, "The Tide of American Economic Thought," *Reports of the Proceedings of the American Economic Association, Fourth Annual Meeting,* 1890, p. 24.
[26] *Ibid.,* p. 27.

edition of *First Lessons in Political Economy,* a high school textbook (but not significantly easier, it is interesting to note, than the college texts). Wrote Walker, "There can be no question, I think, that if the community chooses to claim rent, it has a clear and a full right to it."[27] However, the government must pay compensation, because if it had recognized the individual's legal right to land and its rent, it would be sheer robbery if it suddenly denied that right. Landowners have a vested interest in the land which society is bound to protect even though, with economic progress, "a larger and still larger share of the product of industry tends to pass into the hands of the owners of land, not because they have done more for society, but because society has a greater need of that which they control."[28] This demand for compensation was to bob up again and again.

A little later, Walker informed his young readers that there was an increasing number of educated and experienced gentlemen who believed in the nationalization of the land, although they were still in the minority. Nevertheless, he advised his students to place themselves with the majority until the opposite side had been proved beyond a shadow of a doubt. (p. 212.)

To lengthen that shadow, Walker then listed two principal objections to the national ownership of land, under which appellation he erroneously included the single tax. First was the administrative objection, that the amount of political machinery and officeholders required to administer all the lands and the immense opportunities for corruption and favoritism involved would make the scheme unworkable. An army of officials was pictured crossing the land, fixing and re-fixing rentals, and making

[27] Francis A. Walker, *First Lessons in Political Economy,* p. 208.
[28] *Ibid.,* p. 209.

insecure a man's ownership of improvements upon the land.

This, to, was to become a familiar argument. In rebuttal, supporters of George's proposal pointed out that it could be administered locally rather than nationally and would in no way require more officials than already administered the real estate tax. In fact, the opportunities for corruption would be narrowed since buildings would no longer be taxed. The title to land would remain in private hands, thus safeguarding improvements.

Walker's second objection concerned the conservation of the fertility of nationally owned agricultural land. He said that conservation was of great historical importance, pointing out that there were several ancient lands which once supported rich civilizations but because of soil exhaustion no longer could do so. Walker maintained that land nationalization would be harmful to soil conservation, for what farmer, he asked, would conserve the fertility of soil he did not own?

This argument reflected the growing interest in the conservation of natural resources, and was a much-used weapon against the Georgists in the years to come. In order to evaluate the criticism, one should know the Georgist reply. The Georgists pointed out that even under the existing system of land taxation, the fertility of the soil had been wasted. Vast areas of America, fertile not so long ago, were now sandy wastelands. Absentee farm ownership was an important contributory cause of this, for wherever it existed the tenant-farmer was truly not farming his own soil, and might well take a careless attitude toward long-run fertility. Under land value taxation, however, absentee farm ownership would be eradicated, thus abetting the cause of soil conservation.[29]

[29] Absentee farm ownership in the United States is more widespread than we are apt to think. Aside from the ubiquitous tenant-

A prudent farmer would not ruin the fertility of his soil under any tax system because farm improvements are not easily moved; if the soil became worthless, almost all his improvements would depreciate in value. Under land value taxation the security of his ownership of these improvements would be greatly increased because they would not be taxed.

The great advances made in soil conservation in recent years have come about largely through government action. The Soil Conservation Service, the county agent system, agricultural zoning, a greater public awareness of the problem—all of these highly effective approaches would be helped rather than retarded by a land value tax system.

The Criticism of Other Conservative Economists

In the late nineteenth century, economics in America was dominated by a small group of rather conservative economists, of whom Walker was only one, although perhaps the most prominent. This conservative group dominated the field until the 1930's, and almost to a man they opposed the single tax vigorously. An examination of their arguments will indicate how well they understood the single tax doctrine and the extent to which their knowledge was first- or second-hand. We may also discover some views which, although long forgotten, still have current application.

Henry Fawcett was one of the elder statesmen of this group. Although British, his *Manual of Political Economy* was a leading textbook on this side of the Atlantic. He observed that "although Mr. George writes in a style

---

farming and sharecropping, it should be borne in mind that practically all farms bear substantial mortgages. The farmer may hold the legal title to the land, but economically, the mortgagor, usually a bank, is the real landowner to the extent of the mortgage.

which is often particularly attractive, yet we have frequently found it extremely difficult to arrive at the exact character of his proposals."[30] Perhaps this will explain why Fawcett committed the rather frequent mistake of confusing George's proposal with the land nationalization scheme of Alfred Russel Wallace. Yet Fawcett did not doubt that the state rightfully owns the land of the nation, that in theory it should not have alienated the land it once owned, and should not now sell land it still possesses. But alas, now nothing could be done about the matter. Confiscation could never be justified—not even the Marxist International advocated it!—and compensation was financially impossible.

Arthur Latham Perry was another member of the group of conservative economists. His book, *The Principles of Political Economy,* was an extremely popular textbook of the 1880's and 1890's. Professor Perry taught History and Political Economy at Williams College and was an ardent free trader, advocate of the free economy, and also a well-known historian.

An example of Perry's approach to economics was his statement that no general glut of exchangeable products is possible in this world under conditions of free competition.[31] This was the only reference to depressions that appeared in his thick book. The consequences of 1873 went unexplained. In George's day, all too often economic writing was divorced from economic reality.

Like Fawcett, Perry misunderstood George's viewpoint. He wrote that ". . . George is wholly wrong in his view,

[30] Henry Fawcett, *Manual of Political Economy.* London: Macmillan, 1887 (first edition 1863), p. 283.
[31] Arthur Latham Perry, *The Principles of Political Economy.* New York: Scribner, 1891, pp. 139, 140.

that there is Value in lands as God made them . . ."[32]
Actually, along with practically all other economists,
George maintained exactly the reverse.[33] Perry went on to
state, in contradiction to subsequent economic thinking,
that land values were created by the landowner *per se*
rather than by society's demand. He also believed that
land was a form of capital, and if George did not want the
government to confiscate capital he should not ask it to
confiscate land. It might well be argued that this position
was logically untenable. After all, if a man wishes to distinguish between land and other capital on the grounds
that the former is nature-produced and the latter man-
made, he ought to be allowed to do so. He should be
judged primarily on his logic and not on his definitions.

Edward Atkinson, another member of the conservative
group, wrote no textbooks, nor did he hold any academic
position, but as a prominent businessman he wrote frequently on the subject of economics and was highly
regarded by other economists of his day. In 1890, he
engaged in a widely read debate with Henry George in
The Century Magazine, and the views he expressed were
typical of his conservative *confreres.* One of his chief
objections to Georgism was that the land value tax could be
shifted to consumers in the form of higher prices.[34] Raise
the tax on land and tenants will pay more and so will purchasers of the products produced on land. How, then, can
the land value tax be of any great benefit to society? However, this is contrary to the view now accepted by practically
all economists, who reason that a land value tax cannot
increase the price of land—i.e., rent—because it cannot

[32] Arthur Latham Perry, *The Principles of Political Economy,*
p. 147.
[33] Henry George, *Progress and Poverty,* pp. 235 ff.
[34] Edward Atkinson, "A Single Tax on Land," *Nineteenth Century,* July 1890, pp. 387-88.

decrease its supply. What Atkinson failed to realize was that a tax on land value diverted land rent from the private landowner to the government and in no way affected the total amount of land rent.

Atkinson also felt that a landowner needed great skill if he was to manage his land well, and therefore he was entitled to a return for his efforts. George's view was that a landowner *per se* does nothing more than merely hold title to his land and collect the rent; if he manages the land, he does so in the capacity of laborer or capitalist and the return which he justifiably gets is properly called wages, interest, or profits.

This question worried Atkinson: "How would existing titles be extinguished, and how would the land then be redistributed?"[35] Certainly, the single tax involves no such insurmountable task.

Atkinson also asserted that the single tax had failed when applied in France by the Physiocrats.[36] This is not so; it was never tried in France.

Atkinson concluded his article by saying that the single tax agitation was not all misspent effort because it had focused attention on certain unnamed abuses in our tax system.[37]

The arch-conservative of all the economists in this group was J. Laurence Laughlin of the University of Chicago. In his major textbook, *The Elements of Political Economy* (1887), he accorded George the unanswerable criticism of neglect by not once mentioning him. Nevertheless, Laughlin had the reputation of being anti-George, and his article in the first issue of the *Journal of Political Economy* (December 1892) bears this out. In referring to

[35] *Ibid.,* p. 391.
[36] *Ibid.,* p. 393. Atkinson later rescinded this statement in a subsequent issue of *Nineteenth Century.*
[37] *Ibid.,* p. 394.

the attitude of the Homestead Steel strikers, he denounced their claim to the "unalienable right to continuous employment" and attributed their views to their "one-sided reading" of and exclusive attention to Henry George.[38] It is highly questionable whether George ever had such influence on the working class. His followers were recruited primarily from the middle class, especially by the 1890's.

Arthur T. Hadley's textbook on economics (published 1896) enjoyed a huge sale in the colleges. He was an economist who had done much valuable work on the subject of railroads and eventually became president of Yale. He was one of the many university figures who had participated in a testimonial dinner for Henry George in 1889 when George left for a trip to Australia; other future college presidents in attendance included Seth Low, E. Benjamin Andrews, and E. J. James. This would indicate a certain measure of approval on Hadley's part. Later, after his retirement, Hadley was reliably reported as being among the number of economists in the academic world who endorsed the principle of land value taxation.[39] Nevertheless, Hadley was definitely anti-George in his 1890 textbook. Here is a pattern of personal support coupled with official coolness or opposition duplicated again and again by other academic supporters of Henry George.

What does Hadley's textbook actually say about George? On page 150 appeared the statement that Henry George favored collective property in land!

On page 288, Hadley asserted that the private collection of land rent was justified as a reward for risk. It

[38] J. L. Laughlin, "The Study of Political Economy in the United States," *Journal of Political Economy*, v. 1, p. 3 (Dec. 1892).
[39] Harry Gunnison Brown, ed., *Significant Paragraphs from Progress and Poverty*, p. 80.

might easily be argued that this is questionable justification for it would justify the activities of gamblers and burglars who take tremendous risks in their chosen occupations. Risk increases the return to income-producing property, but it can hardly justify the ethical right to the ownership of that property.

On page 471, he declared that it was difficult to separate land values from improvement values; how then could the single tax be applied? This was one of the most frequent objections to the single tax, yet the fact is that assessors do separate land and improvement values constantly, and while it is difficult for a layman to estimate accurately the value of land, it is comparatively easy for a real estate man who has made this activity his life's work. Walk down the street with an experienced real estate broker, and he will tell you how much each parcel of land will cost approximately. Assessors find frequent real estate sales a good guide for land prices. While a land value tax might err to some extent and tax part of the improvement value as well (i.e., the assessed value of the land might be higher than the market value), it obviously would not tax improvements nearly as much as does the present real estate tax.

Comparative evidence provides additional light on this matter. The land value tax is the sole source of revenue of many municipalities in Australia and New Zealand, and the system is spreading there, which argues well for its administrability. Many cities in America assess land and improvement separately, one of them being New York. Many of the most valuable buildings in America are built on rented land (cf., the four corners of Lexington Avenue and 42nd Street in New York City are operated on a leasehold basis).

In the case of agricultural land, there is greater difficulty in separating land value from improvement value, but the task is by no means insurmountable, as experience in Australia and New Zealand again shows. Consider the most difficult case of all: the addition of fertilizer to the soil. It is an improvement, yet its value becomes intermingled with the land. To solve this difficulty, the annual cost of fertilizer which a prudent farmer might incur could be deducted from the annual land value tax. Fertilizer costs would then be taxed much less than under the present system.

Hadley also believed that the single tax, by doing away with land speculation, would prevent a profit on real estate investment above the normal interest return. The result? Builders would have less incentive to build. Georgists replied that capitalists in all other fields manage to invest and expand with only the normal return on capital as their incentive; why should real estate builders require the promise of a greater than normal profit (interest on capital invested in the building plus possible increase in land value) before investing? It was surprising and inconsistent for Hadley to maintain this, since elsewhere in his book he alleged that land speculation is a risky business which has led many to financial ruin. In any case, it is hard to see how keeping land from its most productive use through land speculation will encourage building and construction. Yet this argument was repeated frequently in other books.

The casual reader of Hadley's textbook would almost certainly infer that he was opposed to George, so consistently did Hadley offer arguments against the single tax, yet as he neared the end of his section on George, lukewarm praise almost amounting to endorsement appeared. The speedy imposition of the land value tax, wrote Hadley, would amount to outright confiscation and be a real obstacle to the eventual adoption of the proposal. A very gradually imposed land value tax "represents the utmost stretch of possibility in this matter." (p. 472). But George and his followers consistently agreed that gradual imposition was a necessity.

Hadley concluded his section on George by writing that one of the advantages of the land value tax was that it would abolish land speculation, now completely contradicting his previous assertion that it would be socially burdensome! (p. 474).

Another observation appearing in a later section in the textbook commented on the attitude of other economists toward the land value tax view: "Most economists would be willing to agree that more taxes should be levied upon economic rent and less upon improvements."[40] This position is encountered frequently in the writings of economists at the turn of the century.

Simon Nelson Patten, the famous protectionist economist from the University of Pennsylvania, gave a speech before the American Economic Association in 1890 entitled "The Education Value of Political Economy." He accused Henry George of being illogical because George could think of only six alternative remedies to land value taxation, and disposed of them all as impractical in twenty-five pages, "but when it comes to his own it is stated in half a page. He gives no affirmative argument for his remedy. His sole reliance is on the insufficiency of the remedies which others had proposed."[41]

It was true that George devoted approximately twenty-five pages to alternative remedies, but it was not true that the affirmative argument for his own position is limited to

[40] Arthur Hadley, *Economics*, p. 474.
[41] Simon Nelson Patten, "The Educational Value of Political Economy," *Publications of the American Economic Association*, 1890, p. 23.

half a page. In fact, some 221 pages of *Progress and Poverty* were devoted to affirmative arguments for the land value tax. One can hardly escape the conclusion that Patten had not read *Progress and Poverty* carefully or completely.

In 1896, Frank William Taussig published a book on the history of the wage-fund doctrine, with much space and praise devoted to Henry George's refutation of that position. He had something to say about other parts of *Progress and Poverty* as well: "As far as Mr. George is concerned, I am glad to express my respect for his nobility of purpose; while the stimulating effect of his writing on economic discussion during the last twenty years is too obvious to need mention."[42] Although effective with the masses, "his writings exerted no great influence on trained students; a result due in part to the thinness of his thought, but perhaps quite as much to the ruthless sweep of the social remedy which he finally proposed."[43]

Why so thin? Taussig gave an example. He referred to George's statement in *Progress and Poverty* that:

the draughtsman, who, shut up in some dingy office on the banks of the Thames, is drawing the plans for a great marine engine, is in reality devoting his labor to the production of bread and meat as truly as though he were garnering the grain in California or swinging a lariat on a La Plata pampa; that he is as truly making his own clothing as though he were shearing sheep in Australia or weaving cloth in Paisley . . .[44]

This quotation, says Taussig, gives us the "swing of George's style and the quality of his matter." But, observes Taussig, although the draughtsman may, in effect, be making clothing, he certainly is not making *his own;* therefore George was wrong. The distinction was a fine one, and it

[42] Frank W. Taussig, *Wages and Capital.* New York: Macmillan, 1896, p. 283.
[43] *Ibid.*, p. 289.
[44] Henry George, *Progress and Poverty,* p. 29.

would seem that other more telling examples should have been offered.

Why was George's remedy, so mild in the eyes of modern social analysts, considered by Taussig to be so ruthless? Because his remedy meant "virtual confiscation of land on the part of the state."[45] Here, then, was Taussig's real objection to the single tax. In his influential textbook, *Principles of Economics,* he asserted that land rent is indeed unearned and that land should have been taxed from the very beginning of society, but higher than the rights of society and producers are the rights of vested interests. The vested rights of landowners must be protected and therefore the land value tax is unethical.[46]

To get around this *impasse,* Taussig endorsed Mills' tax on the future increment in land values, although with many qualifications. He felt that scrupulous honesty and high intelligence were needed on the part of government officials; general price fluctuations and interest rate changes must be considered, etc. Besides, in a country like America where landownership was widely diffused, such a scheme was probably unnecessary. Nevertheless, Taussig, like many others of his time, observed that such a tax was becoming more popular among economists as a result of George's activities, in flat contradiction of his previous statement that George had had little influence on "trained students."[47]

Taussig listed certain economic objections to a tax on land values. There was the usual one about the difficulty of separating land value from improvements (but would not this objection apply with equal force against Mills' tax on future increment which Taussig endorsed?). Taus-

[45] Frank Taussig, *Wages and Capital,* p. 283.
[46] Frank Taussig, *Principles of Economics.* New York: Macmillan, 1911, v. 1, pp. 100, 102; v. 2, p. 576.
[47] Frank Taussig, *Principles of Economics,* v. 1, pp. 75, 104, 106.

sig challenged George's statement that the land value tax was not a burdensome tax, pointing out that although it imposed no burden on future purchasers, it did impose a burden on present owners. This was essentially correct, but when George said that the tax was not burdensome he was referring to the fact that it imposed no burden on the productive process.[48]

Sometimes Taussig was inconsistent. On the point that land value taxation forced land into immediate use, he denoted this as an advantage in one place and as a disadvantage in another.[49] George asserted that since rent measures the social demand for land, a full tax on rent would force land to be used as fast as social needs require. At other times Taussig was uninformed, as when he stated that land value taxation had never been tried, thus ignoring events in Australia and New Zealand.

Taussig summed up his views on George's proposal with this statement:[50]

Though the principles which underlie it are among the most settled in the theory of economics, they bring a shock to the common notions about the sanctity and the stability of real property; and their application involves a disturbance of the common ways of dealing with real property. The movement for taxing the unearned increment on urban sites is certain to grow in strength, and to bring results in legislation; but the precise mode in which it will proceed will be affected by compromises and half measures.

Again it appears that Taussig's primary objection to the single tax was not economic but moral.

We come now to that bellwether of conservative economics for almost fifty years, John Bates Clark. Although the Austrian concepts of marginal utility had been introduced into this country before he published in 1899 his

[48] *Ibid.,* v. 1, p. 73; v. 2, p. 569.
[49] *Ibid.,* v. 2, pp. 575, 576.
[50] *Ibid.,* v. 1, p. 106.

key work, *The Distribution of Wealth,* he translated these concepts into the language of American economics, and it was his version of marginal utility that dominated economic thought in the United States until Keynes' time. Clark overshadowed even such worthy competitors as the German historical school and its close cousin, the Veblenian school of economics.

Clark opposed George vigorously while admitting that "it was the claim advanced by Mr. Henry George, that wages are fixed by the product which a man can create by tilling rentless land," which led him to the discovery of his famous marginal law of wages and interest.[51]

Nevertheless Clark seems to have an incomplete understanding of George's law of wages. He wrote that, according to George, Swiss peasants on a mountainside would set the wages of highly skilled Swiss watchmakers working in modern factories. To use Clark's words, "it puts the man in a shanty into a position that is so strategic as to enable him to dominate workmen of every class, to fix the amount of their wages, and so to control the level on which they live."[52] Actually, George's law does not state that unlettered peasants working on marginal land with but the crudest of tools set the wages of highly skilled watchmakers working with modern equipment. What George really said was that backward peasants working on no-rent marginal land determine the wages only of *similarly unskilled* laborers. Other workers would get an increasingly higher wage depending upon their degree of skill, the agreeableness or disagreeableness of their work, the easiness or cheapness of training, the constancy of employment, responsibility, risk, status of the occupation, etc.[53]

[51] John Bates Clark, *Distribution of Wealth.* New York: Macmillan, 1899, p. viii.
[52] *Ibid.,* p. 89.
[53] Henry George, *Progress and Poverty,* pp. 210-12.

With Clark, as with Taussig and so many other conservative economists of his day, the underlying objection to
the single tax was ethical rather than economic. In an 1890
letter to Richard Ely he wrote, "Confiscation is the whole
of the single tax, and that I can never see as anything but
an inequity."[54]

A few months later, Clark delivered a speech before the
American Social Science Association in which he maintained that under the present system of private land ownership, everyone has an equal right to land insofar as
everyone has an equal right to buy land.[55] In the same
speech he also asserted, somewhat contradictorily, that in
actual fact the community rightfully owns the land because
"the community has created the value that resides in land,
and whoever usurps the ownership of it deals a blow at the
community."[56] However, he quickly added that if the community should not alienate the land for ethical reasons, it
should certainly do so for practical reasons.

And what are these practical reasons? The single tax,
he said, would require the state to seize the homes of poor
men just emerging from the sweated proletariat.[57] He also
claimed that a pioneering farmer needed to own land because his chief income, at least in the beginning, comes
from land speculation: "He starves now, that he may be
independent hereafter."[58] Thus one finds that Clark exaggerated the certainty and reward of land speculation on
the frontier in almost Turnerian fashion. The Turner

[54] Joseph Dorfman, *Economic Mind in American Civilization*,
v. 3, xxviii, quoting Clark's letters to Ely, 1/24/88, 11/13/90, Ely
Papers.
[55] John B. Clark, "Single Tax Debate," *American Social Science
Association,* Sept. 5, 1890, p. 26.
[56] *Ibid.,* p. 21.
[57] *Ibid.,* p. 27.
[58] John B. Clark, "Single Tax Debate," *American Social Science
Association,* Sept. 5, 1890, p. 23.

critics of today would argue speculation in western lands, by the 1880's at any rate, benefited very few people, and could not rightfully be transformed into a national virtue. In any case, boosting the price of frontier land through speculation hardly seems the proper way to encourage people to settle on the frontier. Was not cheap land the attraction that drew people out west?

As for the state "seizing the homes of poor men," this was a rather elementary misinterpretation of how the single tax would be applied. The single tax effected homes only by "untaxing" them.

It is hard to see how Clark could justify the private ownership of land by arguing that everyone possessed an equal right to buy land. If everyone had an equal right to buy the stock of a corporation engaging in monopoly practices, would that right in itself justify the corporation's activities? It is dangerous to assume that "right" and "opportunity" are synonymous.

The treatment accorded George by the conservative economists of his time forms a consistent pattern. Serious misstatements of George's views often characterized their criticisms, particularly because they lacked a clear conception of how the single tax would be applied. Nearly all of them criticized the single tax because they felt it would raise too much revenue, thus giving the government incontrovertible power over the lives of its citizens. Although they were highly critical of George and his ideas, often emotionally so, by the end of the period occasional tributes to his high nobility of purpose and his influence in popularizing the study of economics may be found creeping into the discussion. Even when the emotional tide of their writing ran most furiously against George, one can discern a widespread tendency to concede the validity of some of his ideas, usually in tacit or lukewarm fashion. Sometimes conservative critics would endorse his ethics, sometimes the land value tax (although never as a single tax), almost always a tax on the future increment of land values (over and above their present value). Economists were being influenced in spite of themselves.

The Confiscation Question Considered

A hallmark of the opposition of the conservative economists to Henry George was its extreme vociferousness. They tended to regard him as a dangerous enemy to society and as a foe to private property. Rather contradictorily, he was often accused of being both an anarchist and a communist. The reason for this unusual attitude was the feeling that the single tax amounted to confiscation of vested property in land. More than any other criticism, this charge of confiscation hindered the adoption of land value taxation in America. In our day, we have gotten used to confiscation by taxation, but even yet the argument has considerable impact.

George did not help his cause any by his unorthodox use of terminology in *Progress and Poverty*. On the first page of the chapter entitled "The True Remedy" he wrote:[59]

This, then, is the remedy for the unjust and unequal distribution of wealth apparent in modern civilization, and for all the evils which flow from it:

We must make land common property.

Seventy-seven pages follow to show why private property in land *as now constituted* is unethical. Finally the reader learns how "the true remedy" is to be applied—not by the confiscation of land by the government, which George's

[59] Henry George, *Progress and Poverty*, p. 328.

terminology might have led him to expect, but by the taxation of land values:[60]

It is not necessary to confiscate land; it is only necessary to confiscate rent. . . . we may put the proposition into practical form by proposing—
To abolish all taxation save that upon land values.

The rest of the book deals with land value taxation, but nevertheless a hasty reader could easily get the impression that George favored government ownership of land. Indeed, this was the most universal misconception of the nine conservative economists reviewed so far in this study. Yet whenever the issue of government ownership of land was raised, George vehemently opposed such a scheme as being unnecessary and undemocratic. In no uncertain terms, he thoroughly endorsed private ownership of land *provided* its rent was collected by the government in taxation.[61] A careful reading of *Progress and Poverty* makes this crystal clear.

Does the single tax involve the unjust confiscation of private property? Does it unjustly confiscate private land-rent income? The Georgist reply to this common accusation may be summarized under the following headings:

1. In actual fact, there is no confiscation of property involved at all, for under the single tax system the title remains in the hands of the landowner. Not only could he improve the land as he wishes, but his improvements would not be taxed; thus, his title to the land would be even more complete.

2. Each man is entitled to all the fruits of his own labor; slavery would be the only alternative. If, then, labor is the sole justification for the private ownership of any-

[60] *Ibid.,* pp. 405-6.
[61] *Ibid.,* p. 405.

thing, then land, which is not produced by labor, is not justifiably private property; hence, neither is rent. Furthermore, land is a gift of God or Nature to all mankind, and if all men are indeed created equal then everyone should have an equal right to the use of land. Since distributing an equal share of land to everyone is obviously impossible, then we must distribute an equal share of land rent to all. Only the land value tax can do this. If compensation is to be paid at all, then landowners should repay society for the past loss of society's rightful income.

3. Land values are a social product, produced solely by the presence of society, and thus society should take what it produces and leave individuals free from taxation in order to enjoy the full fruits of their own labor.

4. It is not usual for the government to compensate people for the taxes they have to pay. All taxation is confiscation; why object so strenuously to this particular tax only, especially if it is gradually imposed and is one tax among many? After all, we are faced with the choice of having the government "confiscate" land rent, an income which rightfully belongs to all, or having it "confiscate" personal incomes, which are individually produced. Which alternative is more ethically preferable?

5. When the present real estate tax is increased, the tax on land values goes up also, yet we hear no cry of confiscation or compensation.

6. The government is constantly making adjustments that harm some people but benefit society at large, yet no claim to compensation is recognized or even broached. For instance, the government has prosecuted monopolies to the detriment of those investors who bought the stock of the monopoly with the expectation that they would collect a monopoly profit. Utility rates are lowered by public service commissions, tariffs are lowered, the gas and

tobacco taxes are increased and the government offers no compensation to the individuals whose vested interests are harmed. The Eighteenth Amendment was imposed, yet the liquor interests were not compensated. Are we never to reduce the farm subsidy because by now the farmers have obtained a vested interest? When the government changes a defense contract with a private concern, are the stockholders to be reimbursed if their financial interests suffer? Almost any reform will hurt someone's pocketbook; are we then never to have reform?

7. The total tax load on owners of well-improved land —and this would include most factory and home owners— would actually decrease with the imposition of the land value tax; their only loss would be in the selling price of their land if they wished to sell. But if they sought to buy another piece of land, its price would be similarly deflated and they would suffer no loss. If they became apartment-house dwellers, they would find that the land value tax had reduced the rent they would pay the landowner. This is because there would be no building tax to be passed on to them in the form of higher rent.

8. The only people who might suffer from the land value tax would be those who rent out space, those who have insufficiently improved their land, slum owners, and speculators in empty lots. As for the latter, they may have deserved their fate as they have made improper or unsocial use of their land. As for apartment-house owners, although in the long run they stand to lose their rental income from the land, in the short run they stand to gain because their total real estate tax bill will have been greatly reduced. This is so because while the tax on their land will increase, the much higher tax on their more valuable buildings will gradually disappear altogether. Not only that, but as land values increase with the passage of time, the assess-

ment will lag behind market value even in the most efficiently run city; this would be another "frictional" advantage the apartment-house owner would reap. In any case, because the land value tax would be increased gradually, all real estate owners would have sufficient time to make the necessary adjustments in order to protect themselves.

9. Gradual imposition of the land value tax amounts to compensation. This important point is not generally realized. Gradual imposition accomplished over a period of forty years is exactly equivalent to immediate compensation. If 3 per cent interest on the unpaid balance were paid, then sixty-four years would be necessary.[62] This factor reduces the compensation problem to much smaller dimensions.

So far, only the rational arguments of both sides on the confiscation issue have been presented, but the emotional ones are not to be slighted. In George's time, land had a

---

[62] An example will illustrate: on a $10,000 investment in land, the rental income will be about $500 a year, or 5 per cent. If the tax is imposed over a period of forty years, then in the first year only $12.50 will be taken in taxation, then $25, and so on. This is equivalent to confiscating the whole $500 but returning $487.50 in compensation the first year, $475 the second, and so on. At the end of forty years, the annual compensatory returns will equal the original $10,000. If compensation is paid by a forty-year government bond, then $250 will be paid to the original owner the first year instead of $487.50 as under the gradual land value tax, and $250 will be paid for the next forty years, whereas under the tax the annual compensation would decrease. Under both forms of compensation the *average* annual payment will be $250.

This is how to calculate the 3 per cent interest payment: the average annual unpaid balance under the gradual land value tax plan is $5,000. Multiplied by forty years, it becomes $200,000. Three per cent interest on this is $6,000. Since the average annual compensation under the land value tax would be $250 per year, it would take twenty-four additional years ($250 × 24 = $6,000) for gradual imposition to pay 3 per cent interest on the unpaid balance. Therefore, the total compensation would take sixty-four years to accomplish (24 + 40 = 64).

certain special sanctity that no other type of property possessed. He and his contemporaries were not far removed from the feudal idea that the ownership of land conferred a certain distinction upon the owner and gave him a claim to being a gentleman. Solid citizens owned land, it was thought, and it was less than a century since only landowners could vote or hold political office in most of the country. The farming life was regarded as sacrosanct and peculiarly American. Henry George's single tax proposal somehow seemed to threaten all this; did it not threaten land, the very basis of private property? Hence the bitter antagonism he encountered.

The Views of Liberal Economists

So far, only conservatively oriented economists have been discussed. But even that small yet growing group of liberal economists who advocated an increasing government role in the economy had ethical objections to the single tax. For instance, there was Richard T. Ely, a founder of the American Economic Association in 1885 and a key figure in American economic thought clear into the 1930's. "On what ground of justice or ethics shall the landowner be singled out for taxation?"[63] he asked. Why should the rich man go tax-free while the landowner, who may be either rich or poor, is taxed to the point of confiscation? Ely maintained that the only just grounds for taxation was the doctrine of "taxation according to ability to pay." Therefore he strongly favored the income tax.

Ely had practical as well as moral objections to the single tax. It would be difficult if not impossible, he wrote, to apply land value taxation because we cannot separate the value of the bare land from the value of the improvements on it. Unlike Walker, who made the same objection,

[63] Richard T. Ely, *Outline of Economics* (1893), p. 462.

he concerned himself with urban land, and asked how we could separate from the bare land value such capital improvements as grading, landscaping and installation of sewers, streets and utilities.[64]

Ely was one of the first to broach the charge of inelasticity, which was to appear again and again in the writings of numerous single tax opponents. He felt that the amount of land rent in a community did not necessarily equal the amount of revenue required by the government of that community. At times the land value tax might yield more than the government needed, and at other times it might yield less. In times of emergency, such as depression or natural disaster, the land rent fund would decrease at just the moment that more taxation was needed.[65]

To this indictment the single-taxers replied that the land value tax would collect so much revenue that all possible governmental needs would be satisfied, and if you did not want to collect all the land rent you did not have to. They also argued that the government should live off its own rightful income just as any individual or corporation does, and therefore should limit its expenditures to the socially produced land-rent fund. They reasoned that a government expenditure should create an equivalent amount of land value because it increased the desirability of living in the area served by the government; this increased desirability depended upon location, and the value of a particular location is expressed in land rent. Hence, if a government expenditure did not increase land rent by an amount at least equal to the expenditure itself, then it was uneconomic and wasteful.

Today, we moderns would doubt the sufficiency of the

[64] Ibid., pp. 445, 460.
[65] Ibid., p. 460.

single tax to pay for all government expenditures, and as for the single-taxers' "rightful income" argument, while it might hold true in a utopia where all men are rational and no one infringes upon the rights of his fellow man, it does not hold true in our present non-utopian world. In a utopia, huge outlays for defence and police would not be necessary. But today, the size of such outlays is determined by urgent practical need rather than by the amount of land values they might create.

However, it should be realized that the inelasticity criticism applied only to the single tax, and did not apply to a land value tax imposed as one tax among many. But somewhat unaccountably, Ely and many other professional economists refused to consider the land value tax as anything else than a single tax. Yet there was no real reason why it could not be advocated as one tax among many. Many of George's followers did just this, and George himself welcomed them within his ranks.

Ely's argument that it is practically impossible to separate urban improvement values from bare land values was not borne out by the experiences of many municipalities which even in his day were assessing land and improvements separately. The assessors were and are doing what he claimed was impossible. Pittsburgh and Scranton, which tax land values at double the rate of improvements, do not experience the assessment difficulty to which Ely refers, nor do the Australian and New Zealand cities which support themselves wholly by a tax on land values. Only the costs of land grading and other types of site development present a really difficult problem, but solutions exist. One good method is to spread land development expenses over a number of years and treat them as annual land value tax deductions, thus compensating the the land developer.

How did George answer the "taxation according to

ability to pay" argument? He maintained that all taxation was wrong and that the so-called single tax was a misnomer in that it was not really a tax at all. It was merely the collection of the rent from land by its rightful owner, society. To George, ordinary taxes were revenues to which the government was not morally entitled.

But when he used the word "tax" in the broader and more conventionl sense, George held that it was better to tax a special privilege like rent rather than a special ability like business acumen or inventiveness. Why fine a man by taxing his ability when by using it he cannot help but benefit society? A modern proponent of land value taxation might add that we should tax land values because it is a good tax, and if we still wish to "soak the rich," we could have other taxes for that purpose.[66]

[66] The income tax is not as much of a "soak-the-rich" tax as many people think. There are many loopholes in the income tax law and rich men can employ able accountants and lawyers to find them. Most large incomes are derived from capital gains, which are taxed at only 25 per cent. Income splitting among family members, a loose interpretation of business expenses, income from tax-exempt government bonds, deferred compensation plans, profit-sharing trusts, stock options, etc., are legal means of tax avoidance. In addition, it is well known that tax evasion is widespread at the medium and high income levels, whereas salaried employees must pay their full share and more of the tax load.

In 1955, 84 per cent of the income tax revenue was derived from the 20 per cent basic rate which all taxpayers pay, and only 16 per cent of the revenue was derived from the progressive rate (which ranges from 22 per cent to 91 per cent). How much more progressive (i.e., based on income) is the income tax compared to a national sales tax?

Census figures indicate that in 1955 the highest income-tenth received 29 per cent of the national personal income before federal income taxes and 27 per cent after. The highest income-fifth received 45 per cent before and 43 per cent after (see Gabriel Kolko, *Wealth and Power in America*, p. 34).

Since the more valuable land is owned almost entirely by rich people, a land value tax would fall much more upon them than upon the poor. In the light of the above statistics, there is a real possibility that the land value tax would be more progressive than the income tax!

Charles B. Spahr was another liberal economist who, like Ely, abjured socialism but favored the income tax and more government interference in the economy. Spahr never held an academic teaching post, but as an editor, author, and publicist, he was influential in many social reform movements. He criticized the single tax extensively in an article in the *Political Science Quarterly* of December 1892.

Many Georgists had maintained that since the growth of population increased land rents, these rents rightfully belong to the people at large. Spahr criticized this view, saying that some people create more land values than do others. A law-abiding citizen increases land values, but a criminal may actually decrease them. An industrious Anglo-Saxon, he wrote, would increase the value of land more than the usual immigrant from southeastern Europe. If the Georgists were to be consistent, then they should give more of the publicly collected land rent to the Anglo-Saxon than the new immigrant.[67] Spahr's argument was weakened by racism, but he put his finger on a weak spot in the Georgist ethical argument.

Later in his article, Spahr argued against the single tax on grounds that it would not provide sufficient revenue for the government. This was the first time for such a doubt to be expressed, though it was to recur as time passed. Generally, this charge came from left-of-center economists dedicated to an expensive welfare state and unhampered by ethical considerations concerning the source of government revenue. Later, practically all economists reached a similar conclusion. In the nineteenth century, conservative economists tended to oppose the single tax on the grounds that it would provide the government with too

[67] Charles B. Spahr, "Single Tax," *Political Science Quarterly*, Dec. 1891, p. 634.

much revenue, a viewpoint which virtually disappears after 1913.

Spahr further claimed that George's proposal would burden farmers more than any other economic group. He presented figures to bolster this position. Georgists of his day found other figures to prove exactly the reverse.[68]

Many poor people owned land, Spahr felt, and why should they be taxed? Income or inheritance taxes would be far more ideal. If the income tax should prove too radical for most people, he suggested a national 2 per cent property tax in its stead. The inheritance tax rate likewise would be set at 2 per cent.

Spahr's criticisms merit serious consideration. His doubts about the sufficiency of the land value tax revenue were well founded, as time and warfare eventually proved. However, this argument has less validity when the land value tax is considered not as a single tax but as one tax among many.

Would farmers suffer? A paucity of statistics prevents a definitive answer, although this much can be guessed: farmers with a large investment in improvements and machinery (the most efficient) would benefit, while those whose main investment is in land (usually the least efficient) would suffer, since man-made wealth would be untaxed and land rent would be more heavily taxed. In any event, if the land value tax were to prove a heavy burden on certain farmers, and if this were to be regarded as undesirable, there are other alternatives. For example, the tax might be applied only in urban areas, or farmers in the affected locality could receive special tax deductions. Unfortunately, most economists, including Spahr, thought of the single tax only on a national all-or-nothing basis.

[68] See Charles Fillebrown, "The Farmer and the Single Tax," a pamphlet.

What of the poor people who own land? Georgists replied that if such persons owned land, it would necessarily be land of slight value. Hence, they would be lightly taxed for the small privilege they possessed, while many other more onerous taxes would be abolished or reduced, with a net gain resulting.

Not all left-of-center economists were anti-George, by any means. John R. Commons, the well-known historian and economist, favored the income and inheritance taxes, for instance, but could still write in his textbook, *The Distribution of Wealth* (1893):[69]

If the size of fortunes is taken into account, it will be found that perhaps 95% of the total values represented by these millionaire fortunes is due to those investments classed as land values and natural monopolies, and to competitive industries aided by such monopolies.

Time mellowed his views, but Commons always remained a fairly consistent supporter of the land value taxation principle.

As a rule, George's *academic* supporters were almost as lukewarm in their enthusiasm as his academic opponents were vociferous. For instance, E. Benjamin Andrews, president of Brown University and an announced supporter of Henry George, in a speech before the American Social Science Association at Saratoga in 1890, asserted in his very first paragraph that "the proposition to lay the main tax on land impresses me as just, safe, accordant with the best canons of public finance, and in fact every way excellent."[70] He then spent the remainder of his speech in showing how dangerous such a tax could be. His listeners might easily have gotten the impression that Andrews opposed George completely.

Another example was David Starr Jordan. He co-

[69] John R. Commons, *The Distribution of Wealth*, p. 253.
[70] E. Benjamin Andrews, "The Single Tax Discussion," held at Saratoga, Sept. 5, 1890, *American Social Science Association*, p. 29.

authored a book in which he vigorously criticized the single tax, but near the end of the book appeared his statement, "that the least offensive form of taxation is through land value I am inclined to think true."[71] He was later quoted as saying, "the taxation of economic rent appears to me as a sound and just policy."[72]

Why did the public expression so frequently run one way and the nominal private endorsement the other? Perhaps it was because the single tax seemed like a one-shot gimmick, although the underlying principle (land value taxation) was regarded as practical and moderate. Perhaps there was a fear of losing one's job or possibly a promotion for espousing what at that time sounded like a radical cause. No doubt, the extreme enthusiasm bordering on fanaticism of some of George's adherents embarrassed his academic supporters. Professors hesitated to endorse George for fear that they would be classed with the emotional amateurs.

George's Treatment by the Historians

Historians of George's day hardly mentioned him at all. This is scarcely surprising when one reflects upon the matter, for nineteenth-century historians rarely wrote contemporary or recent history, and when they did, they concentrated on military and political events. If George had succeeded in any one of these fields, then he surely would have received some notice. Thus, the only reference to him in the histories of his day concerned the New York City mayoralty campaign of 1886. It was the closest he ever came to making political history.

For the contemporary historians George cuts an im-

[71] Dr. J. H. Stallard and David Starr Jordan, *The True Basis of Economy*, p. 126.

[72] Emil O. Jorgensen, *The Next Step Toward Real Democracy*. Chicago: *Chicago Single Tax Club*, 1920, p. 105. The source and date of this remark are not given.

portant figure only in the history of American thought. His great influence upon his own generation and on the progressive reformer of the generation following earn him an undeniable niche in that type of history. However, it was not until the 1940's that intellectual history became important, growing out of the literary-economic emphasis of the 1920's. And so, until the twenties, George received only sporadic mention by historians.

By 1897, American economics had developed sufficiently to attract at least one extensive paper titled "Tendencies in American Economic Thought." The author, an historian named Sidney Sherwood, stated that "the influence of Henry George has been much greater than professional economists are generally willing to admit, although it has been largely an educational rather than a strictly scientific influence. He has done more to popularize the science of political economy than any other economist. He has imparted to several of our young economists their first impulse toward the study."[73] This follows the observations of Taussig and Ely.

Sherwood went on to add that more than any other person George had stimulated the trend toward municipal control of public utilities and pointed out the folly of granting municipal franchises to private companies without adequate recompense. This was indeed part of George's general anti-monopoly program and it was a big issue in those days. George performed a great service to society, said Sherwood, by advocating public ownership of public values. He concluded by giving land value taxation a mildly favorable review.

Not long before this, Frederick Jackson Turner had

[73] Sidney Sherwood, "Tendencies in American Economic Thought," *Johns Hopkins Studies in History and Political Science*, p. 607.

published his famous frontier thesis, which might be considered the opening salvo in American intellectual history. Yet Turner was anticipated in his main idea by Henry George in *Progress and Poverty*. On page 390 of this work one reads:

The general intelligence, the general comfort, the active invention, the power of adaptation and assimilation, the free independent spirit, the energy and hopefulness that have marked our people, are not causes, but results—they have sprung from unfenced land. This public domain has been the transmuting force which has turned the thriftless, unambitious European peasant into the self-reliant Western farmer; it has given a consciousness of freedom even to the dweller in crowded cities, and has been a well-spring of hope even to those who have never thought of taking refuge upon it. The child of the people, as he grows to manhood in Europe, finds all the best seats at the banquet marked "taken," and must struggle with his fellows for the crumbs that fall, without one chance in a thousand of forcing or sneaking his way to a seat. In America, whatever his condition, there has always been the consciousness that the public domain lay behind him; and the knowledge of this fact, acting and reacting, has penetrated our whole national life, giving to it generosity and independence, elasticity and ambition. All that we are proud of in the American character; all that makes our conditions and institutions better than those of older countries, we may trace to the fact that land has been cheap in the United States, because new soil has been open to the emigrant.

George went on to predict that the open frontier would end before the turn of the century, and with its ending would come a host of social evils if our land tenure system were not improved.

Here was the frontier thesis of Turner right down to the key safety valve idea. Even though submerged in the "evils of land ownership" argument, one could find it repeated again and again in single tax literature. It could hardly have failed to attract Turner's attention, and indeed, recent historical scholarship has put the matter beyond speculation. Turner's biographer, Dr. Fulmer Mood of the University of Texas, discovered that Turner owned a copy of *Progress and Poverty* and that the young historian had read and marked the book in 1888-9 while a graduate student at Johns Hopkins; in the same year Turner took part in a seminar discussion of the book.[74]

So it might be said that as George passed on the idea of marginalism to John Bates Clark, the seminal figure in American economics of the early twentieth century, so did he present the germ of the frontier thesis to Frederick Jackson Turner, the seminal figure in early twentieth-century American history.

[74] Charles A. Barker, *Henry George*, p. 301.

2

HENRY GEORGE IN THE PROGRESSIVE ERA, 1897-1916

THE YEAR 1897 FOUND HENRY GEORGE AGAIN INVOLVED IN A New York City mayoralty campaign. He took this step not so much to gain political office—one wonders what he would have hoped to accomplish as mayor—as to gain a public forum for the wider discussion of the single tax. But two weeks before election time, after furious campaigning, he died, a martyr to the cause for which he had labored so long. Since the single tax was not generally accepted by Americans, the magnificent public funeral he received, the like of which had scarcely been seen in this country since Abraham Lincoln's death, would indicate that in the public mind Henry George was regarded not only as the father of the single tax but as an elder statesman, a great moralist and a herald of the Progressive reform era just then surging into existence.

George's death accelerated changes that had been taking place in the Georgist movement ever since 1890. When he was writing *Progress and Poverty* in 1879, it was the evil character of private landownership that excited him most, even more than the details of his remedy. If only men had equal access to God's gift of land, then would the Kingdom

77

of Heaven on earth be possible. The coming of the reign of justice would bring the elimination of poverty. This was his message during the 1880's, but after 1887, when he entered politics and began establishing organizations to propagate his ideals, he gave increasing emphasis to the means by which the great reform was to be accomplished, namely the single tax. After his death, this trend was accelerated because few of his followers could castigate the evils of landownership or verbally slay the dragon of poverty as effectively as could he. Moreover, as single taxers gradually became involved in political campaigns for the single tax—in Delaware, Colorado, Oregon, California and elsewhere—they naturally found it necessary to concentrate on concrete method rather than abstract philosophy. Voters are interested in exactly how a reform proposal is to be applied and what its immediate effects seem likely to be, rather than in ethical concepts or possible long-run benefits. The up-and-coming atmosphere of pragmatism in the new century also furthered this trend of emphasizing the practical over the speculative considerations.

How much progress was the single tax actually making in the early years of the twentieth century? There was much public discussion, many ventures into politics, much hope, but little or no actual accomplishment. Writing in a 1902 issue of the magazine *Independent,* Joseph Dana Miller, editor of *The Single Tax Review,* was fairly optimistic about the progress of his movement, saying that single-taxers were "less uncompromising" than formerly, that they had made good progress in educating the public about their aims and methods, and that all this would obviously pay off in the near future. Nevertheless, Miller could not point to any state or locality in the U.S. which had adopted the land value tax.

In 1914, Charles H. Ingersoll, writing in *Survey* maga-

zine on the same subject, could point to real accomplish-
ments only in other countries such as England, Germany,
Denmark, Canada and especially Australia and New Zealand. The only single tax progress he could claim in this
country was the fact that over 400,000 people had cast
votes for single tax measures in various states (none of
which passed, however), and that many prominent people
and even some magazines were in favor of the idea. Yet the
tone of his article was clearly optimistic, and he was not
alone in feeling that the single tax day was yet to come.
Even many opponents seem to have accepted the possibility
that the movement would eventually make some sort of
progress somewhere, some time. Yet the Georgist leaders,
always on the verge of success, never quite could enter the
promised land.

George's death did not improve the poor relations that
existed between the single taxers and the professors. As
Miller phrased it, single taxers progressed "not always
with perfect tact, but with high sincerity and splendid
zeal."[1] Charles Fillebrown, a Boston businessman and the
leader of the moderates in the Georgist movement, even
wrote a pamphlet about the matter in 1914, and his explanation deserves attention:[2]

Unquestionably there has been among the professional economists a tendency not so much to attack as perhaps to ignore
the Single Taxers. Among the various causes for this attitude
one might be assigned as a certain pronounced air of bump-
tiousness often observable on the part of single tax advocates.
. . . Jealous for their champion and sharing his sensitiveness to
the indifference of the professors, Single Taxers have allowed
themselves even in scattered times and places to generate and
foster a spirit of animosity sufficient to keep the opposing lines
well defined.

[1] Joseph D. Miller, "Is the Single Tax Movement Making Progress?" *Independent,* 1902, v. 54, p. 2194.
[2] C. B. Fillebrown, "Henry George and the Economists," a pamphlet, p. 5.

Fillebrown then went on to state that like all reformers, single-taxers were militant, although he personally believed that "militancy is on the wane. . . . Many war phases of a few centuries ago are extinct today [sic]."[3] And then:[4]

It would be interesting to know if there be any considerable number of the many public lecturers and speakers for the Single Tax who have not at some time spoken slightingly of an economist or of his profession? It would be interesting to know what Single Tax organs have not frequently or infrequently spoken disparagingly of the professor of political economy?

Few would wish to dispute Fillebrown's view that such an attitude was certain to antagonize rather than to persuade or convert.

Soon after George's death, a new period in American history was ushered in—the Progressive Era. After forty years of intensive industrialization of the country, the American people had slowly begun to realize that *laissez faire* might not be adequate to protect the ideal of equal opportunity which is the cornerstone of democracy. Henry George, Henry Demarest Lloyd, Edward Bellamy, the muckrakers and others had awakened America's social conscience, and soon reform was to follow reform.

The connection between George and the era that followed him is quite direct. We have seen much writing about how greatly Henry George and *Progress and Poverty* influenced many Progressive leaders in their thinking about social problems, even if only a few became out-and-out single taxers. But it is also revealing to see how closely the Progressive reforms reflected proposals or attitudes that George had set forth a generation before.

For example, there was the idealization of the Jeffersonian ideals, and the feeling that it was possible to return to the unspoiled past despite industrialization. Jefferson had been a life-long hero, and George even named his last

[3] *Ibid.*
[4] *Ibid.*, p. 6.

political party after the great Virginian. Again, there was the insistence that the people should rule the government directly, and that government should be freed from boss rule. George had fought the bosses in 1886 and 1897 and at other times too, and he had been instrumental in bringing the Australian secret ballot to this country. His followers were often in the forefront of direct democracy campaigns. William S. U'Ren had hoped to bring the single tax to Oregon via the referendum and initiative. Aid to the underprivileged was an important facet of the Progressive idea, and it had been an important theme of Henry George. He always envisioned the single tax as supporting the kind of government that would do many of the things municipal governments began to do during the Progressive Era. Many conservationists, as we will see, took their basic philosophy that society had certain transcendent rights as to land use from *Progress and Poverty*. Lower tariffs, an interest of many Progressives, was a cause second only to land value taxation with Henry George. The government regulation of utilities and natural monopolies—Progressive reforms both—was Henry George's third great cause after land value taxation and free trade.

Thus, we see that many of the important Progressive reforms drew support from *Progress and Poverty* or George's later works. All except one: instead of adopting the land value tax, the Progressives adopted the income tax. Of course, there were many other sources for Progressivism in addition to George, such as the Greenbackers, Mugwumps, Populists, muckrakers, pragmatists, etc.

The Views of Seligman and Other Public Finance Economists

One of the newer trends in economics during the 1890's was the development of specialization. Economists became experts in such special areas as finance, transportation, foreign trade and public finance. Land value taxation falls within the confines of this latter field of study, and although the opinions of all economists after 1900 are important in matters of taxation, naturally the opinions that carried the greatest weight were those of the public finance economists. It was from their college courses that city managers and administrators got their tax ideas. It was these professors who were called upon to act as advisers to government tax commissions. But unfortunately for George, the land value tax got even less support from public finance economists than from economists at large.

One of the foremost experts in public finance in America for almost fifty years was Edwin R. A. Seligman, the same person who had taken the lead in opposing George at Saratoga in 1890. Seligman's output of books, articles and speeches was truly remarkable, and he did not spare himself in opposing George's proposal at every turn. His criticisms were more comprehensive and incisive than any offered by his contemporaries, and they demand detailed consideration. One finds them conveniently summarized in his well-known *Essays in Taxation*. First came the criticisms of George's ethical system. Wrote Seligman:[5]

the Single Tax theory of property is the labor theory—the theory that individual human labor constitutes the only clear title to property. . . . Yet individual labor, it may be said, has never by itself produced anything in civilized society. Take, for example, the workman fashioning a chair. The wood has not been produced by him; it is the gift of nature. The tools that he uses are the results of the contributions of others; the house in which he works, the clothes he wears, the food he eats (all of which are necessary in civilized society to the making of a chair), are the result of the contributions of the community. His safety from robbery and pillage—nay, his very existence— is dependent on the ceaseless co-operation of the society about

[5] Edwin R. A. Seligman, *Essays in Taxation*, Ch. 3, "The Single Tax," as reprinted in Edna Bullock, *Selected Articles on the Single Tax*, p. 141.

him. How can it be said, in the face of all this that his own individual labor wholly creates anything? . . . Nothing is wholly the result of unaided individual labor. No one has a right to say: This belongs absolutely and completely to me, because I alone have produced it. Society, from this point of view, holds a mortgage on everything that is produced.

In other words, Seligman believed that the labor theory of property was self-contradictory and therefore invalid, because while it purported to justify the individual ownership of producible goods, it could also justify their ownership by society.

It is possible to take issue with Seligman's arguments. Wood is not a gift of nature. A wild tree might be, but wood is a product of human labor. Someone, probably many people, took the trouble to cultivate a tree, cut it down, sawmill it, and transport the cut wood to the chairmaker. The wood is indeed the product of human labor; if not the chairmarker's, then of others who voluntarily transferred their just title to the chairmaker.

As far as his tools, house, clothing, food and safety are concerned, the chairmaker satisfies his obligations to the society that provided him with these things by paying for them. Should he pay twice, once by reimbursing the original owners of these goods and services and then again by turning over a share, perhaps the whole share, of his own chairmaking income? It would seem that one payment to society and its members should be morally and practically sufficient.

Seligman had also advanced the time-honored proposition that since land is bought with the fruits of human labor, the labor theory of property can justify the private ownership of land. But one wonders how this can be, since land is scarcely producible by human labor. Exchange or purchase cannot make an unjust title just; after all, one might buy stolen property or a slave and yet a rightful title would not be acquired by such purchase.

While it is true that "nothing is wholly the result of unaided individual labor," it is possible to separate each individual's contribution from the social total. A competitive wage market does this very thing. It determines the demand for an individual's labor, hence the price which he can charge for his labor, i.e., his wages. If the market is truly competitive, it will distribute the product fairly according to the principle of "to each the fruits of his labor." It is the government's job to see that the wage market be truly competitive, with neither employers nor employees having special privileges.

Seligman continued his attack on George by justifying non-land value taxation on the grounds that the individual receives benefits for the taxes he pays. This may be so, a Georgist would respond, but each individual does not necessarily use or want those benefits in direct proportion to the taxes he pays. Furthermore, he would point out, ordinary taxation is not just justified because the element of force is involved. Force makes such taxation immoral. Individual rights are thus violated and individual liberty is restricted. Would it be just for an automobile salesman to approach us with gun in hand and say: "Let me have $3,000. Here is a fine new car worth just that price in the open market. You can't complain. You're getting equal value for the money you are parting with."

Seligman had his own view as to what constituted the proper justification of private property. It was the pragmatic social utility theory, which held that private property was justifiable only insofar as it benefited society. This idea did not originate with Seligman, but he was one of its most effective advocates. The social utility theory was commonly accepted in his day and certainly in ours.

This theory, as it is usually stated, is somewhat vague because different people have different standards by which they measure benefit to society. Some people emphasize material welfare, others social peace, others liberty, equality of opportunity, security of vested interests, and so on. "Social utility" can be a catch-all phrase, a slogan, which hides our real values. George, for instance, measured social utility by the degree of social justice that exists, and by social justice he meant respect for natural rights. He argued that all social benefits such as those just mentioned would result from the single tax.

It would seem that the labor theory of property provides a sound long-term goal consistent with the needs of society. To each the fruits of his labor: if society moves in this general direction, it will indeed be making social progress. Thus, there may be no real difference between the social utility and labor theories of property, except in the matter of emphasis. The labor theory provides the distant goal, and the social utility theory, considering as it does the political realities, emphasizes the means by which that goal may be achieved.

Seligman naturally addressed himself to the practical as well as to the moral aspects of the single tax. He objected to the single tax on the grounds that social taxes such as those on opium, oleomargarine ("to ensure the purity of butter"), and liquor would be impossible. He also criticized it because it was inelastic, that is, the amount of the land rent could not be changed to meet the increases and decreases the government's budgetary needs might require. These, of course, are valid objections against the land value tax as a single tax, but not if it were one tax among many.

Seligman believed that farmers would suffer under the single tax and presented statistics to prove that the tax burden on farmers would be increased. This criticism has often been voiced by other academic critics. Fillebrown and Hirsch, both single taxers, offered statistics to prove that the reverse was true. Today, it would seem that farmers who have a heavy investment in buildings, improvements, equipment and livestock would benefit from a land value tax (and they are in the majority), while those farmers whose chief investment is in land would be paying more taxes. In the first category would be dairy and corn farmers, and in the second category would be certain truck and fruit farmers. Thus, with the accelerating trend of farm mechanization, fewer and fewer farmers would be adversely affected by a tax on land values. In any case, it is possible to apply the land value tax only in cities, where the main land values are.

In our time, we are suffering from a surfeit of farm produce, and no doubt of farmers as well. The efficient farmer with his heavy investment in capital equipment would certainly benefit by a shift of taxation from improvements to land; the inefficient might not, but perhaps he should be persuaded by every means, including that of taxation, to switch to more economically desirable endeavors. On the other hand, if farming is to be regarded as a sacred occupation and farmers as the most American of Americans, then special exemptions on lands used for argricultural purposes would be possible, as under our present tax laws.

Supporters of the land value tax aver that it would actually help the farmers solve two of their foremost problems: first, the bloated mortgage burden on farmland (from an economic point of view banks own almost as much farmland as do farmers), and second, the tremendous investment required by young farmers who would like to start their own farms. The land value tax would solve these problems by gradually reducing land prices to almost zero, thus necessitating a smaller investment and a smaller mortgage.

Seligman had many doubts as to whether the land value tax could actually be applied. Land is graded before being built upon, he said, and this cost adds to and is inseparable from the value of the land. However, those parts of the world which have successfully applied the tax over a long period of years—Australia, New Zealand, and the city of Pittsburgh—have not found it insuperably difficult to separate land and improvement value. For example, where the grading cost is known, its cost can be spread over the expected life of the building as a deduction from the land value tax.

Another of Seligman's objections was that the more land values are taxed, the smaller is the selling price of land. If the selling price decreases, the percentage taken by the land value tax will decrease, and so less value will be obtained. "Does it not seem, then, to be a very questionable scheme to endeavor to raise more revenue by narrowing the base of taxation?"[6]

This is a real difficulty which can, however, be overcome. As the assessment falls, the government can raise the tax rate again in order to collect the land rent. If the land value eventually gets too small to be accurately assessed and taxed, then the local government can do what Canberra, Australia does, which is to assess on the annual rent rather than on the selling value and tax that.

Seligman wrote that in his time business loans were granted to builders by the banks in proportion to the value of the land. If a heavier land value tax reduces the selling value of the land, then fewer loans would be granted by the

[6] Edwin R. A. Seligman, "Halving the Tax Rate on Buildings: Pro and Con," *Survey*, 31:697-702, March 7, 1914, as reprinted in Edna Bullock, *Selected Articles on the Single Tax*, p. 158.

banks and fewer buildings would be built. However, it is
conceivable that banks could adjust their lending to any
new tax system. They could base their loans on the value of
improvements, for instance.

Seligman continued: "There is no fund floating about
in the air which can be brought to earth simply by the
imposition of the Single Tax; the amounts to be laid out in
houses must be taken from the capital now invested in
some other form of productive enterprise."[7] This displayed
the rather static view of economics that was commonly held
by economists of Seligman's day, but it overlooked the
probability that if our tax system were remade so as to
increase incentive, increased production would surely follow. Under such conditions, an increase in the money
supply would provide the greater amount of needed
capital, while increased production would prevent an inflation. As long as the land value tax is beneficial for real
estate, banks with the aid of government will always find
ways to increase their loans to real estate developers.

Seligman might also have given consideration to the
fact that builders would have more money to construct
buildings if they did not have to sink part of their funds
into the purchase of land. This they would not have to do
under the single tax since the price of land under such a
system would approach zero. To paraphrase Seligman,
then, the amounts to be laid out in houses will be taken
from the capital now invested in land.

In an article written a few years later Seligman contradicted himself by stating that the imposition of a land
value tax would cause a building boom which would last
until a new equilibrium between housing and population

[7] Edwin R. A. Seligman, *Essays in Taxation*, Ch. 3, "The Single
Tax," as reprinted in Edna Bullock, *Selected Articles on the Single
Tax*, p. 158.

will have been reached.[8] It is interesting to note that the advocates of the land value tax promise even more than this. If the government is collecting the full rent from land, then the land must *constantly* be put to its most efficient use, because the improvement must at least pay for the tax on the land and yield a reasonable profit besides, which is not the case if there were no land value tax. Thus, there would be a constant pressure to prevent buildings from becoming slums.

Seligman had still more criticisms. One of the benefits claimed for the land value tax is that by reducing the tax on buildings, rent to the tenants would be decreased. Seligman said no, the building tax is not always passed on to the tenant in an economy where many things are taxed. Here was a new view, not commonly shared by the economics profession, and in any case Seligman later contradicted himself by saying that the present real estate tax at least makes "the big banks, the big trust companies, the big lawyers, the big financial and business enterprises of all kinds" pay the expenses of government because the tax is being shifted to them as tenants of downtown skyscrapers, whereas the land value tax would not be felt by them.[9] Both views could hardly be true at one and the same time.

Seligman also took issue with the claims of land value tax advocates that their measure would relieve urban congestion, arguing instead that it would cause builders to utilize land plots more intensively by building taller structures.[10] This quite creditable criticism was rebutted by

[8] Edwin R. A. Seligman, "Halving the Tax Rate on Buildings: Pro and Con," *Survey*, 31:697-702, March 7, 1914, as reprinted in Edna Bullock, *Selected Articles on the Single Tax*, p. 164.

[9] Edna Bullock, *Selected Articles on the Single Tax*, p. 158 (Seligman, *Essays* . . .), p. 170 (Seligman, "Halving the Tax Rate . . .").

[10] Edwin R. A. Seligman, "Halving the Tax Rate on Buildings: Pro and Con," *Survey*, 31:697-702, March 7, 1914, as reprinted in Edna Bullock, *Selected Articles on the Single Tax*, pp. 167-68.

Georgists on four counts. In the first place, they suggested that a land value tax would force into greater use much unused or partially used land, making congestion unnecessary. Secondly, a land value tax does not necessitate the erection of an Empire State Building on every plot of land. It requires only an improvement that would pay the tax and provide a reasonable profit in addition. Thirdly, if the problem still persisted, then zoning regulations could be employed. Fourthly, the problem seems not to have arisen in those communities which already tax land values rather than buildings.

Basically, Seligman objected to the land value tax because it was not based on the "ability to pay" principle. He felt that the tax would fall heavily upon the homeowner, increasing his tax burden. He pointed out that a poor man's cottage would escape taxation but so would his rich next-door neighbor whose mansion would also be untaxed. Rich man and poor alike would be paying the same tax on their land, a situation which Seligman and many other Progressives regarded as being inequitable.

There is no doubt that the land value tax benefits the landowner who utilizes his land most fully. This is desirable, say the followers of Henry George. If the government wishes to tax the rich, it can always levy other types of taxes, perhaps an income tax. As for homeowners, they would evidently be benefited by land value taxation, if we are to believe R. M. Haig's study in 1915 and such recent investigations as the Lehigh University study of land value taxation in Bethlehem, Pennsylvania.[11] That homeowners benefit is also indicated by actual experience

[11] For the Haig study, see A. N. Young, *The Single Tax Movement in the United States,* p. 226, and the report on it which follows later in this chapter. For the Lehigh University study, see Eli Schwartz and James E. Wert, "An Analysis of the Potential Effects of a Movement Toward a Land Value Based Property Tax," a pamphlet.

with land value taxation in Australia and New Zealand.

Seligman also averred that the hardest hit of all home-owners would be those who with the progress of time found that the city had moved their way, thus increasing the value of their land. Under land value taxation they would have to pay higher taxes than they could afford. Such homeowners would be forced to move at great financial sacrifice because their land would have lost all selling value and so would their houses—for the houses generally are not removable and the next purchasers, intending to tear them down and perhaps build an apartment house or commercial structure, would be unwilling to pay much if anything for these improvements.

Here Seligman had struck upon a valid objection. How-ever, this unfortunate situation might be remedied by requiring the new purchaser of a piece of real estate to pay the previous owner at least the appraised value of his im-provement. In this way, a homeowner engulfed by the rising tide of progress could escape without losing the investment in his improvement. If houses were easily mov-able, then such a legal provision as this would be unneces-sary, but as this is not the case, land value tax advocates would have to recognize that homeowners are entitled to protection from the unforeseeable whims of the future. The homeowner might also be protected by appropriate zoning regulations.

Surprisingly, despite his many objections to the land value tax, there were times when Seligman could find some sympathy with single taxers. He felt that the single taxers had performed a social service by their opposition to the personal property tax which he, too, opposed. Even more, in March 1915 he wrote that heavier taxes on urban land "may be entirely legitimate from the social, rather than

the individual, point of view."[12] By this he meant that even
if the moral arguments for the land value tax based on the
natural rights of the individual were specious, the tax
might still be justified on the pragmatic premise that the
needs of society would be well served by it.

Before leaving Seligman, it is interesting to compare his
approach to that of Francis A. Walker in an earlier period.
Walker had attacked George's views on the causes of depressions and poverty, i.e., that rent absorbed the benefits
of progress, especially through land speculation. Seligman
dealt more with the single tax as a possible means of
municipal reform, not as a remedy for such all-encom-
passing economic evils as depressions and poverty but as a
possible new approach to the problems of municipal land
planning, taxation and housing. As Walker was typical of
the general approach to George in the 1880's, so did Seligman personify the changing emphases of the early twentieth century.

Seligman was not alone in establishing public finance
as a recognized branch of economics. There was Carl
Plehn, for instance, a professor at the University of California, a president of the American Economic Association,
and popular textbook writer in the field. During the 1890's
he opposed the single tax bitterly although his opposition
mellowed as the years went by.

In his principal textbook (1900), he discussed George's
proposal under the heading of "The Dream of a Single
Tax." On page 85 he wrote that "such a tax could probably
be administered and could be made to yield ample
revenue."[13] Yet on page 88 he stated that he doubted that
the scheme was administratively feasible, and on page 86

[12] Edwin R. A. Seligman, "Newer Tendencies in American Taxation," *Annals of the American Academy*, March 1915, v. 58, p. 5.
[13] Carl Plehn, *Introduction to Public Finance*. Chicago: A. C.
McClurg, 1915, p. 85.

HENRY GEORGE IN THE PROGRESSIVE ERA, 1897-1916   93

he doubted that it would yield sufficient revenue for government needs.

In the last analysis, Plehn's objections to George were based on a moral judgment: the landowner should not be taxed to the exclusion of others.

Charles Bullock, Professor of Political Economy at Harvard, was also prominent in the field of public finance. In one of his textbooks (1900), he considered Henry George in a chapter with the rather misleading title of "Land Nationalization."[14] He offered little in the way of new ideas not already encountered in this study and leaned heavily on Walker's approach. Bullock charged that George's scheme meant confiscation of private property in land but apparently contradicted himself by later writing that land rent is an unearned increment.[15] He conceded that a tax on the future increment in land values would be wise because the community would collect what municipal growth creates—land values—and it would reduce the pressure of taxes upon business enterprises. "It would, moreover, be in line with some of the existing tendencies in municipal finance."[16] Many other economists of the 1900-1920 period observed that the future increment tax was growing in popularity, although it was never to be employed in this country. John Stuart Mill originated the idea of this tax, but George's agitation had made it mildly popular.

Henry C. Adams, Professor of Political Economy and Finance at the University of Michigan, was another bitter opponent of the single tax. In his principal textbook he claimed that the single tax "may be classed as a proposition

[14] Charles J. Bullock, *Introduction to the Study of Economics*. Boston: Silver, Burdette, 1900 (1897), p. 458.
[15] *Ibid.*, p. 240.
[16] Charles J. Bullock, *The Elements of Economics*. Boston: Silver, Burdette, 1913 (1905), p. 329.

to replace the system of free holdings by the tenant system,"[17] a statement sure to mislead his readers. Without any qualification he equated the single tax with state proprietorship of the land,[18] and also stated that "its acceptance would be the reversal of eight centuries of the history of the English-speaking people."[19]

Among his numerous objections, many of which have already been considered elsewhere in this study, he stated that the single tax would not affect other unearned increment coming from capital and natural monopolies, securities speculation, and inheritance. George for the most part had never objected to inheritance since he felt that if a man owns wealth, he has the right to give it to anyone he wishes. He did not consider securities speculation socially harmful, and as far as monopolies were concerned, he was in the forefront in arousing the public to an awareness of the monopoly evil. The establishment of a single tax did not preclude a fight against monopolies.

With the exception of Seligman and one or two others, the public finance writers seem to have been a very conservative group, so much so that most of them opposed the income tax with considerable vigor until after it was adopted. Few were more conservative, however, than Winthrop M. Daniels, author of a textbook entitled *Public Finance,* who not only opposed the single tax on the grounds of confiscation, but was consistent in opposing the regulation of natural monopolies because confiscation of property rights was involved here also. If we limit the return on a utility's investment, he reasoned, then many stockholders would suffer.[20]

[17] Henry C. Adams, *Science of Finance.* New York: Henry Holt, 1892, p. 253.
[18] *Ibid.,* p. 414.
[19] *Ibid.,* p. 254.
[20] Winthrop Daniels, *Public Finance,* p. 85.

George and the Economists

Let us now move to the field of general economics, which at the turn of the century was much influenced by the disconcerting theories of that man from another planet, Thorstein Veblen.

Veblen was born in 1857 on the frontier, one of twelve children of Norwegian immigrant parents. From the first he was regarded as odd and different even by his own mother and especially by his contemporaries. When his family moved to a new farm in Minnesota, he was involved in a fist fight on his first Sunday in the new community.

Not only was Veblen different from his neighbors within the community, but his community set itself apart from the rest of America. His family, no matter how often it moved, lived always in Norwegian neighborhoods where only Norwegian was spoken and only Norwegian customs prevailed. In fact, Veblen learned English as a foreign tongue. The Norwegian community was regarded by native-born Americans as rank foreigners, and thus the young Veblen was doubly alienated from the American culture and economy he was to analyze in later life. This alienation gave him breadth of perspective which other more Americanized economists lacked.

It was not until he was seventeen that Veblen left the tight little life of the "Norwegian frontier" to attend Carleton College, an institution more identified with the American mainstream. *Progress and Poverty* appeared while he was a student there and he let it be known that he supported it. Perhaps his support was more emotional than intellectual, for his teachers opposed the book with great vigor, always a challenge to the perverse Veblen. Whatever his early enthusiasm may have been, later on the single tax incurred his scornful criticism.

Perhaps only a man so isolated from the world he lived in could possess sufficient perspective to detect the reality beneath the accepted platitudes and rationalizations of his day. Veblen's main contribution to economic thought was that social custom influenced our economic behavior, a fact generally overlooked by the classical economists. He claimed that many of our customs conflict with economic efficiency. Profit is not the true measure of efficiency, he said, because as often as not the man who makes the most money is frequently the one who restricts production, eliminates competition, decreases efficiency, and adulterates the product.

Thus, Veblen maintained that the social institution we call capitalism is in large measure irrational. He preferred the feudal virtues of ferocity, self-seeking, clannishness and a free resort to force and fraud. Capitalism, he felt, thwarts the "instinct of workmanship" with its antisocial values of "conspicuous waste" and "conspicuous consumption," to use Veblen's own well-known phrases (moderns might add "planned obsolescence"). He urged that economists study the workings of social institutions at least as much as they study the workings of that abstraction called the "economic man." The closest Veblen ever came to proposing solutions to the problems he analyzed was his belief that the engineers and technologists should be allowed to run the economy unhampered by the businessmen and financiers. Then we would really have industrial efficiency. The technocrats who enjoyed a brief vogue during the 1930's based their theories largely on the Veblenian approach.

With such a philosophy, Veblen could hardly be expected to maintain his early advocacy of *Progress and Poverty*, a book steeped in classical economics. In his own *Theory of Business Enterprise* (1904), he stated that the middle class makes excursions into "pragmatic romance, such as Social Settlements, Clean Politics, Single Tax, Arts and Crafts," which touch only symptoms and are therefore a waste of time and effort.[21]

His criticism of the moral position of the single tax in an article written in 1908 is more serious, namely that the concept of the unearned increment should be applied not only to land but to capital goods in general. All productivity is the outcome of the community's age-long experience, and hence the community has a valid claim not only to land but also to capital.

This is an interesting argument; it was first advanced in America by Edward Bellamy and is not unlike similar sentiments that were expressed by Seligman. Opponents argued that the community's age-long experience is a fund which belongs equally to all, to use or not to use as each person sees fit. Those who make great use of it are entitled to a greater reward than those who are less industrious or ingenious; men who make no use of this fund are not entitled to any reward because they have not benefited society in any way. For the discovery of the New World we credit Columbus because he actually undertook an expedition, not the thousands of other mariners of his time who had available to them the same age-long experience of the community. Is it right to give to the laggards part or all of what skilled workmen have produced on the grounds that all citizens have had available to them the opportunity provided by the community's age-long experience? The community receives its reward for this fund because to the extent that each of its members makes use of the fund, to that extent do they render service to the community. An efficient carpenter benefits society more than his less

[21] Joseph Dorfman, *Thorstein Veblen and His America*, p. 233.

efficient competitor. Society is benefited without laying claim to the fruits of individual labor.

Although Veblen altered the course of the mainstream of American economic thought, during the 1897-1916 period the citadels of economics remained under the control of the more orthodox classical or neo-classical theoreticians. Professors Frank Fetter of Princeton and Henry R. Seager of Columbia are more closely identified with this dominant group and are of interest because their writings on George summarize practically all the principal criticisms of their day, namely:

   a. The social utility theory is superior to the natural rights doctrine,

   b. Land and improvements are difficult to assess separately,

   c. Private ownership of land is inviolable,

   d. Poverty does not necessarily go hand in hand with progress,

   e. Land rent does not absorb the benefits of material progress,

   f. Land rent might be inadequate for government needs,

   g. Land value taxation means confiscation.

   h. The single tax rests upon faith rather than reason,

   i. The single tax is inelastic.

All of these arguments, in one form or another, have been considered in earlier pages. Both Fetter and Seager were convinced that the single tax agitation was performing some social service, and perhaps the words of Fetter best summarize the consensus of most economists of the time:[22]

While the single tax plan is defective in principle, its wide discussion has served to direct attention toward the need of reform in the taxation of land. Some proposals looking toward

[22] Frank Fetter, *Economics*, p. 297.

this end are widely favored by opponents as well as by advocates of the single tax. Such are the following:

(a) The abandonment of the taxation of mortgages.
(b) A more correct assessment, in accordance with the present laws, of lots and lands held for speculative purposes, which in usual practice are now greatly under-assessed.
(c) More adequate special franchise taxation upon corporations for special privileges in the public highways.
(d) Exemption, in value equal to the costs, of improvements on land, such as buildings, drains, fences, and fertilizers, for a limited time after they are made, perhaps five years.
(e) The separate assessment of urban lands used as mere building sites and of the buildings on them.
(f) Taxation of the increase (increment) of urban land values, periodically or on the occasion of transfer of ownership.

By 1914, public discussion of the single tax had reached something of a climax, and *The Atlantic Monthly* ran a debate between F. W. Garrison, a lawyer and grandson of the abolitionist (pro) and Alvin Saunders Johnson, an economics professor at Cornell (con). It is not easy to imagine such a debate in the *Atlantic* of today.

At one point in his article, Johnson stated that the land value tax would discourage construction because it would do away with the incentive afforded by the unearned increment. However, in the next page we read that the land value tax would cause over-intensive use of the land, with higher buildings covering more of the urban area and a housing boom far exceeding the demand for housing space.[23]

Johnson showed some confusion as to the application of the land value tax when he wrote that the time might eventually come when the state would "become the universal landlord, provided that it has evolved to the point where it can manage so colossal a landed estate more efficiently than can private landowners."[24] The land value tax involves no such radical change.

[23] Alvin S. Johnson, "The Case Against the Single Tax," *Atlantic Monthly*, January 1914, pp. 35, 36.
[24] *Ibid.*, p. 36.

Johnson was worried about what the land value tax would do to the farmers and the middle class: "Transform our four million rude farmers into tenants of the state; despoil an equal number of our middle class townsmen of their one solid possession, and the expropriation of the remaining private owners of property will be easily accomplished. Despite the sentimental antipathies of their respective adherents, then, the Single Tax and Socialism are closely related. Their relation is that of means and end."[25]

Although there generally was more criticism than commendation expressed by the economists of the early twentieth century, one should not overlook the latter. The single tax got little or no support from academic ranks, but many professors endorsed the land value tax as one tax among many. Yet support was reticent and cautious. Take Irving Fisher as a case in point. Even though he favored heavier taxation on land values than on improvements, in his textbook *Elementary Principles of Economics* he did not mention the subject except for a one-sentence reference to the " 'single tax' propaganda."[26]

During this period, Professor Herbert J. Davenport of Missouri and Cornell Universities was the chief academic defender of Henry George and his ideas. Because he had academic degrees from rather unorthodox educational institutions, he found it difficult to find a desirable professorship. It is easy to speculate that his unorthodox early career conditioned him to be sympathetic to the academically unorthodox views of Henry George.

This sympathy, however, was not particularly evident in a high school text he wrote prior to becoming a college

[25] *Ibid.*

[26] Harry Gunnison Brown, *Significant Paragraphs from Progress and Poverty,* p. 77, and Irving Fisher, *Elementary Principles of Economics,* p. 413.

professor. He was disturbed by the confiscation aspect of George's proposal, writing that "society would possibly have done well in reserving these [land] values to itself had it started early enough. It would probably now do well, if it is practicable, to take steps to secure to itself any future increment in land value, and particularly the increases which take place in urban lands (city lots); but wholesale appropriation of accrued values is wholesale robbery."[27]

By 1910, however, when Davenport wrote an article for the *Quarterly Journal of Economics* entitled "The Single Tax and the English Budget," the confiscatory aspect of the land value tax no longer seemed to interest him particularly. It had now become more important to attack monopoly and privilege wherever it might exist. The change in his thinking probably reflected the shift in the general climate of opinion, which by 1910 was more liberal and much affected by the muckraker exposures. Now he poked fun at the argument that it was unfair for the single taxers to oppose only one unearned increment and let other forms go scot-free. People who argue this way, Davenport sarcastically commented, to be consistent must object to interference with highway robbery while burglary so obtrusively flourishes.

Later in the same article he expressed his view as to why the single tax received the treatment it did at the hands of economists:[28]

It may be said with approximate accuracy that the economists have never seriously attacked the theoretical validity of the single tax program. In the main, in fact, they have come nearer to ignoring than condemning. They have not been interested; or they have regarded its application of dubious practicability,

[27] Herbert J. Davenport, *Outlines of Elementary Economics*, p. 247.
[28] Herbert J. Davenport, "The Single Tax and the English Budget," *Quarterly Journal of Economics*, p. 279. (Feb. 1910.)

a hobby of doctrinaires and enthusiasts, a program not yet fully within the range of practical discussion, and bidding fair to deserve attention—if ever—only when more serious matters of the plan shall have been considered. . . . the single taxers have appeared to be men with a bee in the bonnet, akin to the anarchists and the socialists and to other disturbers of the king's peace and the scholar's calm. Folk like these are not to be foregathered with by thinkers solicitous of their good repute. Economists of all people dread the stigma of radicalism. Far better it is to elucidate and emphasize the excellent aspects of things as they are; otherwise, one may seem to question the economic harmonies, or to doubt the validity and the beneficence of natural law, or to bring in question the deft guiding of the divine hand.

In 1913 came another temperature change; the single tax received a rather cool reception in Davenport's chief work, *The Economics of Enterprise,* a textbook published in that year. It was hardly mentioned except in one paragraph where Davenport stated that the single tax on land was "tragically inadequate" in attacking all the forms of unearned increment and as a single tax was unworkable. On another page there occurs a slightly more sympathetic reference to the single tax program.[29]

Back swung the pendulum in the March 1917 issue of the *American Economic Review.* Davenport now came out squarely in favor of the land value tax with no ifs, ands, or buts. He began by writing, "I set out with a confession of faith—I am a land value taxer." He then plunged into a consideration of the problem of confiscation, the same problem which had bothered him twenty years earlier. In this article he favored gradual compensation: ". . . payments could well be fixed at the present worth of ground rent charge for approximately the expectation of life, or even for the possible duration of life, of the actual owner. The principle of escheat or of the

[29] Herbert Davenport, *The Economics of Enterprise,* pp. 522, 527.

inheritance tax carried to its ultimate logical extreme would take care of the residue of value."[30]

Davenport offered an unusual reply to those who complained that the land value tax was not based on the ability-to-pay principle. He wrote that this tax was in reality not a tax at all but a charge for privilege—the privilege of exclusive use of a piece of land to which all members in society have equal rights. Accordingly, single taxers should really be called "no taxers."[31]

Throughout the long article, Davenport constantly took occasion to direct pointed barbs at the more dogmatic single tax amateurs whose extremism was hindering the acceptance of their ideas. In his conclusions he was extremely circumspect, obviously fearing that like so many others of his persuasion he might appear doctrinaire and fanatical. He was careful to mollify those whose ideas he attacked, observing philosophically: "Not less perhaps for us single taxers of the looser observance than for our fellows of the stricter faith, is it to be desired that we continually exercise ourselves in the amenities of discussion."[32]

One is struck by the fact that Davenport was so laudatory of the single tax in magazine articles yet so reticent about it in his textbooks. But Davenport was not unique in this respect. The single tax received harsher treatment in textbooks than in any other form of economic literature. Perhaps textbook writers felt a duty to stick to the tried and true, to the accepted and non-controversial.

The years immediately preceding American entry into World War I proved to be a relatively high point of Georgist success in politics. For instance, in 1913, the

[30] Herbert J. Davenport, "Theoretical Issues in the Single Tax," *American Economic Review*, March 1917, p. 2.
[31] *Ibid.*, p. 12.
[32] *Ibid.*, p. 30.

Pennsylvania legislature passed a law allowing Pittsburgh and Scranton gradually to increase the tax on land and decrease the tax on buildings so that by 1925 the tax rate on land would be double the tax rate on buildings, although county and school taxes fell equally on both land and buildings. In 1915, single tax forces in New York City managed to get a similar bill introduced in the state legislature. It received serious consideration. Dr. Robert M. Haig of Columbia was appointed to supervise two studies which were to provide information useful in considering the proposed change. Haig had been an outstanding student of E. R. A. Seligman—indeed, Seligman had obtained this assignment for him—and was unsympathetic to the land value tax.

Haig's reports discussed how the proposed law would affect various types of property in New York City. Most of his views were those of his mentor, plus one new and interesting point. Haig suggested that the land value tax would bring no benefit to prospective real estate owners, even though they would pay practically nothing for land when they acquired real estate, because the higher land value tax to be paid in ensuing years would offset this immediate advantage.

This conclusion is questionable. Many real estate purchasers today go to great lengths to avoid tying up their capital in real estate, as exemplified by the growing popularity of the sale-leaseback arrangement. This plan permits an owner to sell his real estate while at the same time agreeing to lease it back for a long period of time. Many of our finest buildings, for example the four corners of Lexington Avenue and 42nd Street and the Empire State Building, are built on leased land. As a result of these arrangements, businessmen find that they have more working capital for use in their own businesses, where presumably a higher rate of return can be expected. All these advantages would come automatically to every real estate purchaser under the land value tax because land prices would approximate zero. No real estate purchaser would be required to tie up large amounts of capital in land, nor would he be required to incur the considerable expense of interest on a land mortgage.

In an attempt to learn what the land value tax could achieve in actual practice, Haig visited western Canada. Here many municipalities had instituted a real estate tax system exempting improvements from taxation, so that the only tax was upon the land. In the early years of the century, western Canada experienced a real estate boom hardly equalled anywhere else. A tremendous population increase of 260 per cent from 1901 to 1916 fed the boom. Railway expansion was another factor—it was estimated at the opening of World War I that there were more miles of railways in all Canada per 1000 inhabitants than in any country of the world, and the situation was even more extreme in western Canada. Municipalities built expensive public improvements such as streets and sewers in anticipation of the wonderful future everyone expected.

It was at the beginning of this expansion period that the partial or full exemption of improvements from taxation was introduced. Naturally, single taxers were quick to point with pride to this rapid economic growth, ascribing it to the newly introduced tax system. While the boom lasted, it was an effective argument, in no small measure responsible for the prominence of the single tax prior to 1914. But in that year the war abruptly stopped immigration and commercial growth. The land speculation bubble broke overnight and land prices plummeted. Real estate speculators went bankrupt and also many municipalities whose tax revenue dried up while fixed expenses incurred

in the days of prosperity remained the same. The municipalities were forced to condemn many land parcels due
to non-payment of tax arrears. Now it was the opponents
of the single tax who had their day, claiming with equal
exaggeration that the tax on land values was responsible
for this unfortunate situation. However invalid the argument may have been, it was very effective and constituted
an important factor in the single tax decline after 1915.

It was the post-1914 situation in western Canada that
Haig investigated in his second report. He was surprised
to discover that it was the real estate speculators who were
in control of the municipal governments and who in-
stigated the tax exemption for improvements and the corresponding shift of the tax burden to the land. The reason
for this apparent paradox was that assessments trailed far
behind market values, and the full land rent was never
collected by taxation even though the municipalities collected no other taxes except those on land values. For this
reason, speculators paid little regard to land taxes during
the period of prosperity when the future looked rosier
every day. "Taxes, if he took them into account at all, he
thought of as a bothersome but insignificant type of fee
which he had to pay to the public treasury for the privilege
of speculating. Receiving no returns from the land, it was
necessary for him, of course, to draw upon his income from
other sources to pay his taxes, but the prize for which he
was playing was normally so large in comparison with this
fee as to render it of slight importance."[33] Said one real
estate speculator Haig interviewed: "As an owner of vacant
property I am strongly in favor of as much single tax as I
can get. If the rate can be made high enough to induce the

[33] Robert M. Haig, "The 'Single Tax Limited' in War Time," a
speech delivered before the National Tax Association at Atlanta, Ga.,
Nov. 15, 1917, p. 378.

holders of real estate to build sooner or better, so much more rapid will be the increase in the value of the vacant property which I buy and sell."[34]

While the speculative prosperity was raging, then, the tax was not an important factor and cities financed their budgets by collecting much less than the full land rent. When the depression hit, the real estate interests in control of the municipal governments were able to lift the tax exemption on improvements in many municipalities so that the land speculators could get some relief.

To what extent did Henry George or his followers influence the tax system in western Canada? One thing stands out—they had little to do with its inception. The voters were unaware of George and were influenced almost entirely by practical considerations. Haig summarized an interview with an Edmonton alderman thus: "The sytem was originally adopted in Edmonton because it offered a weapon which the people could use against non-residents and the Hudson's Bay Company [which had huge landholdings in the area]. It was not adopted because of its theoretical attractiveness. The people in Edmonton in 1904 did not know whether Henry George was a horse or a dog."[35] Of course, once the idea of exempting improvements from taxation caught on, single taxers became active propagandists in western Canada and attempted to give the movement a theoretical underpinning.

The same situation prevailed in Australia, New Zealand and other parts of the world where land value taxation had been instituted. It would not have helped the single tax cause any in these places if George's feelings about the immorality of private landownership had been widely

[34] Robert M. Haig, *The Exemption of Improvements from Taxation in Canada and the United States*, p. 68.
[35] *Ibid.*, p. 103.

known. For the same reason, it may very well be that even today the reputation of Henry George is such as to be an obstacle to the adoption of the land value tax.

What conclusions did Haig draw from his study? He admitted that the system stimulated building and discouraged land speculation (although it did not eliminate it).[36] On the other hand, he felt that the sytem had very undesirable effects where its introduction involved a material decrease in the tax base. Haig pointed out that it was difficult to compare the boom and bust land speculation in western Canada with the relatively stable real estate conditions in New York City, and he inferred that any reasonable tax sytem has little effect upon business conditions compared to such other factors as population growth, social custom, business cycle, etc. As far as the tax exemption of improvements is concerned, he quoted a Vancouverite as saying that it was "neither a plague nor a panacea."[37] Haig's conclusion was mildly antagonistic to this new tax idea, and played a part in the failure of the 1915 bill to institute a heavier land tax in New York City to obtain passage.

Two years after the submission of his report, Professor Haig made these remarks in speaking before the National Tax Association at Atlanta, Georgia:[38]

It should be carefully noted that nothing which has been said affects the attractiveness of the policy of exempting improvements during periods of prosperity. Conditions in Western Canada are at present admittedly abnormal. Indeed, there is every reason both from the economic and ethical points of view why the advantage gained through the assertion of the public's claim to a large portion of the ground rent should be preserved.

[36] Robert M. Haig, *The Exemption of Improvements from Taxation in Canada and the United States,* pp. 272, 278.

[37] *Ibid.,* p. 280.

[38] Tax Policy League Symposium, *Property Taxes.* New York: Tax Policy League, 1939, p. 147.

During the late 1930's, Professor Haig repeated his opinion that the taxation of land values had not been given a full or adequate test in western Canada. He considered it to be a matter of far-reaching importance that in Australia and New Zealand, cities both large and small had tested it for a much longer period and during boom and depression eras. Nevertheless, his earlier views conveying an opposite impression reached a far larger audience at a more critical moment.

It may be pertinent here to note that the exemption of improvements from taxation coupled with a heavy tax on land values is still very much in evidence in western Canada, although less widespread than in 1914. The tax exemptions range from one-third to one-half of the total value of improvements in practically all the municipalities. A few communities exempt improvements completely. In addition, the province of Alberta levies a tax on oil royalties which provides the revenue for about one-third of the province's budget. In the rural municipalities of Saskatchewan, "land taxation has always been and still is almost the sole revenue source." Most interestingly, in all four provinces there are substantial exemptions, in many cases 100 per cent, for farm improvements. Here as elsewhere, the land value tax has found its most widespread application in farming areas.[39]

[39] H. G. Brown, Harold Buttenheim, Philip Cornick, Glenn Hoover, editors, *Land Value Taxation Around the World* (New York: Robert Schalkenbach Foundation, 1928), Herbert T. Owen, "Canada," pp. 61ff. A rose by any other name may smell as sweet, but in politics a deftly chosen name for a new proposal can often mean the difference between acceptance or rejection. More accurate and understandable than the title "land value taxation" is the title "land *rent* taxation," for it is the rent from land and not its total selling value that George wished the government to take in taxation. However, from the political point of view "tax exemption of improvements" is a much more attractive title. It shifts the emphasis from taxation to exemption.

Yetta Scheftel, another economist of this period, wrote a useful and exhaustively detailed history called *The Taxation of Land Value*. Although the tone is highly antagonistic to George and his followers, we find nevertheless that Miss Scheftel gave her lukewarm endorsement to the idea of a land value tax as a fiscal measure.

She carefully documented her opinion that neither Henry George nor his followers were responsible for the initiation of the land value tax in Australia, New Zealand and Canada, although they may later have been effective proselytizers of the tax.

After analyzing vast seas of statistics, Miss Scheftel came to the conclusion that "in so far as the efficiency of the land can be gauged at all, the results of the levy have been more or less beneficial economically and socially."[40] As far as the experience in western Canada was concerned, she judged that the sharp ups and downs of the business cycle had made it impossible to determine the social effects of the tax, but "as a fiscal measure, the tax has responded adequately to the needs of the communities, since it is not only a productive source of revenue but also since it is least burdensome to industry and capital."[41] Concerning Australia and New Zealand, she stressed that ". . . in no case has there been a repeal of the tax except to extend its operation . . . the adoption of the tax by one state after another, by the local bodies, and recently by the federal government of Australia, argues in its favor and for its expediency in that country."[42]

Would the tax increase the burden on farmers and rural areas in general? Miss Scheftel answers with a qualified yes, although noting that in Australia, New Zealand, and

[40] Yetta Scheftel, *The Taxation of Land Value*. Boston: Houghton, Mifflin, 1916, p. 119.
[41] Yetta Scheftel, *The Taxation of Land Value*, p. 299.
[42] *Ibid.*, p. 120.

western Canada the tax was adopted more often by rural than by urban communities, at least at the beginning. (In Denmark, too, where a strong single tax party exists, its support comes more from the farmers who originated it than from city people.) In any case, she noted that local option could prevent farmers from being excessively burdened.[43]

She concluded her volume by saying that as far as America was concerned, the immediate prospect of land value taxation was remote, but if it could ever rid itself of the single tax onus its long-run prospects would be bright. This view was shared by many others in 1915.

George and the Historians

How did historians of the 1900-1916 period deal with Henry George and his ideas? While historical scholarship in the earlier period had almost completely disregarded him, the increasing emphasis on non-political history after the turn of the century produced a steadily growing interest.

In 1907, Gustavus Myers published his monumental *History of the Great American Fortunes*. This book suffers from the author's extreme partisanship—he was an ardent socialist—but continues to be rather widely read. Myers documented in great detail George's thesis that privilege—particularly monopoly—was responsible for the great private fortunes. Although landownership was only one of the privileges Myers considered, he gave it a fair degree of prominence. Generally speaking, Myers regarded George quite favorably.

One of the leading historians of this time (and indeed for the next thirty years) was Charles Austin Beard. In some of his books he expressed approval of land value

[43] *Ibid.*, pp. 345, 346.

taxation as one among several needed reforms. For example, in *American City Government* (1912), Beard devoted eight pages to land value taxation although the burden of the argument was borne by quotations from others, particularly Frederick C. Howe. Beard quoted this ardent Progressive and Georgist extensively to the effect that land value taxation would result in a well-planned city by eliminating land speculation. This unfortunate phenomenon causes large land areas to be kept out of use, or in only partial use, by urban real estate speculators, thus intensifying the pressure upon other areas and resulting in serious congestion. Residential areas are separated from business centers by vacant or poorly improved land, roughly the ecological phenomenon that we call urban sprawl today. Sewer systems, transportation facilities and utility lines stretch past empty lots. Taxes on buildings inhibit the replacement of old buildings by new ones. High land prices force landlords to crowd their tenements with as many tenants as possible in order to recoup their high investment, and for the same reason builders are driven to construct taller buildings. Land speculation, in short, leads to congestion in some areas while others remain under-developed. "By the shifting of a large portion of the burden of taxation from improvements to land, the holding of vacant lots would be discouraged and a decided stimulus would be given to the building of tenements and residences."[44]

Despite his endorsement and exposition of Howe's views, Beard's approval of land value taxation was cautious and reserved. If he really believed Howe was correct, one wonders why he devoted such a small and incidental section of his book on city government to the land value tax. Beard

[44] Charles A. Beard, *American City Government*, p. 378; see also p. 383.

concluded his section on George's tax proposal with this quotation from Professor Henry R. Seager. Perhaps it represents his true views.[45]

There is reason to think that especially in large cities absentee landlordism is becoming more and more the rule for the simple reason that more and more people are coming to live in tenements and apartment houses. If this is the case, there may be good ground for the contention that the system of private property in land is ceasing to serve any useful purpose in cities which the system of public ownership would not serve as well and that the time is right for a gradual transition to the latter.

The years around 1912 were the high water mark of the Georgist agitation, a time when Beard could write that "there seems to be no doubt that the principle which it embodies will steadily gain adherents until it will become in one form or another a part of the law of New York City."[46]

In 1915, Benjamin P. DeWitt brought forth the first history of the Progressive Movement. The book was a detailed factual narrative of the times in which the author lived, and if it lacks the perspective which more recent works on the same subject display, this is no more than one would reasonably expect. DeWitt's book is especially useful because it shows what aspects of the Progressive Movement seemed most important to the people of that era and elucidated the attitudes and opinions then prevalent.

Unfortunately, DeWitt's treatment of land value taxation was riddled with misconceptions and contradictions. For instance, he declared: "Because of the obvious practical difficulties involved in taking all land in a city from private individuals and turning it over to be managed by the com-

---

[45] *Ibid.*, p. 384. At one point, Beard says, in his own words, that "without subscribing to the 'single tax' theory or any other general philosophy it must be obvious to every one that land values in a city are mainly created by society itself." (p. 141.)
[46] *Ibid.*, p. 138.

munity as a whole, the single tax in its original form, is very rarely adopted."[47] George had contemplated no such confiscation.

DeWitt listed three main objections to the land value tax. First, it would reduce land values and eventually there would be nothing left to tax.

Secondly, a building boom would ensue if the tax on buildings were reduced, but it would be of very short duration because it would cause the price of building materials to jump, thus bringing on "a reaction toward fewer buildings."[48] It is a novel argument but of doubtful validity, for an increased demand for building materials would bring about an increased supply, thus keeping prices at the same level.

Thirdly, the tax would lead to more intensive use of land, increasing urban congestion. In this, DeWitt seemed to contradict his previous assertion.

DeWitt approved a tax on the future increase in land values such as Mill had advocated, even though he did not explain why his earlier objections would not apply equally to Mill's variation of the land value tax.

That the land value tax would become increasingly important as a Progressive reform at the municipal level, DeWitt had no doubt. In this he shared the general conviction of his time. More and more, he stated, the progressive movement advocated "community use of community values for community purposes."[49]

The year 1915 witnessed the publication of two Ph.D. theses on the single tax. *The Single Tax and the Labor Movement,* by Peter A. Speek of Wisconsin, was covertly favorable to the idea and noted that it was gaining in

[47] Benjamin P. DeWitt, *The Progressive Movement.* New York: Macmillan, 1915, p. 358.
[48] *Ibid.,* p. 359.
[49] *Ibid.,* p. 357.

popularity. Speek agreed with John R. Commons' view that George was probably counted out at the polls in 1886 by the Tammany gang then in control of New York City politics. It seems unlikely, however, that the full facts will ever be known. He also noted that "the Georgists were very active in the ensuing years in bringing the Australian [secret] ballot system to America."[50]

The other Ph.D. thesis was of major importance. It was Arthur N. Young's *The Single Tax Movement in the United States,* written at Princeton and still considered the authoritative history of the subject. It was completed under the supervision of Professor Frank Fetter who, as we have seen, was generally anti-George, despite the fact that he, like many other economists of his day, had originally been impelled to study economics by having read *Progress and Poverty.* Young was opposed to the single tax idea although he displayed a certain sympathetic fascination with it.

Both Henry George, Jr., and Charles Albro Barker have since written better and more complete biographies of Henry George, but no one has equaled Young in the description of the single tax movement after George's death. His was the product of extensive research.

Particularly interesting is the detailed chapter about the California in which Henry George formed his economic ideas. Young describes the concentration of land ownership due to the huge old Spanish-Mexican land grants, the fighting over mining claims, the tremendous land speculation in both urban and rural areas due to the obviously inevitable growth of the state, the harshness of the 1873 depression and its disruption of social conditions in California. It has often been said that George's thinking was particularly influenced by the special economic conditions

[50] Peter A. Speek, *The Single Tax and the Labor Movement,* Ph.D. thesis, University of Wisconsin, p. 157.

he experienced in California, but no one had documented
the thesis as carefully as Young.

Young noted that a split had developed in the ranks of
George's followers. There was the more orthodox group
that closely followed the single tax doctrine as delineated
by Henry George, and there was another group which advocated the land value tax but not necessarily as a single
tax. This latter group, for which Charles Fillebrown was
the chief spokesman, was always quick to emphasize that
their tax involved no confiscation of land titles. Young disagreed with Fillebrown *et al* on this key point, writing:
"It is difficult to follow Mr. Fillebrown in seeing an essential *economic* difference between private property in land
and private property in the rent or the value of land."
(italics mine.) He quoted Professor Haney in support of
his position—"Who wants the orange after the juice is
squeezed out?"[51]

To Georgists this analogy would be inapplicable because
the title to land would still be important to a landowner
even if he could collect no rent; his title will enable him to
do whatever he wished with the land and still have secure
tenure in the improvements thereon. Nor would these improvements be taxed, which could only serve to improve
the security of his tenure. The land title, they argued,
would still have an important economic meaning.

Young criticized the single taxer's reliance upon the
"natural rights dogma." "The single tax may or may not
be a good thing, but single taxers can make their case only
by showing that it is *just* and will promote the general
welfare." (italics mine.) He quoted Ely in support of this
statement, "rights are acquired in and through society."[52]

[51] Arthur N. Young, *The Single Tax Movement in the United
States*, pp. 273, 274.
[52] *Ibid.*, p. 303.

Might not Hitler or Lenin, Batista or Castro, have agreed with Ely's statement? One wonders what Young means by the term *just*. The natural rights philosophy, with its labor theory of property, is one definition of that term. It presumes to be based on the reasonable observation that all men are created equal. Of course, both Ely and Young were undoubtedly democratic in spirit, but that was because they instinctively (if not verbally) used natural rights as a basic consideration in their judgment of what social utility is.

In his concluding summary, Young pointed out that the single tax agitation had brought good effects, even if the land value tax itself was not one of them. Single taxers had been influential in obtaining a better application of the real estate tax, were prominent in getting the odious personal property tax abolished in many places, had popularized the study of economics, helped bring natural monopolies under public control, and were "among the most persistent and influential advocates of conservation."[53]

Concerning this last point, Young noted that Henry George in his first book, *Our Land and Land Policy* (1871), eloquently criticized the policy of federal and state governments by which the country's land, forest and mineral wealth were recklessly squandered for the benefit of a fortunate few. Although many single taxers of the more libertarian view felt that the government should rent out all its land for private use, George's doctrine that the land is the common heritage of us all did provide a ready-made philosophy for many conservationists.

"The most vital message of Henry George's life and work," Young concluded, "was the urgency of social reform. Whatever be the fate of the remedy for which he so earnestly contended, one thing is sure. Henry George made

[53] *Ibid.*, p. 319.

it plain that no true civilization can avoid the duty of finding a means to 'extirpate poverty' and 'to lighten the burdens of those compelled to toil.' "[54] More and more Americans of the Progressive Era were gradually coming to accept this estimation of Henry George.

[54] *Ibid.*

3

THE COLD WINDS OF CONSERVATISM, 1917-1933

BY 1917 THE PROGRESSIVE ERA HAD PETERED OUT, FOR reasons which historians are still debating. Perhaps it was because Americans had exhausted reform ideas consistent with the still dominant free enterprise and small government philosophy of the time; the welfare state would need the impetus of a full-scale depression. No doubt our entrance into the war had much to do with it, for the reform spirit was converted into a martial spirit.

In the new era of the silk shirt and the fast buck, in the changed atmosphere of isolation, immigration restriction, high tariffs and our first anti-communist hysteria, all reforms suffered, especially that frail flower that was the single tax movement. With the coming of war, governmental budgets rose far beyond what a single tax on land could apparently provide. The tide of public discussion about the idea receded from the popular magazines to the scholarly economic journals, and by the end of the 1920's it was rare indeed to find articles anywhere. Practically all the single tax magazines dried up for lack of support, and the movement appeared to have lost all contact with the general public. Single tax organizations withered and died, and the membership of the few that remained became increasingly dominated by the old and graying veterans of earlier single tax battles. The movement seemed in danger of becoming an historical relic, something like Bellamy's New Nationalism.

An indication of the uncongenial post-war environment in which the single tax and other reform movements had to work is shown by the following incident. John R. Commons, one of the best known economists of the time, wrote an article in the March 1922 issue of the *Political Science Quarterly* favoring a proposed Wisconsin law to institute a progressive tax on land values. This law provided for an increasing tax rate on land values in excess of $10,000. The editors of the magazine took the unusual step of prefacing Commons' article with the statement that "in accordance with the custom of the Political Science Quarterly, the Editors disclaim responsibility for theories or policies advocated by contributors."[1] No doubt this was their policy, yet no such disclaimer is to be found for any other article in the issues for 1922, although many controversial issues were discussed. Evidently, the single tax was still considered to be a most radical plan, mild as it may seem today. However, there was little need for editorial concern, since the Wisconsin bill did not pass.

Views of the Economists

In economics, the immediate post-war era saw two new developments. Marginal utility analysis achieved dominance and resulted in such great concern about the precise mathematical expression of economic forces under pure competition that the old problem of monopoly and the new phenomenon of oligopoly were given only casual attention. The search for absolute and universal laws con-

[1] *Political Science Quarterly,* March 1922, p. 53.

cerning the distribution of wealth into rent, wages and interest—a search that was the main concern of George and his fellow classical economists—was beginning to seem old-fashioned. A high regard for natural law was considered by the newer economists to be somewhat medieval.

Another development in economics, stemming from the writings of Veblen, was a new emphasis on statistics. Economists began to feel that they did not possess enough facts about the economy they were analyzing and that an empirical approach was needed. The old classical theorizing, based on speculative and unmeasured assumptions, was not a sufficiently scientific approach.

One result of this line of reasoning was the organizing of the National Bureau of Economic Research to gather economic statistics. One of the Bureau's publications dealt directly with matters that concerned Henry George. Wilford I. King, in his N.B.E.R. book entitled *The Wealth and Income of the People of the United States* (1915), estimated after much statistical research that the share of the national income going to landowners as rent remained remarkably steady, fluctuating around 8 or 9 per cent over a sixty-year period, while wages and profits absorbed most of the increase in income made possible by rising productivity.[2] This hardly bore out George's theory that as a result of material progress land rent increases faster than total production. Nor did it support his contention that an all-devouring land rent caused poverty and depressions while wages sank to the subsistence level. What was more, as the years went by and additional statistics became available, it became apparent that the share of rent decreased to 6 per cent of the national income in 1929 and to only 3 per cent in 1951.[3] Since 1951 the land rent percentage has risen slightly, but the inferences drawn from these

[2] W. I. King, *The Wealth and Income of the People of the United States,* Chap. 7.

[3] Robert Heilbroner, *The Worldly Philosophers,* p. 181.

statistics were that the land value taxers were making a tempest in a teapot, that they were talking about an insignificant part of the economy, that the land reform they proposed could not promise enough benefit to be worth all the effort necessary to get it adopted.

In George's own day, it had not been felt that he was raising a tempest in a teapot. Land was considered to be an important factor in economics, and the rent from land was thought to be a major part of the gross national product. Many conservatives had even thought that a land value tax would provide the government with so much revenue that despotism would be made possible. As late as 1913, Herbert Davenport was writing that as much as "five-ninths of the durable wealth reported by the [1904] census is made up of privately appropriated social wealth," by which he meant land rent and other monopoly profits.[4] King himself demonstrated by statistics that although the land rent fund would have been large enough before the Civil War to pay for all government expenses nearly twice over, by 1910 it would have been barely sufficient as a single tax.[5] But the monumental expenditures of war plus the growing demand for increased governmental welfare services soon convinced most people of the post-war era that the land value tax could not be a single tax.[6]

As a result of King's work in national income analysis, the writers of economics textbooks began to lose interest in land and its rent, and gradually both these terms disappeared from chapter headings.[7] The distinction between land and capital became blurred, and rent began to be

[4] Herbert Davenport, *Economics of Enterprise*, p. 521.
[5] Wilford I. King, *The Wealth and Income of the People of the United States*, pp. 160-62.
[6] However, this may not be the case in underdeveloped areas, where the land rent to G.N.P. ratio is much higher than in the U.S.
[7] See H. E. Batson, *Bibliography of Modern Economic Theory, 1870-1929*, p. 84.

treated as interest. For these and other reasons, economics textbook writers of the post-war decade were more anti-George than were the economists at large, thus continuing what could be termed a long and well-established tradition. Not surprisingly, their texts were often marred by inaccuracies, some new and some old, when dealing with George and his theories. For instance, one high school textbook writer, Fred Rogers Fairchild, a well-known economics professor at Yale, informed his readers that "the single tax is ultimately land nationalization" which he had previously defined as government ownership of the land.[8]

L. A. Refener, professor of economics at the University of West Virginia, demonstrated that he had given the subject of the single tax much thought, but he was unable to come to a final verdict. Single tax ethics were right, he said, but confiscation was wrong. Land rent was unearned income, but on the other hand it was received mainly by the poor or middle class. By reducing the selling price of land to almost zero, it would tend to abolish land speculation, reduce absentee landownership, and make it easier for workers to own their own homes. Yet such a tax would be difficult to administer. Refener compromised by favoring a tax on the future increment of land values, although it is difficult to see how this tax would have been any easier to administer.[9]

Henry George in the History of Economic Thought

During the 1920's, an aspect of economics that received increasing attention was the history of economic thought.

[8] Fred Rogers Fairchild, *Essentials of Economics.* New York: American Book Co., 1923, p. 526.
[9] L. A. Refener, *Principles of Economics.* New York: Houghton, Mifflin, 1927, pp. 212, 222, 224, 227, 228.

The most popular text in that area, and one still in use today, was written by two Frenchmen, Gide and Rist. Unfortunately, the references to Henry George were not accurate.

For instance, the term "land nationalization" was misleadingly used to describe Henry George's scheme. Henry George himself was classified as a Christian Socialist, despite his firmly held belief in the beneficence of industrial competition. The authors wrote that because land can be exchanged for the fruits of one's labor, its private ownership was justified, a view very much open to question. They chided George for not taking into account the unearned decrement of land value as well as the unearned increment, but George *had* taken this into account by advocating that the selling value of land he reduced to almost zero through taxation; no landowner could suffer much from an unearned decrement then.[10]

In criticizing *Progress and Poverty,* Gide and Rist suggested that the book "has all the liveliness of journalism and the eloquence of oratory, but has neither the precision or the finality of a work of science," no doubt a widely held view of the time.[11] No doubt critics today would share the authors' conclusions about rent not absorbing the benefits of progress. Yet it would have been helpful had Gide and Rist rested their assertions upon some concrete evidence, either theoretical or empirical.

Lewis Haney's *History of Economic Thought* (1921) hardly mentioned Henry George at all. When he did, Haney equated George with the agrarian socialists—entirely without warrant—and wrote that the modern single tax idea is quite different from the plan of the French

[10] Charles Gide and Charles Rist, *History of Economic Doctrines.* New York: D. C. Heath, 1948 (first edition 1909), pp. 156, 537, 591, 592.

[11] *Ibid.,* p. 588.

Physiocrats. "The latter recognized the rights of the land-owner and would have guaranteed property in land. Nor did they aim to seize an 'unearned income.' "[12]

This physiocratic analogy was decidedly misleading. While it was true that the Physiocrats did not consciously and purposefully aim to seize an unearned rental income, both they and George advocated the same proposal—a single tax on land values. Both George and the Physiocrats would have inviolably guaranteed private property in land. The real difference between the two lay not in their economic proposals but in their analysis. They reached the same conclusion, but for different reasons.

One source of confusion was semantic. The Physiocrats thought of the landowner as a farmer or agricultural entrepreneur and regarded him as the only true producer of wealth because he made something useful come about, namely crops, which had not existed before, whereas manufacturers and merchants merely reshaped or transported already existing wealth. Georgists, on the other hand, defined a landowner as anyone who holds legal title to a piece of land, and without producing anything, pockets the land rent; thus Georgists regarded landowners as idlers and parasites preying on the true producers of wealth, labor and business owners.

There was another important difference in economic analysis. The Physiocrats believed that a tax on land values could be passed on from the landowner to the consuming public in the form of higher prices. Every economic authority today agrees with George's contention that this is not so; the landowner cannot shift the land value tax to others.

One wonders to what extent class distinctions played a part in determining the different attitudes displayed at the

[12] Lewis Haney, *History of Economic Thought*, p. 179.

time toward the Georgists and Physiocrats. The latter were regarded as gentlemen and scholars by Haney and those who thought like him. In contrast, Henry George and his followers were predominantly self-educated enthusiasts who were easily pictured as low-class fanatics and even revolutionaries.

Views of the Public Finance Economists

Merlin Hunter's *Outlines of Public Finance* appeared in 1921 and contained many of the standard anti-George arguments then current. The single tax did not affect all the unearned incomes, just one. It would force the building of skyscrapers, it was inelastic in that the revenue it produced bore no relation to the amount the government might need, it was difficult if not impossible to administer, it would hit farmers hard, and apportioning the single tax revenue between the various city, state and federal governments would be a problem. Notice that the single tax alone was referred to, not the land value tax; perhaps a textbook on public finance should have given more emphasis to the latter. Hunter pointed out the usual benefits to society of the single tax agitation: more emphasis on better assessment methods and the publicizing of the evils of the general property tax.[13]

Hunter borrowed from Alvin S. Johnson in saying that the unearned increment in land values was a chief incentive to the western pioneer (hardly important in 1921, even if true), and he borrowed from Seligman in saying "that every material thing is based on some gift of nature." Hunter also asserted, without any foundation in historical fact, that the single tax had been tried in France with disastrous results during the time of the Physiocrats and was soon abandoned.

[13] Merlin Hunter, *Outlines of Public Finance*, pp. 367ff.

One argument that Hunter advanced demands considerable attention. He stated that individual landowners may
create the value of their lands and are therefore rightfully
entitled to own them. As examples, he cited Gary, In-
diana, and Pullman, Illinois—cities created by corporations out of marsh and farm lands. Were not the increases
in land values in these towns brought about primarily by
these corporations, which would then be morally entitled
to keep them? One could cite the similar but more recent
examples of Levittown in Long Island and the Bell Lab-
oratories in Nutley, New Jersey.

This was a compelling argument, to which the Georgists
replied that if the lands increased precipitously in value
after enterprising corporations built upon them, it was
because certain corporation leaders recognized that these
lands had a potential location value unrecognized by
others, and higher profits were the reward of their sagacity.
They attracted people to these lands and it was these people who enhanced the land values. People would scarcely
have come if the lands possessed no potential location
value. Had the corporations put up similar improvements
in an isolated desert, it is doubtful that there would have
been much of an increase in land values. Economic value
is determined solely by social demand where supply is
fixed, as in the case of land.

It is possible to maintain that Hunter's objection (which
can be traced back to Seligman, incidentally) is irrelevant
because if we are trying to determine who should rightfully own land, we should not be concerned with how its
value is created. If labor creates the sole just title to private
property, then land, which is not a product of labor, should
not be privately owned unless the owner pays for the
privilege in the form of land rent. Similarly, if all people
should have equal access to nature's opportunities (i.e.,

land), then land should not be privately owned unless society receives payment for the privilege in the form of land rent, which measures exactly what the privilege is worth.

G. Findlay Shirras, Harley Lutz, and Leon Edie also wrote a popular textbook on public finance which deprecated the single tax. Their arguments are familiar: revenue would be insufficient for government needs, the burden of taxation was not distributed equally, it was an inelastic tax, it affected only one type of unearned income, and it meant confiscation of private property. It would be difficult and expensive to collect—"how would valuation on such a scale be made?"[14] As usual, the authors were discussing a national single tax and not the more practical local land value tax. They repeated the old argument that incentive to improve land would be lessened if there were no unearned increment. It might be, however, that if a man did not have to buy land, he would have more money for improving it. There was no mention in this textbook of the successful Australian, New Zealand and western Canadian experiments.

Favorable Viewpoints

One might get the impression that Henry George's ideas were unpopular with every economist of the 1920's, but this is not so. Raymond T. Bye, economics professor at the University of Pennsylvania and author of two popular economics textbooks, took a mildly favorable view. In his chief textbook (still in use) no mention of George appeared, but in another, *Applied Economics* (1928), he devoted an extensive section to the man. However, so much space was devoted to pointing out the inadequacies of the single tax that the casual reader could easily over-

[14] G. Findlay Shirras, *Science of Public Finance*, p. 333.

look his endorsement of the land value tax. We have noted this phenomenon before and will see evidence of it again.

According to Bye, "authorities on public finance are now generally tending toward the view that land is a more suitable object for taxation than the improvements erected upon it."[15] Perhaps this was so but it is pertinent to add that these particular authorities were generally less dedicated than were those opposed to the idea.

Bye also advanced an interesting method by which the land value tax could more easily find popular acceptance. He suggested that it be made part of the already instituted inheritance tax, ". . . the law of inheritance to be so changed as to provide that all lands transferred at death should henceforth be subject to a tax sufficient to appropriate the rents thereof."[16] Herbert Davenport had earlier made a similar suggestion.

Among other economists of the era who supported land value taxation were, paradoxically enough, both conservatives and socialists. While their economic views were generally diametrically opposed, they could find different points of agreement in George's philosophy and proposal. The socialists were more enthusiastic about the man because they, as well as he, were dissenters from the prevailing opinion and were attacking established institutions. The cry of "Confiscation!" did not disturb them; indeed, they interpreted George's public collection of land rent as an acceptable alternative to government ownership of the land. Professor Scott Nearing, for instance, an ardent socialist economist, wrote that landowners have a monopoly power which enables them, with increasing population and progress, to place an ever-increasing tax upon the ac-

[15] Raymond T. Bye and William Hewett, *Applied Economics,* p. 547.
[16] *Ibid.*

tivities of the community. He regarded land rent as a form of surplus value.[17]

Conservative economists, though they might deprecate George's sympathy with the underdog and his upsetting reformist attitude, could still find agreement with the individualistic aspect of his philosophy—his emphasis on pure competition and no taxation of or government interference with capital or labor. Some conservatives realized that free enterprise could not be morally defended unless it was truly free, free from monopoly and free of unearned incomes.

Thomas N. Carver, professor of economics at Harvard and perhaps the arch-conservative of his time, devoted a whole chapter to the single tax in his *Essays in Social Justice* (1915). Nine-tenths of his exordium paraded the usual arguments against the single tax and only at the very end did his reluctant endorsement of some form of land value taxation shine through.

He was very critical of the single tax argument that the community should own the land because the land gets its value from the presence of the community.

To Carver, social justice meant a community organized to further his favorite virtues of hard work, abstinence and high productivity. In the last analysis, he was won to the land value tax, despite his stated dislike for single taxers, because he felt it might further these virtues. It would make idle land productive, it would un-tax initiative, and it would force many of the idle yet talented rich to go to work.

Apparently Carver was the first person to make the important point that the land value tax would divert much-

---

[17] Scott Nearing, article in the "Single Tax Section," *Annals of the American Academy*, p. 157. (March 1915.)

needed savings from the unproductive investment in land
to the more productive investment in capital. "Instead of
buying land, men would buy other sources of income, that
is, other means of production."[18] This point has become
particularly significant in the case of underdeveloped countries today.

Of all the economists who have passed through the halls
of Academia, none have more vigorously defended Henry
George than Harry Gunnison Brown, indefatigable economics professor at the University of Missouri. From his
pen came a torrential flow of books and articles on tax
reform. An untiring polemicist whose impact was strongest
during the 1920's, his books bristled with caustic criticisms
aimed at detractors of Henry George.

Brown's viewpoint is representative of the more sophis-
ticated single tax group. He completely laid aside *Progress
and Poverty's* all-devouring rent thesis though he emphasized the great importance of land rent in our economy.
Nevertheless, he may be classified as a modified single
taxer because with the exceptions of the inheritance tax and
such taxes as on gasoline he opposed all taxes except those
on land values. However, as time went by he realized that
the land value tax would probably be insufficient for
government needs.

Capitalism he embraced wholeheartedly, so long as competition remained unhampered by monopoly and incen-
tive-thwarting taxation. He railed against his fellow economists because they preferred, to use his own words, a
type of taxation "tending to weaken the incentives of
capitalism and going at least part way in the communist
and Marxist direction as regards tenets that, carried sufficiently far, are utterly irreconcilable with an acceptable

[18] Thomas N. Carver, *Essays in Social Justice,* p. 302.

functioning of capitalism. *Is an unpublicized fear the Achilles heel of capitalism's answer to communism?*"[19]

Brown has never changed his position significantly throughout his career. Therefore it is interesting to note that in 1924 he directed his arguments against the conservative economists, whereas by 1958 he had found it necessary to attack the liberals.[20] Although George was considered radical in his own day, his followers were forced to take an increasingly right of center position because they could not countenance the taxation required to finance a welfare state. George himself had envisioned a welfare state, but one which was financed by land value taxation. The locus of history had moved in a leftward direction past the Georgists.

No discussion of the position of Henry George in economic thought during the 1917–1933 era would be complete without mentioning two lists of his academic endorsers. One list was compiled by Emil O. Jorgensen in his *Next Step Toward Real Democracy* (1920), and contains about twelve names of pro-George professors who have not been discussed previously. Many, however, were in fields outside the social studies.[21] Harry Gunnison Brown's list, compiled in 1928, is more impressive.[22] Perhaps the views of all the economists listed by Brown are best summarized by Irving Fisher's statement.[23]

I cannot agree that land value should be the sole source of public revenue. Nevertheless, premising that so important a

[19] Harry Gunnison Brown, "The Effective Answer to Communism and Why You Don't Get it in College," a pamphlet, p. 99.
[20] Compare *ibid.* and Brown, *The Taxation of Unearned Incomes*, p. 119.
[21] Emil O. Jorgensen, *The Next Step Toward Real Democracy*, pp. 105-6.
[22] H. G. Brown, editor, *Significant Paragraphs from Henry George's Progress and Poverty*, pp. 77-80.
[23] *Ibid.*, p. 77.

change should not be made abruptly, I favor the gradual reduction so far as possible of taxes on the products of labor and
taking instead the economic rent of bare land.

Frank D. Graham, professor at Princeton and later senator from North Carolina, presented the dubious argument that "society creates the value and should secure it by
taxation."[24] Professor Glenn Hoover of Mills College and
later a very active proponent of land value taxation, conceded that the claims of landowners to some compensation
were indeed entitled to consideration, but felt that such
claims would be met by the gradual imposition of the tax.
Wrote Hoover: "why [these claims] should serve to perpetuate among future generations, a system which is as
unethical as it is unsound economically, is beyond me."[25]

Other endorsers were Paul H. Douglas, then professor
of economics at the University of Chicago and at present a
U.S. Senator from Illinois, and the Rev. Dr. John A. Ryan
of the Catholic University of America. Ryan, a liberal in
his church, opposed land value taxation in many books
written during his earlier years, but favored it in his later
writings.

Perhaps the most important endorsement and at the
same time the most enthusiastic came from the renowned
philosopher John Dewey. He wrote:[26]

It would require less than the fingers of the two hands to
enumerate those who, from Plato down, rank with Henry
George among the world's social philosophers. No man, no
graduate of a higher educational institution, has a right to
regard himself as an educated man in social thought unless he
has some first-hand acquaintance with the theoretical contribution of this great American thinker.

[24] H. G. Brown, editor, *Significant Paragraphs from Henry
George's Progress and Poverty*, p. 78.
[25] *Ibid.*, p. 79.
[26] *Ibid.*, p. v.

George and the Historians

During the 1917–1932 period, the historians took an increasing interest in Henry George. Previously few had devoted much space to George because history was still being written with a heavy political emphasis and George made very little political history. However, during the 1920's there was a gradual shift in emphasis to economic and social history, areas in which George had made a far greater impact. Toward the latter part of the decade, intellectual history—the history of ideas—assumed great prominence, especially with the publication of Parrington's *Main Currents in American Thought* (1927). George's influence upon reform thinking, and hence upon the course of American history in general, now became a fact of greater interest to historians. Nevertheless, the heyday of intellectual history lay still some ten to twenty years in the future.

The incident in George's life which appeared most frequently in general histories written during the 1917–1933 period was still the 1886 election in which George ran for mayor of New York City. Although he was defeated, the election was close and George had received more votes than the Republican candidate, one Theodore Roosevelt. In a sense, the election climaxed a period of rising labor agitation in New York which gave many worried moments to the conservative defenders of the status quo of the time. Yet its only tangible political result was to frighten the legislators in Albany into passing some pro-labor laws. This election gained mention only because it was the closest Henry George came to making political history. Not only George but such other reform thinkers of his day as Bellamy, Lloyd, Veblen, and even the muckrakers received light treatment at the hands of the historians.

Unfortunately, errors frequently marred even these limited historical treatments. For instance, the ordinarily reliable textbook writer, David S. Muzzey, referred to George as the editor of the San Francisco *Times*—actually it was the *Post*—and more importantly, stated that George called labor the chief factor in the production of wealth; no such thought can be found anywhere in George's writings. It was probably a confused notion of George's labor theory of property.[27]

In 1926 Thomas Beer wrote *The Mauve Decade* in the popular debunking style typical of the era. He referred to the single tax as "the reduction of real estate to common property by an imposition of a tax equal to the total rental value of the land." He also stated that George supported the Populist Party in 1896 whereas the exact reverse was true.[28]

It is possible to take issue with many of the statements made by the well-known conservative historian, James Ford Rhodes. In his *History of the United States from Hayes to McKinley, 1877–1896* (1928), one part of his multi-volume series on American history, Rhodes flatly stated that George's 1886 campaign was made possible by the Haymarket Affair and the railroad strike in the southwest. No proof of this novel view was given and the facts would seem to point in the opposite direction, for the Haymarket Affair hurt rather than helped George by temporarily frightening many people away from all reform movement. I have never seen any reference to the south-

[27] David S. Muzzey, *The United States of America*. New York: Ginn, 1924, v. 2, p. 192. Quite a few writers mistakenly accused Henry George of holding to the Marxist labor theory of value. In fact, George's labor theory of value was entirely different, as was his labor theory of property.

[28] Thomas Beer, *The Mauve Decade*. New York: Knopf, 1926, pp. 11, 38.

western railroad strike in connection with George in either primary or secondary sources.

Rhodes also asserted that George wanted "virtually to confiscate all the land." This belief, although still commonly held, is inaccurate. To Rhodes, George represented "the incarnation of a demand that the world should be made a better place to live in than it is "today" as well as being an "apostle of discontent among the industrial workingman." However, although George's following was swelled by "boycotters, socialists, anarchists and cranks," Rhodes conceded that *Progress and Poverty* was, withal, the work of an honest and sincere man.[29]

Lewis Einstein's 1930 biography of Theodore Roosevelt stated that in 1886 George ran on a socialistic platform.[30] The fact is that George ran on his own single tax program. Although he did have the grudging support of the socialists in 1886, constant quarreling between single taxers and socialists destroyed George's party within a year.

Charles E. Mirriam, a prominent political scientist and occasional historian of this period, gave some attention to the influence of Henry George in his *American Political Ideas, 1865–1917* (1920). He reviewed *Progress and Poverty* sympathetically but felt that a large number of independent landowners in the United States "made it difficult to secure widespread adherence to the new doctrines."[31] Other obstacles he noted were the opposition of farmers and tax limitations imposed by state constitutions. For these reasons, said Merriam, the single tax has made more headway in other lands like England and Germany.

In Merriam's opinion, George's philosophy had a greater

[29] James Ford Rhodes, *History of the United States from Hayes to McKinley, 1877-1896.* New York: Macmillan, 1928, p. 286.
[30] Lewis Einstein, *Roosevelt, His Mind in Action.* Boston: Houghton, Mifflin, 1930, p. 39.
[31] Charles E. Merriam, *American Political Ideas, 1865-1917*, p. 42.

impact upon American political thought than did his tax proposal: ". . . throughout his writings ran a strong current of democratic sympathy and democratic idealism, which beyond doubt, was as broadly influential as his arguments in the field of public finance. His goal was as attractive to many as the road he indicated."[32]

Another political historian, Fred E. Haynes, sociology professor at the University of Iowa, published *Social Politics in the United States* in 1924. The purpose of the book was to outline social and economic factors in political history, and as a result Henry George received some mention. There was one reference to the single tax as a form of agrarian socialism—highly incorrect—and George was likened to a founder of a new religion.[33] He observed that single taxers were mostly middle class, especially professional, and often held key positions in society. Thus, although not numerous, they were able to keep their proposal before the public. He estimated single tax membership at between twenty-five and fifty thousand.[34] Like Merriam, Haynes felt that George was important because he propelled the issue of poverty and the common man's welfare into politics for the first time. "The absolute truth of his principles has nothing to do with the greatness of his achievement as a prophet and preacher."[35]

Some years after the appearance of Haynes' volume, Harold U. Faulkner published his *Quest for Social Justice, 1898–1914* (1931), a highly regarded history of the progressive era. Faulkner typified the new trend among historians by rating George highly as a beneficial influence upon American social thinking, while at the same time giving scant attention to his specific economic theories. George's

[32] *Ibid.*, p. 43.
[33] Fred E. Haynes, *Social Politics in the United States*, p. 117.
[34] *Ibid.*, p. 136.
[35] *Ibid.*, p. 134.

death in 1897, wrote Faulkner, "stilled the voice of the most acute critic of American economic life. Yet the fires of revolt, though burning low, were not quenched. Soon they were to blaze forth into hot and consuming flame," i.e., the flame of Progressive reform.[36] To be sure, Faulkner left the reader wondering why George was "the most acute critic of American economic life," since no supporting explanation was offered. But he did mention many progressive reformers, such as U'Ren, Tom L. Johnson, and Newton D. Baker, who had been directly influenced by a reading of *Progress and Poverty*.[37]

The first major work devoted entirely to the history of American ideas was written, somewhat surprisingly, not by an historian but by a professor of literature at the University of Washington, Vernon Louis Parrington. Parrington's youth in Kansas, with its searing memories of sagging crop prices and mortgaged farms, vitally affected his later interpretation of American life and letters. There were years when corn was often used for fuel, he remembered, "and if while we sat around such a fire, watching the year's crop go up the chimney, the talk sometimes became bitter . . . who will wonder?"[38]

Parrington's social philosophy was the very quintessence of Progressive thought expressed in the biting style of the 1920's. Rapid industrialization had enhanced the power

[36] Harold U. Faulkner, *Quest for Social Justice*. New York: Macmillan, 1931, p. 81.

[37] See George Geiger, *The Philosophy of Henry George* (New York: Macmillan, 1933), p. 465n, which describes a pamphlet published by the Joseph Fels Fund entitled "Tentative List of Prominent Americans Who Endorsed the Single Tax and Those Who Favor the Taxation of Land Values Rather than of Improvements." No date is given, but it probably was published around 1912. This pamphlet contains some four hundred names, almost all well known.

[38] See Parrington's introduction by J. Allen Smith's *The Growth and Decadence of Constitutional Government* (New York: Henry Holt & Co., 1930).

of materialism and greed which was obscuring the Founding Fathers' vision of social justice. A shambling Jacksonian democracy was no longer able to stay these powers, and as the nineteenth century neared its end, perceptive men were beginning to see this: "The America of Fisk and Gould, of Boss Tweed and the *Crédit Mobilier* scandal, was far from satisfying the requirements of any rational civilization. After a hundred years to have come to such heroes, to have bogged down in such filth, was an outcome to the great experiment that one could not contemplate with pride. It was no time to be silent."[39]

The problem which confronted the Progressives of the early twentieth century seemed clear enough to Parrington: there was too much acquisitive instinct, too little social justice. Industrialists and middlemen were thought of as exploiting capitalists who were "quite cynically buying and selling the political state."[40] But although Parrington was long on moral indignation, he was quite short on specific proposals for reform. He was, in fact, disappointed with what his generation had accomplished while committed to its official philosophy.

Like most of his fellow Progressives he seemed to have been looking for a definitive economic or political method for improving human nature; Progressivism was not far distant from the utopian experiments of the Jacksonian era. It is hardly surprising that the too eager search for perfection that characterized the Progressive Era led inevitably to the cynicism of the 1920's. It was in this latter era that Parrington wrote, and though he was not cynical he was disenchanted.

Parrington treated Henry George sympathetically, although he was capable of quite contradictory views about

[39] Vernon L. Parrington, *Main Currents in American Thought,* v. 3, p. 137.
[40] *Ibid.*

him. For instance, on page 12 he could include George with Virginia Woodhull and Tennessee Claflin, "Citizen" George Francis Train, Henry Bergh, Ben Butler, Ignatius Donnelly and Bob Ingersoll as a "goodly company of cranks," but on page 402 he placed George in company with Darwin, Spencer, Mill, Karl Marx, Haeckel, Taine and William James as "masters of which no school in any age need feel ashamed."

Parrington may very well have been mistaken when he stated that "from the classical economists Henry George got little." His substantiation for this was merely that George denied the inevitability of poverty and depressions.[41] One could easily question whether this inevitability was the true views of *all* classical economists, and in any case such inevitability was not basic to their argument. Actually, George borrowed heavily from classical economics and embraced wholeheartedly its fundamental concept of the possibility and beneficence of pure competition. Perhaps Parrington found it difficult to see this because in his day George was so often thought of as a socialist of some sort.

The lengthy section on George in Parrington's book is summarized by a rambling page-long paragraph.[42] George is termed a "brilliant thinker" and is compared to Tom Paine. "In fastening upon monopoly as the prime source of social injustice, he directed attention to the origins of exploitative capitalism. . . . The suggestive principle of unearned income calls for further expansion to embrace other forms than rent, to fit it to the needs of a complex society."

George performed another service, wrote Parrington, in spreading through America a knowledge of the law of

[41] *Ibid.*, p. 131.
[42] Vernon L. Parrington, *Main Currents in American Thought,* pp. 135-6 for all the subsequent quotations from Parrington.

economic determinism. There was some truth in this, although since Parrington's time economic determinism has been deemphasized in favor of cultural, ideological and irrational determinism.

Parrington noted that later academic economists dealt sharply with Henry George "but what have they done to justify their magisterial tone? The science of economics is still cousin-german to philosophy in its fondness for spinning tenuous subtleties; it is still system-ridden, still too much the apologist for things as they are. From its servitude to a class Henry George essayed to deliver it." George's only shortcoming, according to Parrington, was his oversimplification of the problem: "Society is more complex than he esteemed it; individual motives are more complex. It is perilous to subordinate psychology to abstract theory; the ideal of justice is always running afoul of immediate and narrow interest." Selfishness often overrides reason; the single tax has never been successfully instituted because it cannot appeal to any particular economic group.

As can be seen, Parrington regarded Henry George more as a molder of American democratic thought than as an economic reformer, though he was sympathetic to him in both roles.

In 1933, there appeared an important and still highly regarded work on the philosophy of Henry George. George Geiger, a doctoral candidate working under John Dewey at Columbia University, produced this as his Ph.D. thesis. It is a monument to diligent research.

Geiger's book contained an excellent brief biography of George and a useful exposition of his economics and influence, but primarily Geiger was concerned with George as an ethical philosopher. He therefore discussed George's statement of the labor theory of property at great length. The reigning view of Geiger's contemporaries was that in the industrial era all production is completely social, that very few individuals produce a complete product, and that any individual contribution in production becomes an inextricable part of the total product. Geiger replied that however this may be, in the last analysis all the acts of production are performed by individuals. He might have added that the wages an individual receives, if determined in a purely competitive market, measure exactly the value of what he produces, so that even in a monetary and industrial society it is possible to separate the individual's production from the total product.

Geiger attempted to reconcile the labor theory with the social utility theory by saying that "the labor which is the basis of property must be labor that meets the needs of society . . . merely working, e.g., piling up sand in the desert, does not constitute a property claim."[43] This is the labor theory as Marx stated it and the social utility theory as Seligman stated it, but one wonders who is to judge what labor is socially necessary. Certainly, different cultures or different epochs within a single culture would be most unlikely to reach identical answers. If a man wishes to exercise the perquisites of ownership over a desert sand pile—he may have his reasons—why not let him do it? If society is organized on the basis that each man should own the fruits of his own labor, would not the greatest degree of freedom in equality then exist?

Geiger's statement on compensation was interesting. He argued that first we must decide whether private property in land is ethical or not, and then we can deal with the matter of compensation. Once we have done that, he feels that we should treat compensation "not in the uncompromising fashion of George, but with the realization that

[43] George Geiger, *The Philosophy of Henry George*, p. 148.

it constitutes one of those points of adjustment that would be required by any drastic social change . . ."[44]

Geiger concluded that "the work of Henry George, and the intimate connections that it has had with other important social and economic movements, cannot without risk be slighted by the historian of economic theory."[45] While agreeing that George exaggerated the importance of land value taxation, Geiger took issue with those who felt that George should be relegated to the dusty pages of forgotten history for that reason alone. He maintained that almost every intellectual contribution "from a Platonic doctrine of Ideas to a Watsonian behaviorism, has been originally elaborated in an extreme, often bizarre form. Compromise has no place at the initiation of ideas; it enters later, when history has performed its function of erosion."[46] George's intense concentration on his remedy may have been misplaced, but it "cast the brightest kind of focus upon the crucial part played by land in the economic process."[47] It is the duty of the social scientist to extract the usable and reject the exaggerated.

In an epilogue to his book, Geiger deplored the fact that the social sciences, particularly economics, were becoming more engrossed with methodology than with ethics, with means rather than goal or purpose. Social scientists who avoid ethical inquiry were like those pilots who allow their ships to be blown about on the high seas by the four winds with no destination in mind. On the other hand, the social scientists who based their theories on unverified assumptions were like the pilots who set sail without navigational instruments. We cannot divorce empirical

[44] George Geiger, *The Philosophy of Henry George,* p. 148.
[45] *Ibid.,* p. 473.
[46] *Ibid.,* p. 474.
[47] *Ibid.*

from ethical inquiry for "facts without values are blind; values without facts are empty."[48]

When Geiger wrote, the Great Depression was in full swing and he urged social scientists to meet the challenge with the same high ethical purpose Henry George had displayed. His plea recalls similar sentiments spoken by Henry George some fifty years earlier:[49]

The true law of social life is the law of love, the law of liberty, the law of each for all and all for each; . . . the golden rule of morals is also the golden rule of the science of wealth; . . . the highest expressions of religious truth include the widest generalizations of political economy.

[48] *Ibid.*, p. 488.
[49] Henry George, Jr., *Life of Henry George*, p. 279, quoting George's speech on the nature of political economy given March 9, 1877 at the University of California.

4
HENRY GEORGE AND KEYNESIAN ECONOMISTS, 1933-1964

IT WAS A CONFIDENT AMERICA THAT ENTERED THE YEAR 1929. By 1933, however, that confidence had been badly shaken by a business depression more vicious and debilitating than the country, indeed the world, had ever experienced. One out of every four workers was unemployed, businesses went bankrupt one after another, and more and more banks were forced to close their doors. As the grip of the depression enveloped the desperate country, new remedies were sought and daring social experiments tried.

Under such conditions one might expect a revival of Henry George's single tax program. Indeed there did develop a mild renaissance of interest in the movement. New advocates appeared, while older ones could buttress their agitation with that always effective argument, "I told you so." But the renaissance was mild because the pressing problems of the day seemed to call for specific remedies that could promise immediate relief. If private enterprise had caused the great debacle, then the government must intervene. If housing was inadequate, then let the government build houses; if workers were unemployed, let the government employ them; if business could not revive itself, let the government take over the task. The trend of thought was definitely in the direction of the welfare state and away from the free enterprise and natural rights system of George and his followers. The New Deal reformers had an entirely different philosophy than the single taxers.

An interesting by-product of the change in American social thought brought on by the depression and New Deal was that although the single taxer had heretofore been considered a radical thinker, a critic from the left, with the onset of the New Deal he began to be regarded as a conservative. In fact many single taxers today, in their zeal for free enterprise, would have to be classified with the radical thinkers of the democratic right. This shift was very rapid in the thirties and the chief criticisms of the single tax now emanated from left rather than from right wingers.

It was in these changing times that the single tax movement began to assume its modern organization and purpose. All through the twenties its old and graying members, veterans of the limited successes of the Progressive Era, made numerous unsuccessful attempts to usher in the new Georgist day via politics; they met ever-deepening failure. So, too, with such sporadic efforts as magazines (*The Freeman* was originally a Georgist publication), clubs (the old and respected Manhattan Single Tax Club, for instance, was breathing its last), speakers' bureaus and reading circles. The depression might be presenting a wonderful opportunity to the single taxers, but there was no movement, no effective organization, to take advantage of it.

At this critical juncture, Oscar Geiger, father of George Geiger and a one-time acquaintance of Henry George, in

1932 unemployed because of the depression, scraped together his life's savings and established the Henry George
School of Social Science. He offered what eventually became a ten-week course in economics, using *Progress and
Poverty* as the textbook. Advanced courses were later
added, and John Dewey consented to become the first
Honorary President of the school. Geiger eschewed politics
altogether, saying that no political efforts could succeed if
the people were not first educated in Georgist economics.
Today, an additional incentive for staying out of politics
is that all contributions to the school are tax deductible;
this privilege would be denied the school if it engaged in
political activity.

Geiger was able to obtain a charter for his school from
the New York State Board of Regents. All courses were
free but carried no academic credit whatsoever. Most of the
students still come to the school as a result of large-scale
mailings and are adults from literally all walks of life.

Geiger found the going hard at first, but the idea caught
on and the school expanded. Graduates of the program
volunteered to teach new classes without salary and the
school's faculty still operates on this basis today. Contributions came in, particularly from John C. Lincoln, onetime
president of the Lincoln Electric Company in Cleveland.
Eventually, branches were set up in cities throughout
America and even the rest of the world. There are approximately thirty of them today, and the school estimates its
graduates at 100,000.

Another successful Georgist organization is the Robert
Schalkenbach Foundation. Schalkenbach was a wealthy
printer who died in 1924, leaving a trust fund to be used
for the publication of George's books, all of which were
out of print in that year. In recent times, the Foundation
has devoted much effort to the establishment of more

cordial and effective relations with historians and economists in colleges and universities. A greater academic recognition of Henry George and land value taxation has been the result. The Foundation also publishes the *American Journal of Economics and Sociology* and recently sponsored a conference on land value taxation in Boulder, Colorado, which counted among its fifteen participants one college president, two deans, and three chairmen of economics departments in major universities. Thirteen papers were presented, each favorably discussing some aspect of land value taxation.[1]

Georgists who wish to work for more immediate political goals have found an outlet for their energies in Pennsylvania, where recently adopted local option laws permit cities of so-called third-class size (numbering about forty-eight), to tax land heavily, even exclusively. (The revitalized Henry George Foundation is helping in this work as is the Economic Education League and such individual land value taxers as Harry Gunnison Brown and W. Wylie Young.)

If the more recent Georgist organizations cannot as yet match the more spectacular efforts during the Progressive Era, they are at least better organized for the long run, less likely to collapse, and more soundly financed. In the earlier days, soap manufacturer Joseph Fels spent vast sums on political campaigns that in the end proved to be fruitless. Today Georgist organizations tend to live off the income of charitable bequests as well as annual contributions, a mode of operation much more suited to longevity and success.

Economic theory could not help but be affected by the

[1] Arthur P. Becker, Program Chairman (also Chairman, Economics Department, University of Wisconsin), "An Institute on Land-Value Taxation and Contemporary Economic Problems," August 24-26, 1961, mimeographed report.

depression. The old economics of *laissez faire* had clearly failed, however sound it might seem in theory. A new economics was not long in coming, for in 1936 John Maynard Keynes published his *General Theory of Employment, Interest and Money*. His message can be simply stated: in a depressed economy, where men and machines are idle, a government-induced increase in the money supply will not raise prices but will instead increase demand, which in turn increases production and employment. In good times, Keynes said, the government must restrict the money supply in order to combat inflation, but when bad times threaten the government must use deficit financing in order to revitalize production. In such emergencies, the government might well become an employer, a dispenser of much-needed welfare. What Keynes did was to restate an old doctrine in modern economic terminology and make it respectable. He provided a theoretical basis for what was common sense and fast becoming unavoidable political necessity. Voters who have once tasted the fruits of prosperity will not face poverty and starvation with philosophic calm. After Keynes, the new emphasis in economics was on fiscal policy, the economic effects of welfare measures and the measurement of gross national product. As economists became accustomed to this new way of thinking, Henry George still seemed as outdated as ever. This was especially apparent when land values took a sharp drop due to the depression from which they did not really recover until the 1950's (and then with a vengeance).

Views of the Public Finance Economists

Let us initiate our inquiry into the treatment George has received from more recent historians and economists by turning to the public finance experts. Land value taxation falls most naturally into their field of study and it might be hoped that among these specialists, at least, there would be a high degree of careful reexamination and new thinking.

Unfortunately, Clyde King's otherwise excellent textbook *Public Finance,* published in 1935, belies this hope. It repeated the hoary assertion that "Henry George would 'abolish all taxation save that upon land values,' and thus 'make land common property.' "[2] King further stated that "the tax is levied, not to raise money, but to make land, in effect, nationally or state owned."[3] This was an inexcusable error. Revenue was of central import in George's plan, as he made crystal clear in Book IX of *Progress and Poverty.*

After a favorable exposition of the ethical basis of the single tax, King concluded that land values were not the only unearned increments and that the single tax could scarcely do all that Henry George claimed for it.

Although King was antagonistic to the single tax, he had kind words to say about the Pittsburgh graded tax: "The Pittsburgh Plan is, on the whole, therefore, a moderate tax reform carried on in a conservative manner."[4] Yet the Pittsburgh Plan differed only in degree, not in kind, from full land value taxation.

Jens Jensen, Professor of Economics at the University of Kansas, was a highly regarded expert on tax matters. In his *Government Finance* (1937) he carefully differentiated between the single tax and the land value tax—something few other economists had done. He brushed aside the oft-raised objection that the single tax would not suffice to cover all public expenditures by suggesting rather sensibly,

[2] Clyde King, *Public Finance,* p. 273.
[3] Clyde King, *Public Finance,* p. 274. However, King writes that "the single tax would just about meet present fiscal needs."
[4] *Ibid.,* p. 281.

"let it yield what it will, and [we will] be to that extent relieved from more objectionable taxes."[5] He cited the Australian experience to show that "the tax is well established. The fact of long use, and present universal occurrences in that continent, should dispose of the old objection raised to the tax in the United States that it is incapable of administration because it is impossible to assess separately the bare-land value."[6]

But there was one argument against the land value tax which Jensen thought conclusive, except to its dyed-in-the-wool advocates, and that was the charge of confiscation: "The original appropriation was unethical, according to a labor theory of property. But it was the law, the rule of the game, at the time, and has been so since."[7] Only a high degree of necessity could condone the confiscation of privately collected land rents. Jensen's views on this matter were so pronounced that he made extreme statements which could easily convey misunderstanding: "The tax is laid on the landlord, and stays there, and he is *pro tanto* dispossessed, which is the intention of the land-value taxers."[8] However, under special conditions Jensen was willing to adopt a land value tax, particularly to finance wars and prevent post-war land speculation.[9]

Mayne S. Howard, a Commissioner and Director of Research in the Department of Taxation and Finance in New York City, gave land value taxation an extensive treatment in his textbook, *Principles of Public Finance* (1940). He wrote that "the advocacy of the single tax furnishes the one instance in public finance where the discussion approaches

[5] Jens Jensen, *Government Finance,* p. 288.
[6] Jens Jensen, *Government Finance,* p. 290.
[7] *Ibid.,* p. 289.
[8] *Ibid.,* p. 287.
[9] *Ibid.,* p. 438.

that on religion in intensity of feeling."[10] He thereupon
listed eighteen single tax arguments saying that "of these
eighteen arguments, there are probably only two or three
besides the first for which the non-single-taxer has much
respect."[11] The first argument was that since land-rent is
socially created, it should be socially collected. After listing
twelve anti-single tax arguments, Howard wrote, "of the
twelve arguments listed there are probably none for which
the single-taxer has any respect."[12]

Mr. Howard himself took a position opposed to the
tax, if in a somewhat contradictory fashion. Rather than
pay a full tax on land values, he said, would there not be
a massive migration from the cities? Yet, in the next paragraph he implied that land value taxation would cause a
flood of skyscrapers to be erected in order to minimize the
land value tax payment![13] The author concluded by saying that George's idea had nowhere been tested.[14] By so
doing he overlooked the long years of experimentation in
Australia and New Zealand.

Merlin Hunter and Kenneth Allen, both of the University of Illinois, collaborated in a 1940 textbook which
the publishers advertised as a complete revision of Hunter's earlier text reviewed in Chapter III of this study.
The single tax-Henry George section remained essentially
unchanged, except that two new objections are added,
both questionable. The authors claimed that the land
value tax was administratively unfeasible because of the
inseparability of land and building values, and in their
review of the Canadian experiment they remarked that
"the real test came with the World War, when taxes were

[10] Mayne S. Howard, *Principles of Public Finance,* p. 146.
[11] *Ibid.,* p. 147.
[12] *Ibid.,* p. 148.
[13] *Ibid.,* p. 145.
[14] *Ibid.,* p. 150.

increased to an amount equal to the economic rent, and more."[15] No research, either for or against the single tax, appears to support this contention.

Alfred G. Buehler considered the single tax in his textbook on public finance (1948). Some of his views were novel. He charged that the single tax enclaves in the United States had grown very slowly if at all since their inception.[16] For evidence to the contrary, see the discussion on page 174. Buehler claimed that today the income tax collects the "unearned increment," so land value taxation is no longer needed to curb speculation.[17] Yet *House and Home,* the leading trade magazine for the construction industry, believes that land speculation is a major urban problem today (see August 1960 issue).

Another of Buehler's statements is open to question: "Even if it were possible for our cities to live on the income of socialized land, would the public ownership or management of land be preferable to private land ownership and utilization?"[18] Henry George always stated that land value taxation is not land nationalization, nor did he advocate the latter.

William Withers (Queens College) was noncommittal in his brief exposition of Henry George and his ideas, but he must have left many students baffled when he wrote, ". . . [George] believed that unearned increment in the value of *real estate* should be taxed . . ." (italics mine).[19] Neither did Richard U. Ratcliff have much to say about George in his *Urban Economics* (1949), although his

[15] Merlin Hunter and Kenneth Allen, *Principles of Public Finance,* pp. 409, 411.

[16] Alfred G. Buehler, *Public Finance.* New York: McGraw-Hill, 1948, p. 381.

[17] *Ibid.*

[18] Alfred G. Buehler, *Public Finance,* p. 383.

[19] William Withers, *Public Finance.* New York: American Book Co., 1948, p. 157.

conclusion that "the adoption of this plan would revolutionize our land system and the whole institutional framework of private ownership"[20] is unsupportable.

M. Slade Kendrick (Cornell University) presented a high-level analysis of George's single tax in his excellent textbook, *Public Finance* (1951). Although opposed to the idea, he introduced his discussion by writing: "The clear logic with which the case for the single tax is presented, warmed by the fires of conviction, is ample reason for an examination of the issues."[21]

Professor Kendrick acknowledged that the land value tax would result in a more intensive use of land and that improvements which cannot now be made because of an insufficient return after taxes would become profitable under the new tax system.[22] Presumably, this advantage would apply to the long-continuing housing shortage and would have a salutary effect upon urban blight and renewal.

"The single tax has been the butt of many misleading arguments. Few proposals have been subject to greater misunderstanding of theory or effects."[23] Kendrick then proceeded to sweep aside such invalid objections as: the singe tax involves the nationalization of land, the private collection of land rent is an incentive to increase production, and that many incomes other than land rent are unearned and of social creation.

In conclusion, Kendrick presented what he believed to be the real difficulties. First of all, those individuals "who put their savings in land, or who had inherited it, would

[20] Richard U. Ratcliff, *Urban Economics.* New York: McGraw-Hill, 1949, p. 426.
[21] M. Slade Kendrick, *Public Finance.* Boston: Houghton, Mifflin, 1951, p. 233.
[22] *Ibid.*, p. 235.
[23] *Ibid.*

lose their possessions."[24] Some would benefit by the tax change but what of those who would lose? Professor Kendrick was concerned particularly with holders of mortgages on real estate.

How would the land value tax affect such persons, as Georgists see the matter? From a legal standpoint they would hardly be affected at all, since ownership rights would remain untouched. From a business standpoint, mortgages on well-improved real estate would become even more soundly secured because the total tax burden on such property would diminish. As for poorly improved properties, the owners would have time to make the necessary improvements because the tax would be imposed gradually over a number of years. Perhaps it would be desirable for the government to arrange low-cost loans for those real estate owners who would pay a higher tax under George's system and who would therefore be forced to improve their land. This would enable such owners to improve their land to an extent consistent with the use put upon it by the local economy.

Professor Kendrick observed, as an additional objection, that few real estate owners would know how the land value tax, if instituted in their community, would affect them monetarily. However, would it not be quite easy—an exercise in simple arithmetic—for a real estate owner to figure out how he would fare under George's system compared with the present real estate tax? Professor Kendrick complained that in all of the single tax literature there were no analyses of how the tax would work out in actual situations,[25] but in 1958, five professors working under a grant from the Economic Education League provided just such an analysis for the city of Bethlehem, Pennsylvania.

[24] *Ibid.,* p. 236.
[25] M. Slade Kendrick, *Public Finance,* p. 237.

Professor Kendrick's third objection was that the successful application of the land value tax required greater accuracy in assessment than now exists.[26]

His fourth and last objection was that some localities would have more revenues than they need and others less.[27] A practical solution to this difficulty is that those localities which have more could remit the surplus to their residents, presumably for payment of state and federal taxes; those localities which could not provide for all their revenue needs via the land value tax would have to levy additional taxes.

Although some of Kendrick's conclusions might be debated, his discussion of George was fair and objective.

Other public finance textbook writers failed to make a distinction between the single tax and the land value tax, and consequently their treatment of Henry George suffered somewhat. William H. Anderson (University of Southern California) listed four objections to George's tax ideas, but they were all directed against the single tax; a land value tax as one tax among many received no mention. His objections were: the single tax would be inadequate as a revenue-raiser, others besides landowners receive surplus gains, land like everything else must be bought at its full market value, and the single tax ignores ability-to-pay.[28]

In discussing the unearned increments tax, Anderson erred in saying that the Lloyd George attempt to levy such a tax failed because it was inadequate in yield and difficult to administer.[29] Actually, the Conservative ministry that followed Lloyd George's original government refused to

---

[26] M. Slade Kendrick, *Public Finance*, p. 237.

[27] *Ibid.*

[28] William H. Anderson, *Taxation and the American Economy*, p. 460.

[29] *Ibid.*, p. 461.

perform the necessary assessment and the tax was never imposed at all. He also referred to the graduated land tax used in New Zealand and Australia to break up large estates, but he failed to mention the larger, more important and more apropos land value tax which supports most of the local governments in New Zealand and a constantly growing number of them in Australia as well.

E. H. Plank (University of Denver) repeated exactly the same statement as Anderson. He added another, that there is no need for a single tax since the unearned land rent increment is well distributed throughout society. One wonders if this is a sufficient objection, although undoubtedly the situation would cry out for reform if landownership in the United States were concentrated in the hands of a few. Plank then goes on to list the usual objections, including the one about the impossibility of separating "economic and business rents." One of his statements raises eyebrows: "Frequent transfers of various types of land would greatly complicate the problems of effective and equitable administration."[30] Actually, this would greatly facilitate administration because it would make land assessment more accurate (assessment could be more easily compared to recent market prices).

Perhaps the dean of recent textbook writers in public finance has been Harold M. Groves of the University of Wisconsin. The many new editions of his *Financing Government,* originally published in 1939, attest to its continuing popularity. He was familiar with the Australian and New Zealand experience with land value taxation, but comments that the tax there encounters "the very favorable circumstances that many public responsibilities (edu-

---

[30] E. H. Plank, *Public Finance.* Homewood, Ill.: Irwin, 1953, p. 430. Brownlee and Allen, in their *Economics of Public Finance* (New York: Prentice-Hall, 1954), followed closely the reasoning of Anderson and Plank.

cation, for instance) which are borne locally in the United States and Canada are there undertaken by the state or national governments."[31] On the other hand, in none of these localities was land rent being collected fully by taxation; for example, no more than one-half is being collected in Queensland, the province taxing land the most heavily.[32]

A casual reading of Groves' extensive section on land value taxation would leave the reader with the impression that he was opposed to the idea, but careful consideration reveals that he endorses it, although diffidently. Groves writes:[33]

> With the rates moderate, a tax confined to land need not depress land values; indeed, it is argued that the stimulus to city growth resulting from "enlightened" taxation adds more to land values than the tax subtracts. . . . All things considered, it seems to the author that the case for the special taxation of land, particularly urban land, rests on sound ground. It is very doubtful whether cities ever should have allowed the sites within their boundaries to have passed entirely from public ownership. The main sound argument for private property in city sites is that city governments are too corrupt to manage a real estate business. Failing to follow the course taken by the city of Canberra [in which all land is city-owned and rented out on long-term lease], the next best program is to recapture a large amount of urban economic rent through special taxes on land.

Another textbook, *American Public Finance* by Schultz and Harriss (1959), disposed of the single tax on the ground that it could no longer be single, and of the land value tax on the ground that present landowners would suffer indefensible loss. A tax on future increases in land

[31] Harold M. Groves, *Financing Government*. New York: Henry Holt, 1958 (1939), p. 323.
[32] Land Values Research Group, *Public Charges Upon Land Values*. Melbourne, 1961, p. 6.
[33] Harold M. Groves, *Financing Government*, p. 323.

value the authors view favorably, especially in part payment of the new federal highway program, but they feel that assessment difficulties would be a major stumbling block.[34]

So far, this review of public finance textbooks would leave any reader with the impression that Henry George's ideas were unpopular with the tax experts, but there is evidence to the contrary. For instance, in 1936 the Tax Policy League sent a long questionnaire to the senior public finance professors in one hundred major universities throughout the land in an attempt to obtain a consensus on leading taxation issues among the academic tax experts. Fifty-four of these professors responded. Here are the results on three questions which dealt with land value taxation:[35]

Questions	Yes	No	No Opinion
Should improvements be taxed at a lower rate than land?	28	20	6
Should improvements be exempted?	2*	47	5
Special tax on unearned increment of land values?	30	16	8

* Probably these two were H. G. Brown and Paul Alyea.

In answer to the question, "What percentage of unearned increment should such a tax take?" seven responded 10 per cent-50 per cent; six, 50 per cent; one, 50 percent or more; and three, 100 percent. Others answered "substantial amount," "probably high," "nearly all." Thirty-four did not have an opinion.

[34] Schultz and Harriss, *American Public Finance*, pp. 398-400.
[35] Tax Policy League, "Tax Opinion Survey," May 1936, summarized in "Tax Bits," mimeographed bulletin.

This survey indicates a great deal more support for the land value tax (in modified form) than might have been expected from textbook statements. However, neither this survey nor any like it can measure intensity of opinion; it measures inclination rather than conviction, and with very few exceptions those economists who opposed George's ideas did so with more fervor than those who approved of them. For instance, Walter Morton, in his *Housing Taxation* (1950) gives an implied endorsement when he writes: "As a stimulus to new construction, it is wiser to reduce taxes on improvements without reducing them upon the site value of land, because the latter policy, as we have just seen, simply raises net economic rent which is capitalized into land values."[36] This will hardly stir any reader to action, nor is it as forceful as the usual anti-single tax statement in the textbooks, yet it is typical of many pro-land value tax statements.

Mabel Walker, the Executive Director of the Tax Institute, a leading research organization centered at Princeton, is another case in point. In 1938 she wrote and edited *Urban Blight and Slums,* a volume in the Harvard City Planning Studies. She excoriated land speculation as an evil, saying that land prices must adjust to present need if housing blight is to be avoided; a tax shift to land values was suggested as the remedy for this.[37] She quoted Edwin R. A. Seligman, George's old opponent, and Mr. Jesse Isador Straus to the effect that ". . . a heavy tax on land, by keeping its capital value low, makes it more accessible of purchase by those of small means."[38] A tax on future increments in land values was advocated as being superior to special assessments when special public improvements

[36] Walter Morton, *Housing Taxation.* Madison: University of Wisconsin Press, 1955, p. 21.
[37] Mabel Walker, *Urban Blight and Slums.* Cambridge: Harvard University Press, 1938, pp. 110, 253.
[38] *Ibid.,* p. 253.

such as roads, sewers, etc. must be paid for; the latter would be on expected windfalls whereas the former was on actually realized ones.[39]

After having devoted two chapters to a rather favorable treatment of land value taxation and its variants, one would expect that the author's last chapter on "Summary and Conclusions" would include them among its many recommendations, but such was not the case. Instead, only a vague reference to the necessity for "a reformed tax system" was made. Miss Walker's most recent book, *Business Enterprise and the City* (1957), makes no mention of special taxes on land.

Harold S. Buttenheim was a more enthusiastic advocate of George's ideas. Although he never held a teaching position, he was influential in tax matters because of his long editorship of *The American City*, the trade magazine for municipal administrators. Over the years he published many editorials in favor of land value taxation. As with many other advocates, the ethical argument was his strongest incentive in working for the idea. He regarded the Pittsburgh graded tax as a "scientific" system of real estate taxation and argued that it encouraged building and urban renewal.[40]

During the depression, many radical ideas on what to do about urban blight were circulating and so the land value tax lost some of its radical aura. This oblique endorsement came from the 1937 National Resources Committee set up by the New Deal:[41]

State and local authorities should consider the reduction of the rate of taxation of buildings and the corresponding increase of such rates on land, in order to lower the tax burden on home

[39] Mabel Walker, *Urban Blight and Slums*, p. 273.
[40] Dorothy Rosenman, *A Million Homes a Year*, p. 122.
[41] Leon Silverman, "Municipal Real Estate Taxation as an Instrument for Community Planning," *Yale Law Journal*, Dec. 1957, p. 230.

owners and the occupants of low-rent houses, and to stimulate rehabilitation of blighted areas and slums.

In 1956, an objective and scholarly book on Fairhope, the single tax enclave in Alabama, appeared. It was written by Paul and Blanche Alyea, the former a tax economist teaching at the University of Alabama. Much of the land in Fairhope, a town of 4,200, is owned by a corporation which rented out the land and used the revenue to pay the taxes of its lessees. The authors' conclusion was that the experiment has proved successful. The town has grown faster than its neighboring communities, Daphne, Montrose, Battles Wharf and Point Clear, all of which are much older and enjoy special advantages not enjoyed by Fairhope. The part of town which belongs to the single tax corporation has been more highly improved than the other parts, and from an over-all viewpoint it is an attractive place in which to live. It is characterized by an open-mindedness and freedom of thought not usual in the average small town. Fairhope is "less standardized, less tradition-bound, less dominated by any given set of values than other small communities . . . it was not mere coincidence that Mrs. Johnson located her school [the famous progressive School of Organic Education] in Fairhope."[42]

The authors point out that one difficulty, even danger, that the program faces today is that so few of the present residents really understand the single tax idea; indifference can kill any successful experiment.[43]

Once again, in studying the views of economists, we

[42] Paul and Blanche Alyea, *Fairhope, 1894-1954*, pp. 254, 284, 290, 291.
[43] *Ibid.*, p. 269. In the summer of 1954 I visited Arden, Delaware, another Georgist enclave, and spoke to Mr. Don Stephens, an official there. The successes and problems of his community, as he related them to me, exactly parallel the Fairhope story.

encounter the work of Professor Harry Gunnison Brown, public finance professor at the University of Missouri and George's outstanding academic defender. Although now officially retired, he (and his wife) are still quite active in the Georgist cause with frequent articles in economics magazines and speeches in the Pennsylvania campaign to get a city, any city, to adopt land value taxation.

Brown's most recent writings have stressed the success of George's ideas in Australia and New Zealand. For instance, his article on "The Challenge of Australian Tax Policy" in the *American Journal of Economics and Sociology* commands notice. It is a report on a survey taken by Mr. A. R. Hutchinson, who based his findings primarily on published statistics and, where necessary, on personal observation.

This survey arranged the Australian states according to the order in which they tax land values: Queensland, New South Wales, Western Australia, South Australia, Victoria and Tasmania. The states taxing land values more heavily had a greater increase in total area under crops, in new dwellings constructed per one hundred marriages, and a greater inflow of population. The average value of improvements per landholder was twice as great in the states that taxed land values more heavily, their ratio of improvements to unimproved land was also double, and these states also showed a slightly higher average income per capita. In other words, the more land value was taxed, the better the economic situation.[44]

Although these statistics indicate that land value taxation deserves serious consideration form the public finance economists, a point which Professor Brown was

[44] Harry Gunnison Brown, "The Challenge of Australian Tax Policy," *American Journal of Economics and Sociology,* July 1949, pp. 12, 15.

quick to make, a skeptic might very well be entitled to question whether these superior results are due to the tax system or to other more important factors. The three land value taxing states are, in the main, the younger frontier states, and like our own western states are more likely to grow faster than the older and more settled ones.

However, there were other statistics in Brown's article which were less susceptible to this criticism. He reported that those districts in South Australia and Victoria which taxed land values were markedly superior in new dwelling construction. Thus in Victoria, "although at the 1921 census only 16 per cent of the state population was in the fourteen districts rating land values, these districts accounted for 46 per cent of the total increase in dwellings for the State between the two census years [1921 and 1933]."[45]

But his figures on the Melbourne suburbs were even more convincing. Brown found that those suburbs which are about five rail miles from Flinders Street Station in the center of Melbourne and which tax land values, had 50 per cent more dwellings constructed per available acre in the 1928-1942 period than those which did not. Making a similar comparison for suburbs seven miles out, the land value tax suburbs did two and a third times better; for suburbs nine and a half miles out, they did twice as well.[46] As Brown pointed out, these figures certainly seem to demand the attention of all those interested in municipal finance.

Professor Brown's comments about the almost irrational feeling toward Henry George by members of the academic economic fraternity bear mention:[47]

[45] Harry Gunnison Brown, "The Challenge of Australian Tax Policy," *American Journal of Economics and Sociology*, July 1949, p. 13.
[46] *Ibid.*
[47] *Ibid.*, pp. 96, 97.

A well-known economics teacher who had collaborated in the writing of a book in which increased taxation of land values was favored, told me in private conversation that he had, because of this, taken considerable "razzing" from colleagues. Another economics teacher confided to me that when, during his graduate school days, he had made his interest in land-value taxation known to one of his teachers, the latter suggested to him that, as a young economist, he should be careful about committing himself thus to a view not generally held in the profession. . . . And a very able and distinguished economist of my acquaintance, definitely friendly to land-value taxation, who has done most useful work in another field of economics, explained to me some years ago that he does not express this sympathy publicly lest, with the prevailing antagonism among economists, his studies in this other field might have relatively little influence.

Some five years ago, the Economic Education League, a Georgist organization financed by Gilbert Tucker, author of *The Se'f-Supporting City,* sponsored an extensive and highly detailed research project which was to determine what effect land value taxation would have if adopted in the city of Bethlehem, Pennsylvania. This project was directed by The Institute of Research of Lehigh University; Dr. Eli Schwartz, Assistant Professor of Finance, and Dr. James E. Wert, then Assistant Professor of Accounting, were in charge. Their findings were enlightening.

Schwartz and Wert found that in determining the effect of land value taxation on property owners, the ratio of land assessment to total real estate assessment was the key factor. For the city of Bethlehem as a whole, land assessments approximated 27 per cent of the total real estate assessment. Consequently, if improvements are to be wholly or partially exempted from taxation, real estate properties which have a land value greater than 27 per cent of the combined land and building assessment would pay more taxes than they pay now; conversely, those properties having less than a 27 per cent assessment on land would pay less if land value taxation were to be instituted in Bethlehem at the time of the study. The same principle, though of course not the same ratio, would hold true in any other city.

With this in mind, which real estate owners would pay more in taxes and which less if George's proposal were introduced? Schwartz and Wert found that with few exceptions homeowners would pay less in taxes. The exceptions were homes in or close to commercial areas, and, said the authors, "it is questionable whether it is economic for these properties to be used as residences."[48]

Other property owners who would obtain immediate tax relief as a result of improvements exemption would be industrial and outlying commercial properties. Higher tax burdens would be incurred by many owners of commercial properties located in the heart of the city and, of course, by owners of vacant land.[49]

The authors' conclusions were reassuring to the followers of George. Schwartz and Wert felt that a land value tax would lead to a more intensive and modern use of the central commercial districts whose deterioration is such a problem in most American cities today.[50]

The authors also concluded that industrial land would be used in a more extensive manner. "It would pay to use a great deal of single-story floor space (the most efficient type of factory construction); it would be economic to disperse plants and comparatively inexpensive to develop parks and parking places around the plant area. Extensive

[48] Dr. Eli Schwartz and Dr. James E. Wert, *An Analysis of the Potential Effects of a Movement Toward a Land Value Based Property Tax.* Albany: Economic Education League, 1958, pp. 17, 29.

[49] *Ibid.,* p. 34. In a private conversation with me on July 14, 1961, Percy Williams, former Chief Assessor of Pittsburgh, stated that the effects on property owners that Schwartz and Wert observed were also the effects of the graded tax in Pittsburgh.

[50] *Ibid.,* p. 36.

rather than intensive use of industrial land would do much to make industrial cities pleasanter places in which to live and work."[51]

Still another conclusion was that "the tax pressures should induce rapid development of idle land."[52] This would be no small result if the authors' figures are to be taken at face value. They report that although only 1.7 per cent of total taxable property consists of vacant land, that class of land represents 6 per cent of total assessed land value.[53] It is well known that throughout the United States vacant land is greatly underassessed, and Bethlehem was no exception. In fact, for a representative sample of fifty properties, the appraisal-assessment ratio (estimate of present market to actual assessed vaue) was amost five times greater for vacant than for improved land.[54] Idle land or poorly used land, then, was no small factor in Bethlehem's economy, and presumably in the economy of most American cities.

The final conclusion which Schwartz and Wert reached was that "there should be a general flurry of repair and modernization activities" in the older residential districts.[55] On this one item alone, the Federal Housing and Home Administration is spending millions of dollars a year; so are local and state governments.

Recently land value taxation has received enthusiastic support from another outstanding and rather surprising source. The August 1960 issue of *House & Home,* a Henry

[51] Dr. Eli Schwartz and Dr. James E. Wert, *An Analysis of the Potential Effects of a Movement Toward a Land Value Based Property Tax,* p. 36.
[52] *Ibid.*
[53] *Ibid.,* p. 12.
[54] *Ibid.,* p. 28.
[55] Dr. Eli Schwartz and Dr. James E. Wert, *An Analysis of the Potential Effects of a Movement Toward a Land Value Based Property Tax,* p. 36.

Luce publication and the leading magazine for the construction industry, was devoted entirely to the subject of land economics. This issue was researched and written in collaboration with Miles L. Colean, a widely respected housing economist, and two well-known land economists, Professor Ernest M. Fisher of Columbia University and Professor M. Mason Gaffney of the University of Missouri.[56]

This special issue appended no ifs, ands, or buts to its advocacy of land value taxation. One finds this modern publication quoting approvingly Winston Churchill's statement (*circa* 1910) that the landowner collects all the benefits of material progress:[57]

Some years ago in London there was a toll bar on a bridge across the Thames, and all the working people who lived on the south side of the river had to pay a daily toll of one penny for going and returning from their work. The spectacle of these poor people thus mulcted of so large a proportion of their earnings appealed to the public conscience, and agitation was set on foot, municipal authorities were roused, and at the cost of the rate payers the bridge was freed and the toll removed. All those people who used the bridge were saved sixpence a week, but within a very short time rents on the south side of the river were found to have risen about sixpence a week, or the amount of the toll which had been remitted!

One wonders how Churchill would view this statement today. It is reported that once when a Georgist urged him to stand for Henry George's ideas as he had once done, Churchill replied that if the Georgists would muster up the votes, he would sing The Land Song (a Georgist

---

[56] It is interesting to note that in none of Professor Fisher's many previous books, some of which are texts, is there any favorable mention of land value taxation. If there is a reference, it is veiled and vaguely derogatory. This comment applies to his most recent book, published in 1954.

[57] *House & Home,* August 1960, p. 126.

"spiritual" sung to "Marching Through Georgia" with the tag line, "God Made the Land for the People!"), in Parliament if necessary.

Almost completely missing from the eighty-two page, devoted to the land question is the name of Henry George On page 134, his picture appeared along with twelv other endorsers of the land value tax, from Moses to Sun Yat-sen. To one familiar with the history of the tax, his absence elsewhere was conspicuous. Perhaps the editors felt that to identify land value taxation with Henry George might stir up old emotions and half-forgotten antipathies, so that the idea would be retarded rather than advanced. Other advocates of land value taxation who have been active in politics have also found it necessary to mute the name of Henry George in order to achieve quicker acceptance. It seems highly probable that the writings of historians and economists have been of key importance in etching this unfortunate image of George upon the American mind. The web of written history, for all its invisibility, is steel-like in its strength.

According to *House & Home*, since 1950 land prices have soared "anywhere from 100 per cent to 3760 per cent," yet there is no shortage of land.[58] Our principal cities are spotted with vacant lots and speckled with underused land. A thorough land survey in Indianapolis, for example, revealed 4,381 acres (nearly seven square miles) of unused level land zoned for homes in the heart of the city, and 79,000 acres available for housing around the edge of the city (these 79,000 acres add up to more land than Indianapolis can absorb in thirty-five years at the present rate of growth).[59]

Where will all this land hoarding, land speculation and

[58] *House & Home,* August 1960, p. 101.
[59] *Ibid.,* p. 119.

land inflation lead us? *House & Home* points darkly to the history of depressions in America, saying that land speculation and collapsing land price booms were a chief cause. Other ill effects are the increase in investment needed to start a good farm or any industrial venture and the increase in house-building costs.[60]

The editors of *House & Home* have followed up this special issue with frequent editorials criticizing the Federal urban renewal spending program and urging land value taxation as a substitute or at least an addition to the present program (see February 1961 issue).[61] However, Henry George's name is never mentioned.

The Economics Textbooks

As might be expected, the changes wrought by the new Keynesianism on the contents of college economics textbooks meant that even less space than formerly was devoted to the ideas of Henry George. Whereas the older texts stressed the factors of production and distribution value, monopoly and ethics, the more recent texts preferred fiscal policy, national income accounting, problems of depression and inflation, oligopoly and sociology. Although Keynes wrote his masterwork in 1936, it was not until 1948 or 1950 that college texts showed the effects of his thinking. High school economics textbooks seem to have lagged another ten years.

Another reason for de-emphasis was that the single tax movement had small success in this country and little-

[60] *Ibid.*, pp. 123, 124.

[61] The tax also has application to the federal highway program. Professor Mason Gaffney of the University of Missouri reports that Rex Whitton, President Kennedy's Federal Highway Administrator, has suggested that land value increments be taxed to help finance highways, but he hesitated to advocate it strongly because he thought it was his own "pet idea" (see *Henry George News*, January 1961, p. 4.)

known success elsewhere. If Kerensky had triumphed instead of Lenin and if Sun Yat-sen had completed the Chineses revolution instead of Chiang and Mao, then the extensive chapters on communism and socialism might have been replaced with chapters on the single tax, since Kerensky and Sun Yat-sen had strongly endorsed land value taxation.

Not quite half of the dozens of college economics texts examined George and the single tax. Those that dealt with rent, tax shifting and unearned incomes usually discussed George. Except for Broadus Mitchell, Raymond T. Bye, and Harry Gunnison Brown, none of the textbook writers really supported George's ideas; most were in vigorous opposition. Only two of the textbooks referred to the actual use of a land value tax elsewhere in the world. Mrs. Elizabeth Read Brown—wife of H. G. Brown—surveyed seventy-six economics textbooks and found that only forty-one mentioned Henry George, *Progress and Poverty*, or the single tax.[62]

The usual textbook treatment displays a fairly definite pattern. A brief description of George's personal life is followed by a cursory outline of *Progress and Poverty*. Then come the arguments in favor of the single tax (few distinguished between the single and land value tax). There follows a much lengthier exposition of the arguments opposed. The latter usually carry the stated or implied approval of the author.

Textbook arguments for the single tax generally emphasized ethical considerations: the tax falls on unearned increment or income and land values are a social product. Supplementary practical arguments were that the production of wealth would be untaxed, land speculation ended,

[62] Elizabeth Read Brown, "How College Textbooks Treat Land Value Taxation," *American Journal of Economics and Sociology*, January 1961, pp. 147, 148.

and land necessarily put to its best use. But quite often these arguments were presented abstractly and were not related to practical present-day problems. For instance, C. Lowell Harriss concluded his brief section on George by writing, "Removal of taxes on building would encourage construction."[63] But there was no reference to this fact some three hundred pages later, when he discussed the spread of urban blight in these terms:[64]

But there *must* be some possibility of prevention. The years ahead will bring difficult housing problems. The millions of the poor are likely to find slums increasingly expensive. To meet the crude, quantitative needs for our population growth, the economy will be able to build enough housing units though rising land and construction costs will not be easily met by the masses.

In discussing the reduction of the price of land to zero that would ensue from a land value tax, Lawrence Abbott, who favored the idea, made this interesting comment: "Instead of having to pay $10,000 for land with a $600 rental value, the 'buyer' would pay nothing, invest the $10,000 in securities, and use the dividends to pay the $600 tax!"[65]

Some new and untypical thinking on the subject of the single tax appeared in *Applied Economics,* a textbook written by Raymond T. Bye and William W. Hewett, of the Universities of Pennsylvania and Cincinnati respectively. One of their ideas is of special interest: It is possible—and it actually has happened—that material progress can increase production on marginal land at a faster rate than on more valuable land. For example, constant transportation advances can triple the productivity of marginal land although total production may only have doubled.

[63] C. Lowell Harriss, *The American Economy,* 3rd edition, p. 548.
[64] *Ibid.,* p. 842.
[65] Lawrence Abbott, *Economics and the Modern World,* p. 654.

Thus, land rent, being the difference between what could be produced on good land and on marginal land, does not increase as fast as total production (*per* Ricardo's Law of Rent), leaving increasingly more for wages and interest.[66] This analysis is somewhat similar to Walker's, and it is unusual to see George's economic analysis handled in such detailed fashion in a modern textbook. However, it was eliminated in later editions.

Bye and Hewett unmistakably endorsed land value taxation, although not as a single tax. Indeed, they characterized single taxers as "zealots who look upon George's program as a panacea for most of the economic ills that beset society."[67]

Although the authors claimed that the private collection of land rent was unethical, they advocated the compensation of landowners for their investment which society at one time recognized as being permissible. They recommended that the tax be gradually imposed like the graded tax in Pittsburgh. Other suggested methods were compensation via long-term low-interest bonds or life annuities, or by changing the laws of inheritance "to provide that all lands transferred at death should henceforth be subject to a tax sufficient to appropriate the rents thereof."[68] Of all these methods, according to the authors, the one considered politically most feasible is gradual imposition.

At this point, it is worth while to review the more common arguments against the single tax found in current textbooks.

(1) Confiscation is still number one, although it no longer elicits a strong emotional reaction. No doubt, the

---

[66] Raymond T. Bye and William Hewett, *Applied Economics*, 1928 edition, p. 545.

[67] *Ibid.*, 1960 edition, pp. 211, 212.

[68] Raymond T. Bye and William Hewett, *Applied Economics*, 1928 edition, pp. 546, 547; 1960 edition, pp. 211, 212.

heavy taxation we experience today somewhat blunts this argument. Is confiscation by income tax, excise tax, admissions tax, car tax, etc. any less confiscatory than a tax on land rent?

(2) Many authors claim that if the single tax seizes the unearned increment, it should likewise compensate landowners for a drop in land prices, which they liked to describe as the unearned decrement (see discussion on Taussig).

(3) Many authors feel that the income tax falls to a very large extent on land rent, making land value taxation unnecessary. However this may be, land still commands considerable rentals today.

(4) The land value tax is not based on the ability-to-pay principle, a fact nearly always deprecated in the newer textbooks.

(5) George's contention that landowners perform no useful function provoked the criticism of those textbook writers who feel that landowners perform the service of allocating land to its most efficient use.[69]

(6) Another source of concern is the fear that under land value taxation, democracy would suffer. If citizens did not have to pay taxes because the government lived off land rents, the main incentive to participate in government would be removed.

(7) Many authors felt the single tax was defective because it did not affect unearned income other than land rent. Recently, the term "unearned income" has been redefined to mean any income derived from property rather

[69] For instance, see Theodore Morgan, *Introduction to Economics* (New York: Prentice-Hall, 1956), p. 362. Land value taxers consider this the job of the improvers or users of land, the landlord *per se* merely letting out his land to the highest bidder. The only service the landowner performs is that of rent collector, for which even George was willing to pay him a commission of up to 3 per cent.

than labor and which is not strictly needed to elicit production.[70] This might be called "G.N.P. ethics." By this definition, income from securities and inherited personal ability (such as musical talent) would be considered unearned, and since Babe Ruth might have worked just as hard if he had received $10,000 a year, any income he received in excess of that figure is "unearned."[71] Naturally, most textbook writers who put forth this revolutionary definition shrink from its full implications. In George's opinion, income from securities is earned because securities are justifiably subject to private ownership; as for Babe Ruth, he was entitled to whatever anybody in a free market was willing to pay him.

Garver and Hansen, in their *Principles of Economics*, questioned whether further development of mines and water power would be discouraged by the government collection of land rent. Oil wildcatting and mine prospecting involve the risking of huge amounts of money with the strong possibility of ending up with nothing but a dry hole. Do not wildcatters and prospectors deserve the extra incentive of being able to engage in a little land speculation?[72] This argument has been taken very seriously by the United States Congress (cf., the much-criticized oil depletion allowance). Professor Harry Gunnison Brown suggests that we treat a natural resource prospector exactly as we do an inventor: we should give him a monopoly of limited duration by allowing him to collect the land rent,

[70] According to this ethical viewpoint, anything is ethically permissible so long as it increases economic production. To be consistent, those who profess such ethics would have to embrace communism if eventually the communists should out-produce us.

[71] For instance, see William Kiekhofer, *Economic Principles, Problems and Policies* (New York: Appleton-Century-Crofts, 1951), p. 574.

[72] Frederick Garver and Alvin Hansen, *Principles of Economics*. Boston: Ginn, 1937, p. 436.

untaxed, for a certain numbers of years. Just as patent monopolies, lasting for a few years only, are a sufficient extra inducement to inventors, so would a temporary land rent monopoly be a sufficient extra inducement to prospectors—in addition to the return on their capital and labor. Brown points out that even if the Wright brothers had never been born, we would eventually have had the airplane. Their social contribution was that they gave it to us a few years sooner than "normal" and so they were entitled to patent monopolies for a few years. The same with prospectors. The mines or wells they open would eventually be found anyway; thus they are only entitled to a land monopoly for a few years.[73]

Surprisingly, fewer outright errors are to be found in the general economics textbooks than in the textbooks on public finance. The reason for this paradox may lie merely in the less extensive treatment given George in the general texts as compared to the public finance textbooks. By giving him less space, perhaps the latter had less room for error.

Nevertheless, egregious misstatements did crop up. Melville J. Ulmer wrote, "theoretically, this idea might have worked, but fortunately it was never tried; practically, the administrative difficulties would have been mountainous."[74]

It was common among the older economists to confuse the single tax with land nationalization and with socialism. Modern writers made this mistake much less often, but it did occasionally occur. For instance, William Kiekhofer's widely used text equated public property in land with the public collection of the land rent.[75]

[73] Harry Gunnison Brown, "The Effective Answer to Communism," pp. 34-36.
[74] Melville J. Ulmer, *Economics, Theory and Practice*, p. 512.
[75] William Kiekhofer, *Economic Principles, Problems and Policies*, p. 577.

Using the term "unearned increment" in describing land value taxation could quite easily lead authors astray. Wrote Knight and Hines: "Nor is it necessary for the state to appropriate the whole of economic rent in order to do away with unearned increment. Suppose increments in land values accrued to past owners who did not earn them. This does not necessarily warrant taking rent away from present owners."[76] George's quite different approach maintained that the private collection of land rent by anyone would be wrong because all land rent—present as well as future increments—belongs to society. "Unearned increment" is a term more appropriate to the land ideas of John Stuart Mill; it did not appear in *Progress and Poverty* at all.

Two Princeton professors, William Baumol and Lester Chandler, made a rather astounding statement about the single tax in their otherwise excellent textbook: "Again the argument is weak because a tax on land can affect the supplies available on the market. A land tax of sufficient magnitude may induce landlords to let their acres grow wild or use them as hunting grounds rather than renting them out for industrial building. The less effectively he can shift the taxes on to the person to whom he rents his land, the greater may be the landlord's inducement to hold it back for his own use."[77] Ignored was the problem of how the landlord would be able to pay his land tax, if he had no rental income.

David McCord Wright argued similarly: "If all the increase in land values were taxed away, there would be less incentive to undertake improvements."[78]

The Australian and New Zealand experience with land

[76] Bruce Knight and Lawrence Hines, *Economics*, p. 515.
[77] William Baumol and Lester Chandler, *Economic Processes and Policies*, 1954 edition, p. 666.
[78] David McCord Wright, *A Key to Modern Economics*, p. 479.

value taxation would seem to confute most of these statements. For instance, the taxpayers in Mildura, an irrigation district 351 miles northwest of Melbourne, Australia,
voted 3½ to 1 in favor of land value taxation in August
1956. Two years afterwards, it was reported, "Building in
1957 broke all records. And at the present rate, the 1957
record will be broken this year."[79] The citizens of Wangaratta (Victoria) also voted a land value tax into effect
in August 1956. A June 1958 issue of the *Wangaratta
Chronicle Despatch* reported, "Valuable blocks of idle
land have been sold by auction at 'very satisfactory' prices,
and some derelict buildings have been demolished to make
way for new ones."[80]

Professor Wright also stated that "most countries which
have tried the George thesis have found that the expense
of administering the tax is out of proportion to the collections."[81] Actually, the reverse seems more true. The
Taxation Enquiry Committee appointed in 1947 by the
Kenya government (East Africa) reported that the land
value tax, since 1921 the sole source of tax revenue in
the capital city of Nairobi, is "economical to administer.
. . . From the fiscal point of view and bearing in mind the
present need to encourage development, the Committee
favors the site-value [George] system in the taxation pattern of the Colony and the principle of levying a comparatively high tax on land, thus ensuring that it will
not be left idle or insufficiently developed for long, rather
than the taxation of improvements."[82] Yetta Scheftel concluded that in Australasia the "cost of administration and
collection of the tax constitutes a very small proportion of

[79] *Land & Liberty*, August 1958, p. 156.
[80] *Ibid.*, p. 136.
[81] David McCord Wright, *A Key to Modern Economics*, p. 479.
[82] H. G. Brown, *et al.*, *Land Value Taxation Around the World*,
p. 47.

the revenue collected."[83] And in "South Africa, as in Australia, it was shown that, once the practice of relieving improvements from taxation has been experienced, it remains established for good."[84]

Mrs. Brown, in the article previously cited, had these pertinent remarks to make:[85]

Again, if "the expense of administering the tax is out of proportion to the collection," how could it happen, as Dr. Rolland O'Regan reports: "Some 56 New Zealand communities have adopted land-value taxation, exempting all buildings and improvements, in the last fourteen years?" (This was by vote of property owners 30 per cent of whom had signed "a petition for land-value taxation," resulting in a special election called by the governing body.) Dr. O'Regan commented that "it spreads like a grease spot." It appears unlikely that citizens would request such action—and overwhelmingly vote for it— if other citizens in New Zealand and Australia had discovered through experience that the "cost of administering the tax" was "out of proportion to the collections."

A rather misleading objection concerned the constitutionality of George's proposal. One textbook, written by a committee of 67 professors pronounced it not constitutional because "the Constitution of the United States guarantees the inviolability of property."[86] This completely ignored Pittsburgh, the California Irrigation District and other places in the United States where the law had been applied and accepted. On the other hand, it is true that a few *state* constitutions provided that localities might not grant special exemptions in the real estate tax,

[83] Yetta Scheftel, *The Taxation of Land Value*, p. 95.

[84] H. G. Brown, *et al.*, *Land Value Taxation Around the World*, p. 46.

[85] Elizabeth Read Brown, "How College Textbooks Treat Land Value Taxation," *American Journal of Economics and Sociology*, January 1961, p. 156.

[86] Committee on Principles of Economics, *Principles of Economics*, p. 373.

which has generally been interpreted to mean that the tax on land and buildings must be the same.

Henry George received much the same treatment in high school economics textbooks. The same arguments and the same errors reappear. Few favored his ideas, and few showed awareness of the application of the land value tax in Australia, New Zealand, Pittsburgh, and elsewhere. Although many mentioned tax exemption of improvements in their lists of single tax advantages, few gave space to Henry George's contention that the tax would prevent the twin evils of land utilization—underuse (by ending land speculation) and overcrowding (by increasing the usable supply of land because its price is reduced to zero).

Nevertheless, it may be somewhat surprising to learn that George received more mention in the high school than in the college texts. The explanation for this is that very few of the writers for the high school market dealt with Keynesian issues, thus leaving more room for the ideas of Henry George. Of course, it should be understood that in most instances the discussion of George was so brief and sketchy that it would be difficult for the average student to really comprehend his basic ideas.[87]

A textbook by Broadus Mitchell, an economics professor then at Johns Hopkins University, was unusual and deserves mention. He devoted fifteen pages to Henry George's life and philosophy, endorsing the latter enthusiastically even to the extent of calling rent "the graft of the landlord (it is nothing else)." Could George's tax be "single?" Mitchell answered yes; in times of emergency, the government could borrow. His bibliography on George

[87] Judging from my own experience, a course in modern economic problems would be more rewarding at the high school level than a course in economics. It would be less abstract and less likely to be duplicated by a similar course taken later in college.

was extensive, and it was listed in the text itself, not merely appended at the end of the chapter. He wrote, "The single tax may be called the tidiest of social reform doctrines."[88]

Socialists and Conservatives

At this point, for the sake of perspective, it may be worth while to see what the extreme right and the extreme left were saying about Henry George. Knowing the extremes may bring the center more clearly into focus.

Almost without exception, extremely conservative thinkers are opposed to George, and vigorously so. Socialists, on the other hand, are quite apt to include the ideas as one in their arsenal of reforms. This has been embarrassing to many modern-day Georgists who, except for their advocacy of the land value tax, are conservative economically and have nothing but contempt for socialism.

The conservatives were apt to characterize the single tax as land nationalization, socialism, and confiscation. In the ardor of their opposition they tended to make glaring errors. Dr. Harley Lutz's memorandum to the Tax Committee of the N.A.M. in the early 1950's is a case in point. For instance, Dr. Lutz, a professor of economics at Princeton, stated that there was no readily available critical discussion of the single tax. However, the most casual examination of almost any library will prove the contrary.

Lutz had peculiar notions about what George advocated, so peculiar as to make one wonder whether he had first-hand acquaintance with *Progress and Poverty*. For instance, he doubted that George himself believed in the sufficiency of the single tax as the sole source of government revenue. According to Lutz, George believed that

[88] Broadus Mitchell, *General Economics*, pp. 395, 401, 402.

landowners set their own rent. Lutz further maintained
that landowners perform the useful task of improving
their land; but do they act in their capacity as landowners
or rather as workers or capitalists? He also felt that land
and improvement values cannot be separated and ended
his memorandum by referring to Marx and Engels as the
communist predecessors of George.[89]

Another conservative, Murray N. Rothbard, writing for
the libertarian Foundation for Economic Education,
handled Henry George and his ideas with even less
finesse. He believed, for example, that if the government
collected all the rent from land, land values would sink to
zero, and since the tax is levied on assessed land value, it
would yield no revenue at all;[90] Rothbard made many
other similar errors in his paper on George. Although it
could easily be argued that the land value tax is tailor-
made for the implementation of the conservative philosophy, all the average conservative can see in it is that vested
rights would be confiscated.

The extreme liberal or socialist view is best exemplified
by this statement of Norman Thomas:[91]

The good earth and the minerals under it are, of course, basic
to all our wealth. The desire of a man for a piece of land he
can call his own goes deep and is very widespread. Private
ownership of land should therefore be permitted, but on the
basis of occupancy and use. It is axiomatic that the rental value
of land is a social creation. I may let my lot go to ragweed, but
I can get far more for it than my neighbor who has cultivated
his garden, provided that a town or city moves my way. I think
socialists might well adopt Henry George's principle that the
rental value of land apart from improvement belongs to society

[89] Joseph S. Thompson, "An Analysis of 'The Single Tax.'" pp. 1,
4, 8.
[90] Murray N. Rothbard, "The Single Tax: Economic and Moral
Implications," p. 4.
[91] Norman Thomas, "Democratic Socialism, A New Appraisal,"
p. 29.

and should be taken by a tax. The tax, however, should not be a single tax. This land tax should be supplemented by income and heavy inheritance taxes as the major basis for the support of government and government activities at all levels. A proper tax on land values is no such threat to incentive.

When one ponders the matter, it is equally easy to argue that land value taxation, the cornerstone of George's essentially conservative philosophy, would fit very neatly into a socialist economic scheme. If a socialist government supports itself from the profits of the industries it operates, then prices could easily be forced up and the consumers—all of us—would suffer. This would be the equivalent of the much-reviled excise or sales taxes. On the other hand, practically every economist agrees that the land value tax would not raise consumer prices; a socialist government could therefore live off land value tax revenue without having to raise consumer prices.

Even under socialism, land rent would have to be considered by economists, if only as a bookkeeping item, in order to insure that the land is most efficiently utilized. Under any economic system rent measures the social demand and usability of land.

Views of the Land Economists

Land economics is the economic specialization which deals most directly with Henry George and his ideas, yet a detailed examination of the books in that area reveals very little mention of either topic. The only two extensive references were by pro-George writers.

Mason Gaffney, an associate professor in agricultural economics at the University of Missouri (where Harry Gunnison Brown served for so many years), wrote a fact-filled essay entitled "Urban Expansion-Will It Ever Stop?" for *Land*, the 1958 yearbook of the Department of Agriculture. It attracted much attention. Gaffney's thesis was that the recent spurt in urban land values posed a threat to economic progress. In the past, land speculation had been one of the main causes of depressions and it might prove so again. He pointed out that a real estate boom had preceded every economic bust, with real estate acting as a flywheel of the business cycle.

Gaffney felt that the real estate market was rife with land speculation, which he regarded as a price for the use of land based not on present use only, but on its possible enhanced use in the future. Thus, present users of land may be charged more for the land than it is now worth. This means that less money is available for improvements and the total amount of construction is lessened. It also leads to "urban sprawl," where urban communities hop, skip, and jump over unused or underused land and occupy more space than they need. Sewers, roads, busses and utilities must service the artificially enlarged area at an increased cost. The city thus squanders its chief advantages of cheap distribution and easy access. The high land prices require builders to build more intensively on the land they do utilize.

Gaffney quoted eye-opening statistics on the patchy development of urban centers. For instance, in 53 major central U.S. cities, the undeveloped portion was about 29 per cent. Wrote Gaffney: "If the central city is a little patchy, its outskirts are in shreds. . . . Probably less than half the 4 million acres of urban fringe cited in the census deserves to be called 'developed.' "[92] He added that empty spaces make up even larger portions of the smaller cities.

In building up his case that land speculation set land prices so high as to prohibit present use, he cited the case

[92] Mason Gaffney, "Urban Expansion—Will It Ever Stop?" in *Land,* yearbook of the Department of Agriculture, 1958, pp. 505, 506.

of Cleveland, where "57 percent of the Cuyahoga County Planning Commission's 'suburban ring' and 84 percent of the 'rural ring' were vacant in 1954."[93] In San Francisco, 23 percent of the land was undeveloped in 1955; in the "Peninsula" suburb, often thought of as being "a solid mass of suburbs," 75 percent was undeveloped.[94] In the entire 22-county tri-state New York metropolitan region, "only 21 percent of the suitable land, or 16 percent of the gross land area, was developed for urban use."[95] Nor have the downtown city areas, often thought of as congested or over-built, escaped the blight of underused land. Victor Gruen, the architect, retained to re-plan downtown Fort Worth, found that "the underused or derelict reservoir was large enough to provide space for a belt highway, parking garages for 60 thousand cars, greenbelts, a 300 percent increase in office space, 80 percent in hotel space, and new civic, cultural, and convention centers. . . . Fort Worth is not a special case . . ."[96] A U.S. Census report for 1957 supports these observations by reporting that vacant lots account for 21 percent of all city lots.[97]

Though a few have profited handsomely from land speculation, why should so many speculate in land when it is known to be a risky means of making money? Gaffney replied by quoting Alfred Marshall: ". . . if an occupation offers a few extremely high prizes, its attractiveness is increased out of all proportion to their aggregate value."[98]

[93] *Ibid.*, p. 508.
[94] *Ibid.*, p. 515.
[95] Mason Gaffney, "Urban Expansion—Will It Ever Stop?" in *Land*, yearbook of the Department of Agriculture, p. 515. Land in Westchester is reported as being 63 per cent undeveloped, Bergen 54 per cent, and Brooklyn 44 per cent. These figures are higher than the usual person's estimates derived from personal observation.
[96] *Ibid.*, p. 518.
[97] *Ibid.*, p. 521.
[98] *Ibid.*, p. 516.

Gaffney was somewhat vague in suggesting reforms. Something must be done to bring prices down quickly, he felt, but how this was to be accomplished the yearbook article did not say. He was much more specific in the August 1960 *House & Home* issue on land problems, in which he strongly advocated a land value tax.[99]

Another land economist, Mary Rawson of Vancouver, defended land value taxation in a technical and highly detailed pamphlet entitled "Property Taxation and Urban Development," published in August 1961 by the Urban Land Institute in Washington, D.C. Among other things, she claimed that a legacy of prejudice and confusion engendered in earlier days by controversy over the single tax still impeded objective research on land value taxation. In no uncertain terms, she claimed that the treatment of the land value tax in the books devoted to land economics was decidedly less than accurate. R. T. Ely's writings on the subject were "confused, contradictory and shot through with nonsense," nor were the writings of his followers— G. Wehrwein, E. M. Fisher, and R. U. Ratcliff—much better.[100]

George and the Historians of Economic Thought

The historians of economic thought regarded George as an interesting anachronism of the nineteenth century, an amateur whose attention was focused on a small and constantly diminishing factor in the total economic pic-

[99] Professor Gaffney has reported that Walter Heller, President Kennedy's chairman of the Council of Economic Advisers, has written very sympathetically and knowledgeably about land value taxation in his paper on "The Use of Agricultural Taxation for Incentive Purposes," included in a book published by the Harvard Law School in 1954. See *Henry George News,* January 1961, p. 4.

[100] Mary Rawson, "Property Taxation and Urban Development," Urban Land Institute Research Monograph No. 4, p. 7.

ture. He had spoken with much enthusiasm and was to be commended, perhaps, for bringing to the fore the issue of justice in distribution. George was recognized as having stimulated the thinking of many economists—Clark's acknowledgment that he conceived the marginal utility theory after having read George received frequent mention—but he was judged to have had little influence on current economic thinking. Hardly any mentioned the successful experiments in Australia and New Zealand. They made no effort to extract the usable parts of the theory from the unusable.

George has probably received less mention than is due him in the histories of economic thought published in the last thirty years. It is true that he was a vital influence in the development of American social ideas, as so many contemporaries and present-day historians have maintained, it is hard to see why he received so little space in these textbooks. To this day, economists have been affected by his distinction between earned and unearned incomes, and the taxation of land values is still an important issue to many prominent economists and economic thinkers. Certainly George addressed himself to such important and still current problems as taxation and urban land use. In general, most modern historians of economic thought have continued the old practice of praising and emphasizing the Physiocrats at George's expense, a questionable tactic in view of the close similarity between their respective proposals.

An explanation for this may well lie in the declining role played by the theory of rent in recent theoretical economic discussion. One has to search hard for articles on this subject in scholarly journals. One surveyor of the current economics scene writes, "The idea that rent constitutes a share in distribution functionally attributable to a peculiar factor, as interest is attributable to capital or wages to labor, is probably no longer very generally held. The old fires that burned so hotly have about died out."[101]

In dealing with George, traditional suspicions persist even in this special field. The old charges of land nationalization and socialism crop up, plus new ones, such as when the British Labor Party's Town and Country Act (1947) was described as "interesting evidence of the continued vitality of Henry George's economics in England. It sought to prevent future speculation and unearned increments on land by controlling land use and charging fees for the right to develop it."[102] This is the antithesis of land value taxation and was vehemently condemned by the British single taxers.

George Soule, in his *Ideas of the Great Economists,* ignored all the practical applications of land value taxation in Australia, New Zealand, etc., and stated that the Town and Country act was the only serious use of the tax.[103] He pointed out that George was limited in his thinking by the paucity of good statistics in his day, which consequently forced him to rely only on observation and deductions from assumptions. Soule referred to recent statistical studies which show that wages have at least kept pace with GNP while property income has not increased at the expense of labor. "A complete abolition of 'unearned increment' could not have made an important difference."[104] Therefore, Soule concluded: "The very problem which Henry George set out to solve [why poverty

---

[101] Howard S. Ellis, editor, *A Survey of Contemporary Economics,* p. 45.

[102] Eugene O. Golob, *The "Isms," a History and Evaluation,* p. 286.

[103] George Soule, *Ideas of the Great Economists,* p. 85.

[104] George Soule, *Ideas of the Great Economists,* p. 86.

with progress] therefore did not exist, in the form in which he stated it."[105]

It is worth noting that those histories of economic thought which appeal to a widespread popular audience give more emphasis to George than do the textbooks on the subject. Robert Heilbroner's best-selling *Worldly Philosophers* is a case in point. Like most writers in this field, his view is unsympathetic. In discussing George's courting of Annie Fox, his bride-to-be, he could write:[106]

He eloped with her; she was a seventeen-year-old innocent and he a handsome young lad with a Bill Cody mustache and pointed beard. The trusting young Miss Fox took with her a bulky package on her secret marriage flight; the young adventurer thought it might be jewels, but it turned out to be only the *Household Book of Poetry* and other volumes.

If by this incident Heilbroner was trying to cast aspersions on George's moral character, then he finds no support from George's scholarly biographers nor from any other book. None imply that George had acquisitive intentions on his elopment night; as a matter of fact, Miss Fox's very limited finances were well known.

Heilbroner refers to George's supposed "equation of rent with sin" (not precisely so—it is the private collection of rent that George opposed). Heilbroner concluded his section on George with these picturesque words: "He was a religious man; let us hope that his soul went straight to heaven. As for his reputation—that went straight into the underworld of economics and there he exists today; almost-

[105] *Ibid.* Soule admonishes George for not attempting to analyze depressions. Actually, this is precisely what George did; the subtitle of *Progress and Poverty* reads: "An Inquiry Into the Cause of Industrial Depressions and of Increase of Want With Increase of Wealth." There isn't a chapter in the book that doesn't deal with this theme. We can only conclude that Soule had not read *Progress and Poverty*.
[106] Robert Heilbroner, *Worldly Philosophers*, p. 176.

Messiah, semicrackpot, and disturbing questioner of the morality of our world."[107]

In assessing the single tax, Heilbroner put forth the "tempest in a teapot" argument: "Suffice it to point out that rental income in the United States has shrunk from six per cent of the national income in 1929 to only three per cent in 1951."[108] Other modern writers have pointed out that not only do the statistical facts disprove George's all-devouring rent thesis, not only have real wages gone up, not only would his tax be inadequate in meeting present governmental expenses, but land rent is such a small factor in our industrial economy and its collection would accomplish so little social good that it simply is not worth the tremendous effort needed to get it adopted. The game is not worth the candle; what could a tax on such a small economic factor such as rent accomplish anyway?

These views are shared by many other writers in this field. To support their opinions, they quote the following figures of the National Bureau of Economic Research:[109]

	Land Values	Total Wealth Including Land	% of Land to Total Wealth
1896	$63.4 billion	$164.2 billion	38.6%
1948	78.6 billion	461.8 billion	17.0%

(All figures are quoted in "1929 dollars." In "1952 dollars," land values in the U.S. would amount to $157 billion.)

This shows a trend quite contrary to Henry George's

[107] Robert Heilbroner, *Worldly Philosophers*, p. 182.
[108] *Ibid.*, p. 18.
[109] Robert Clancy, June 1952 Faculty Letter of the Henry George School, p. 1, quoting the N.B.E.R. report, *U.S. National Wealth, 1896-1948*, compiled by Raymond Goldsmith.

analysis, although 17 per cent is no small figure and indicates that land was a more important economic factor than Heilbroner's figures would lead us to believe.

Two Recent Criticisms and the Georgist Rebuttal

Two basic criticisms can be found in recent literature critical of Henry George. One states that land rent is of minuscule importance in today's economy and the other criticizes George's view that poverty has accompanied technological progress. Robert Clancy, Director of the Henry George School, has presented the most praiseworthy Georgist rebuttal of these criticisms.

In commenting upon the N.B.E.R. report just mentioned, he gave great emphasis to the report's concession that "the margin of error in estimated land values is widest for commercial properties such as stores, office buildings, hotels, theatres, warehouses and garages." Commented Clancy: "The margin of error is widest where land values are greatest!"[110]

The Henry George School director also challenged the N.B.E.R. assumption that vacant lots have a somewhat lower value than improved land. He accused the N.B.E.R. of underestimating the value of government-owned lands, which the report readily conceded to be based on earlier data and rough estimates. Such lands are not to be treated lightly, for the Federal government alone owns a land area equivalent to all the states east of the Mississippi River with Louisiana, Texas and Arkansas also included.[111]

Moreover, Clancy pointed out that the N.B.E.R. report omitted from the land value inventory all subsoil assets (land receiving its value from the mineral resources under-

---

[110] Robert Clancy, June 1952 Faculty Letter of the Henry George School, p. 7.

[111] N.Y. *World-Telegram & Sun,* Feb. 12, 1956, second section.

neath it)—a considerable omission.

In addition, Clancy noted that farm land values for 1952 were reliably estimated at $70 billion by the Bureau of Agricultural Economics. He compared this to the $157 billion figure of the N.B.E.R. report and declared it unreasonable to suggest that farm land values total almost half as much as urban land values. "What then can we conclude about the estimate of $157 billion given us?"[112]

Clancy had other arrows for his bow. Corporations ordinarily underassess the land they own, relying on long-outdated estimates. They seldom list land separately in their accounting procedures, including it instead under the general heading of "real estate." Furthermore, urban rent controls, still important in 1948, kept down rents and hence land values. Most important, the imposition of land value taxation, with the concurrent reduction or abolition in other taxes, should greatly increase total production—and with production, rent and land values. For that matter, asked Clancy, why must we take soaring government budgets lying down? Cannot the government live within its rental income without having to poach upon the taxpayers?

N.B.E.R. figures referred to 1948. Since that year a terrific inflation has taken place in land values, a fact to which all the trade journals attest. Land value in inflation has by far exceeded the general price inflation.

A recent article in *Harper's* magazine estimates land values in the U.S. at $600 billion, nearly twice the national debt, six times the federal revenue, almost twice the price of listed stocks, and more than twice the assets of all commercial banks put together.[113] Also, the N.B.E.R. report

[112] Robert Clancy, *Henry George News*, July 1952, p. 7.
[113] Daniel Friedenberg, "Coming Bust in the Real Estate Boom," *Harper's*, June 1961, p. 39.

neglected to include the vast amount of land rent currently being collected by the present local real estate tax. This amount should be added to any estimate of total land rent or land value in the United States. One wonders what an N.B.E.R. report issued today on the same subject would conclude.

Addressing himself to the oft-heard statement that "things are better than ever," that we never had it so good, that there is no poverty with progress, that real wages have increased significantly over the years, Clancy adduced six arguments:

(1) The average U.S. home used to have more spacious accommodations than today: "The 'progress' of our standard of living seems to be in the direction of more and more gadgets, and less and less space for them. We need only look at the new houses being built—little better than streamlined shacks huddled together—and at the highways clogged with traffic, to see that George was right in saying that the high price of land was going to steadily encroach against wages—that is, against the total satisfactions of the wage earner."[114]

(2) Although unions have raised real wages, as George himself admitted was possible, it has been at the expense of the workmen's economic freedom. Corruption, racketeering, strikes and class consciousness have been the unfortunate results.

(3) Minimum wage laws, unemployment insurance, social security, rent controls, parity payments, etc. have ameliorated economic conditions, at least in the short run, but "would these props still be needed if there were not a *downward tendency* to wages—or at least, a failure of

[114] Robert Clancy, February 1960 Faculty Letter of the Henry George School, p. 2.

wages to keep pace with increase of productive power?"[115]

(4) Statistics show that the percentage of corporation stockholders to the total public has decreased in the last thirty years, and that according to a 1952 survey, "less than 1% of all American families owned over four-fifths of all publicly held stocks owned by individuals."[116]

(5) Gabriel Kolko, in his book, *Social Class and the Distribution of Wealth,* presents evidence to show that the distribution of income, wealth, and consumption in America has not substantially changed over the past forty years. In fact, as of 1957, 44 per cent of spending units (families and unattached individuals) lived in what must be called poverty, and 27.5 per cent lived at the bare subsistence level in a constant struggle to survive. Director Clancy quoted Professor Kolko: "The poor remain and will likely increase in the near future. The predominantly prosperous middle class society is only an image in the minds of isolated academicians."[117]

(6) Citing statistics of the National Industrial Conference Board (April 1961), Clancy charged that our recent economic advance has been illusory: after considering the effects of inflation plus federal income and social security taxes (but no other taxes), a 1939 income of $3,000 is equivalent to a 1961 income of $7,000, a $5,000 income in 1939 is equivalent to a $12,000 income in 1961.[118]

Clancy concludes that our problems are not those of an affluent society but of a society plagued by an inadequate and inequitable distribution of wealth. And if this

[115] Robert Clancy, February 1960 Faculty Letter of the Henry George School, p. 2.
[116] *Ibid.*
[117] Robert Clancy, March 1962 Faculty Letter of the Henry George School, pp. 1, 2.
[118] Robert Clancy, May 1961 Faculty Letter of the Henry George School, p. 1.

is true in America, what is to be said of the rest of the world? "The poverty of the world's masses is too well-known to invoke."[119]

Clancy's views are presented here in detail because they are deeply rooted in the philosophy of *Progress and Poverty* and epitomize the views of Henry George's present-day followers.

[119] Robert Clancy, February 1960 Faculty Letter of the Henry George School, p. 1.

5

HENRY GEORGE AND MODERN HISTORIANS, 1933-1964

IN DEALING WITH HENRY GEORGE, MODERN HISTORIANS TEND to pass lightly over his tax idea in favor of his considerable influence on the course of American thought. This can be explained both by the lack of single tax success in this country as well as by his unpopularity with the economic fraternity. If the historians were more familiar with actual land value tax experiments such as Arden, Fairhope, California Irrigation District, Pittsburgh, Australia, or New Zealand, they might find it expedient to revise their consideration of George's specific remedy.

Views of the General Historians

Ralph Henry Gabriel's famous volume, *The Course of American Democratic Thought* (1940), illustrates the recent treatment of Henry George. In discussing the program of the Christian Socialists, Gabriel pointed out that much of it was George-inspired; for instance, their emphasis on social conscience, anti-bossism, municipality-owned utili-

ties, direct democracy, the parks and playgrounds movement, public ownership of railroads and other natural
monopolies, even land value taxation. "Henry George,
rather than Karl Marx, was the patron saint of this socialism. Its essence was gradualism rather than revolution,
brotherhood in a classless society rather than class war."[1]

Gabriel's underlying thesis for the 1865-1900 period in
American history concerns the struggle between what he
calls the "gospel of wealth" and its counterpart, "non-
rationalism." These concepts are not essentially different
from the terms now more generally used, Social and Reform Darwinism. If an historian views history in terms
of such a struggle, then he is bound to stress the contributions of Henry George. Professor Gabriel certainly does.

Gabriel is perceptive when he lists the four chief experiences that conditioned George's philosophy: his early
religious training, the frontier moods of materialism and
individual liberty, personal poverty, and his discovery in
New York City of the social extremes possible in an industrial age. "Though he cheerfully recognized his debt to
English classical economists, his philosophy was essentially
an American product."[2]

There then follows an able and extensive presentation
of George's natural rights philosophy. George's actual tax
remedy is stated sketchily in a single sentence: "George
did not propose the complete nationalization of land but
merely, as a practical measure, the appropriation by the
State of the unearned increment in value which society

---

[1] Ralph Gabriel, *The Course of American Democratic Thought*,
p. 318. Wrote Walter Rauschenbusch in his *Christianizing the Social
Order:* "I owe my first awakening to the world of social problems to
the agitation of Henry George in 1886, and wish here to record my
lifelong debt to this single-minded apostle of a great truth." (See
Henry George News, January 1964, p. 14).

[2] *Ibid.*, p. 200.

itself brings about."[3] Such a brief and general description
might leave many readers in the dark as to precisely what
George advocated. For George wanted to appropriate the
entire rent from land, not just the future unearned increment.

For an historian to place such decided emphasis on the
philosophy rather than the remedy is understandable. The
remedy was never adopted but George's emphasis upon
economic humanitarianism, government economic inter-
vention and the perfectibility of man penetrated the American subconscious: George "was the evangelist of the neo-
rationalism of the late nineteenth century."[4]

The struggle between Social and Reform Darwinism
was emphasized by Eric F. Goldman in his popular
Rendezvous with Destiny (1953) as the dominant theme
for the 1865-1900 period. As a result, Henry George
emerged as a prominent key personage. Goldman went in
heavily for brief biographies of important reform figures,
and his pages are speckled with references showing how
these reformers were originally inspired by Henry George.
His comment about Clarence Darrow is a fair example:[5]

The story of a large number of the group was like that of
Clarence Darrow, who, having been jolted out of conservative
ways of thinking by *Progress and Poverty,* soon tossed aside
its "Problem Solved" chapter. What Henry George did for the
Darrows was to point a way, by a Reform Darwinism of
cankerous power, through the steel chain of conservative ideas.

A reader will look in vain through the pages of *Rendezvous with Destiny* for any description of George's proposed

[3] Ralph Gabriel, *The Course of American Democratic Thought,*
p. 202.
[4] *Ibid.,* p. 204.
[5] Eric F. Goldman, *Rendezvous with Destiny.* New York: Knopf,
1953, p. 98. Professor Goldman lists *Progress and Poverty* among the
thirteen books that have shaped the thinking of living Americans (see
Saturday Review of Literature, July 4, 1953, p. 38).

solution, however. The dominant impression Goldman leaves is that Henry George with his fervent criticism and eloquent exposition of his unexplained remedy "had caught the mood with which thousands of Americans left the depression of 1873" and had instilled Reform Darwinism into their thinking.[6]

Perry Miller of Harvard offers a striking example of the new attitude toward George. While regarding George as the most important exponent of Reform Darwinism, Miller wrote that "in the cold light of history, it seems clear that this ingenious device [the single tax] is impracticable, and one can only lament the time and energy George expended in trying to prove it feasible."[7]

Charles and Mary Beard, in their epic work, *The American Spirit* (1942), advanced still another thesis which placed new emphasis upon George. The Beards suggested that America had succeeded in the past only because her citizens developed social conscience adequate to meet the new demands imposed by population growth and industrialization. They interpreted American history as a conflict between the individual's personal needs and his social duties.

According to the Beards, George put forth the doctrine that society has claims upon the economic distribution of wealth which are as valid as those of individuals: "By declaring that the landlord's ground-rent was a product of

[6] Eric F. Goldman, *Rendezvous with Destiny,* p. 34. On pp. 99-100, Goldman alludes to George's supposed unfriendliness toward Jews. However, the quotation he gives to prove this merely indicates George's reasons why Jews were different. The main reasons, said George, were environmental rather than hereditary. George's close personal ties with Jews throughout his adult life would refute Goldman's thesis.

[7] Perry Miller, editor, *American Thought, Civil War to World War I.* New York: Rinehart, 1954, p. xxv. George's remedy is described as being "a single tax upon all increments in the value of land."

civilization, in society, and that it should be expropriated for public purposes, he hurled into the forums of discussion the vexing issue as to whether other forms of wealth were not in significant respects the products of civilization and society, also properly subject to expropriation in the public interest."[8] Thus did George fasten upon the American mind that the interests of society, or as the Beards' phrased it, "the idea of civilization," must be considered.

No survey of American intellectual history would be complete without a consideration of Merle Curti's Pulitzer Prize-winning *Growth of American Thought* (1943). His remarks about George have been a source of inspiration to many subsequent historians judging from the similarity in style and content between their treatment of George and Curti's. Although Curti wrote at great length about George's personal history, philosophy and influence, he devoted only two sentences to the application of the land value tax, and these were vague if not misleading:[9]

In place of the existing system of taxation George proposed a single tax on all increments in the value of land. This would merely allocate to the public, to all individuals, that part of the value of a given piece of land that the public, or all individuals, had created.

This hardly gives an adequate explanation of the mechanics of the land value tax. Besides, what George actually proposed was that all the value of land be taxed away, not merely part of it. Curti's vagueness about the application of the land value tax affected his evaluation of George's ideas. For instance, Curti wrote:[10]

Moreover, the unearned increments of mines, real estate, and other landed properties were distributed in widely held insurance policies, stocks, bonds, and mortgages. Henry George

[8] Charles and Mary Beard, *The American Spirit*, p. 372.
[9] Merle Curti, *Growth of American Thought*, p. 615.
[10] *Ibid.*, p. 616.

in reality never understood the pervasive nature of capitalistic society. Consequently he provided for no adequate political means for effecting his program. Nor did he understand the obstacles in the way of mobilizing power behind a program that in effect would have entailed a virtual revolution against capitalism.

Did Curti realize that land rent can be separated from other economic factors and collected by the government in taxation? The reader may wonder what political means Curti would regard as adequate for effecting the land value tax, but wherever that tax has been applied the ballot box and the present municipal tax administration have proven quite sufficient. As for the astounding statement that "a virtual revolution against capitalism" would be required, an opinion once expressed by Karl Marx became relevant: he called the single tax "capitalism's last ditch" and an attempt to "rear [capitalism] anew upon a firmer basis than its present one."[11] In misunderstanding the mechanics of George's proposal, Curti and others were led to believe that it would require a complete revamping of our present social and economic arrangements.

Misconceptions about George and his ideas occur in the works of other historians. For instance, Arthur Ekirch wrote that, according to George, the basic source of poverty "lay in the ratio of population to land."[12] Actually, George was indignantly anti-Malthus and devoted four chapters in *Progress and Poverty* to disproving Malthus' contentions. Ekirch believed also that the single tax led to the socialization of the land although George was not a socialist "in the nationalistic sense of the term."[13]

[11] Letter written by Karl Marx to a friend, June 20, 1881, and reprinted in the *People* of June 5, 1892.
[12] Arthur Ekirch, *The Decline of American Liberalism*. New York: Longmans Green, 1955, p. 157.
[13] *Ibid.*, p. 159.

Edward R. Lewis wrote: "it is clear that he [George] was wrong in his theory that wages are the direct result of the contribution of labor."[14] However, this theory is commonly accepted among economists today, and it is not true, as Lewis stated, that Taussig disagreed with George on this point. Lewis also repeated Seligman's objections. It may be said for Lewis that he was one of very few historians to offer a detailed economic analysis of George's theory.

Many modern historians often used "panacea" to describe Henry George's proposal; was the term justified? Those who answer affirmatively can point to this important paragraph in *Progress and Poverty*:[15]

What I, therefore, propose, as the simple yet sovereign remedy, which will raise wages, increase the earnings of capital, extirpate pauperism, abolish poverty, give remunerative employment to whoever wishes it, afford free scope to human powers, lessen crime, elevate morals, and taste, and intelligence, purify government and carry civilization to yet nobler heights, is— *to appropriate rent by taxation.*

This would seem proof enough of the right to use the label "panacea," yet George always denied that he so regarded the single tax. When William Lloyd Garrison (the younger), an avid supporter, told George that he did not believe the single tax to be a panacea, George replied, "neither do I; but I believe that freedom is, and the single tax is but the tap-root of freedom."[16]

Certainly George recognized obstacles to liberty other than the private appropriation of land rent, such as political tyranny, natural monopolies, and the low state of

---

[14] Edward R. Lewis, *A History of American Political Thought from the Civil War to the World War.* New York: Macmillan, 1937, p. 278.

[15] Henry George, *Progress and Poverty,* p. 405.

[16] George Geiger, *The Philosophy of Henry George,* p. 558. See also a pamphlet by Henry George entitled "The Single Tax, What It Is and Why We Urge It," p. 9.

public morals. This issue would seem to hinge upon the reader's definition of "panacea."

Biographers of George

Biographers have not overlooked Henry George. After all, he was a unique figure and his life mirrored the spirit and events of his time. Although a hard man to evaluate, there is drama in his story.

In 1900, his elder son, Henry George, Jr., published the first full treatment, a very detailed and factually accurate biography. George's ardent lieutenant, Louis F. Post, wrote a second biography in 1930 that all too frequently referred to George as "the master" or "the prophet." Albert Jay Nock's work (1940) is a literary-philosophical interpretation. The biography by George's daughter, Anna George deMille in 1949 is a charming work, especially in the passages referring to her father's personal life. It took still more years before all the emotions aroused by George's career had sufficiently cooled so that a biography written by a scholarly historian could be attempted. This was finally accomplished by Charles Albro Barker of Johns Hopkins University, who published his biography in 1955. Elwood Lawrence's *Henry George in the British Isles* (1957) added much new material about an important aspect of George's life.

Another source of biographical information and interpretation concerning George have been books which contain composite biographical sketches of various historical characters. George's life has fascinated many such biographers. Such an example is Gerald W. Johnson's *Lunatic Fringe* (1957), written for a popular audience. Here are sketched the careers of fifteen Americans, from Theodore Roosevelt (who coined the title phrase) to Carry Nation and Coin Harvey. Johnson did a creditable job on every one of these, Henry George alone excepted. After stating that George's ideas still influence current thought, Johnson proceeded to make no less than eleven misstatements about him:[17]

(1) George was a devout Episcopalian throughout his life (actually he was a Methodist in California and an unaffiliated deist later in life).

(2) He was nominated for mayor of New York City in 1884 (1886 is the correct date).

(3) He was persuaded to run for mayor in 1897 against his better judgment (he voluntarily consented to accept the nomination).

(4) George withdrew from the San Francisco *Evening Post* voluntarily because he "simply recoiled from success" (his chief creditor, Senator John P. Jones, called in a loan he had made to George after a serious depression had taken hold in California; George could not pay and was ousted).

(5) George was unaware of Marx (George called him "the prince of muddleheads" at the end of a long analysis of his ideas).

(6) *Progress and Poverty* was published in 1877 (actually 1879).

(7) George's basic principle was "that the survival of capitalism depends on the creation of effective consumer demand" (hardly; George never mentioned consumer demand and more basic were his theories concerning land and its rent).

(8) As he grew older, the importance of the single tax in his mind steadily diminished (he preached it literally to his dying day).

[17] Gerald W. Johnson, *The Lunatic Fringe*. Philadelphia: Lippincott, 1957, pp. 110, 111, 113, 115, 117, 118. For rebuttal to Johnson's statements, see Charles Barker, *Henry George,* and Francis Neilson, *Henry George the Scholar* (New York: Robert Schalkenbach Foundation pamphlet, early 1940's).

(9) "His philosophy rested on the belief that the economic system is a creation of the human mind, not the resultant of universal law." (George was the philosopher of natural rights *par excellence*.)

(10) George's principal claim to fame and influence was his advocacy of rent control, public housing, minimum wages, old-age and unemployment insurance, a graduated income tax, etc. (most of these things he opposed, and the rest were inconsistent with his theories).

(11) George was unaware of American history (his books are peppered with references to it).

Eleven outright errors in one chapter! We are entitled to wonder why an able author who could be so competent in dealing with other difficult figures in American history should err so frequently when dealing with George.

Stewart Holbrook's *Dreamers of the American Dream* (1957), also designed for a popular audience, contains a more sober account of George. He makes only one clearcut error—"the single tax would, in short, reduce all real estate to common property."[18] His vague description of the single tax as a tax on increments in land value would leave the uninformed reader in the dark. Otherwise, Holbrook's account makes useful reading.

His comment on George's personality is interesting:[19]

There was something almost magic about Henry George himself. There was nothing of the intense and often sour fanatic about him. The defeats of a quarter of a century left him the same gentle, sympathetic, affable, and even humorous man he had always been. It is doubtful if any other American radical, unless it be Eugene Debs, appealed so warmly to those who knew or only met him. On one occasion Charles Dana, editor of the New York *Sun*, sent a reporter to interview the single-tax advocate but did not print the result. Instead he called the

[18] Stewart Holbrook, *Dreamers of the American Dream*. New York: Doubleday, 1957, p. 161. On page 163 Holbrook states that *Progress and Poverty* was finished in 1878; the correct date is 1879.

[19] Stewart Holbrook, *Dreamers of the American Dream*, p. 161.

reported into his sanctum, telling him, "You sound like Wendell Phillips reporting Saint John the Baptist. I told you to see a Mr. Henry George."

Holbrook's concluding comment is more cryptically written: "Henry George's failure was in no manner due to any imperfections of his single tax, but to the seductive nature of capitalistic society."[20] One would wish for some elucidation of this "seductiveness," but there is none.

The two aforementioned books were written primarily for the mass market, but historians writing for a more scholarly audience have not overlooked the method of biographical sketches as an effective way to illumine the past. Charles Madison's *Critics and Crusaders* (1947), for instance, contained sketches of twenty-four Americans, including one on Henry George.

Like most contemporary historians, Madison discounted George's economic proposal but praised him as a reformer in the realm of social thought, as an awakener of America's social conscience. Unlike many other historians, however, he has some words of praise for George's analysis of property and depression, which "for all its flaws and 'unscientific' emphasis, [is] an original and positive formulation of a body of principles which has been condemned as a whole or in part by a number of the keenest academic minds but invalidated by none."[21] Unfortunately, Madison did not detail his reasons for this interesting evaluation.

Daniel Aaron, in *Men of Good Hope* (1951), also attributed George's great reforming influence to his eloquent condemnation of poverty while brushing aside "the dubious mechanics of his land tax."[22] The dubiousness is unexplained though frequently referred to.

[20] *Ibid.*, p. 166.
[21] Charles Madison, *Critics and Crusaders*. New York: Henry Holt, 1947, p. 282. On this page occurs the misstatement that George advocated the common ownership of land.
[22] Daniel Aaron, *Men of Good Hope*. New York: Oxford University Press, 1951, p. 71.

A number of minor errors or questionable statements are to be found in Aaron's chapter on George. For instance, Aaron believed that George favored the income tax and listed Condorcet, Comte and Fourier as George's ideological forerunners.[23] He criticized George's dismissal of two aides, M'Cready and Sullivan, from the *Standard*, George's weekly, even though they both moved into George's house uninvited during his summertime absence and issued scurrilous statements about George and the single tax movement.[24] Nor, as Aaron charged, could George's break with Father McGlynn be considered a blunder. McGlynn, the Catholic priest who was temporarily excommunicated for his pro-George beliefs, wanted George to expand their single tax party on a national level even though the party had just suffered a disastrous defeat in New York State. When George refused, McGlynn read him out of the party, after which the party proceeded to collapse. The whirling dervish Anti-Poverty Society, which often embarrassed George by its near-fanatical enthusiasm for the single tax, was founded and led by McGlynn, who can be said to have represented the religious extremists among George's followers.[25]

Saul K. Padover's *Genius of America* (1960) added nothing new to what has already been said of George, but certain discrepancies in his evaluation need pointing out to document the thesis that George has been misinterpreted or misunderstood. Padover stated that the single tax was unconstitutional—an obviously incorrect judgment—then contradicted himself by saying on one page that George advocated the single tax so that it would "give men a chance to buy and own land for personal use

[23] *Ibid.*, p. 75, 89.
[24] Compare Aaron's less documented account to Charles Barker, *Henry George*, p. 537, 605 and Henry George, Jr., *Life of Henry George*, p. 520.
[25] *Ibid.*, p. 513.

and improvement," and on another page that "George himself said that his panacea would turn the state into 'the universal landlord.' "[26] The latter statement was, of course, incorrect, but by citing it Padover raised the spectre of a single tax state which would dominate the livelihood and ultimately the liberties of its citizens. Actually, the government collects rent now through the real estate tax; George advocated that the government collect it all at the same time that we reduce other taxes.

Albert Jay Nock attempted a book-length interpretation of Henry George in 1939. Nock was an essayist with a highly cultivated style barbed with stinging sarcasm. He was a close associate of H. L. Mencken and shared many of that gentleman's views about the "booboisie."

Many writers have traced the genesis of George's thought to his extensive reading of the English classical economists. Others have stressed the importance of his frontier experiences in California. Nock emphasized instead the all-pervading influence of George's early childhood environment in Philadelphia, and his evaluation of it was none too high.[27]

It was marked by a monstrously over-developed sense of expansion [i.e., faith in materialistic progress], a defective sense of intellect, a defective sense of religion and morals, a stunted sense of beauty, a stunted sense of social life and manners; and for a mind eminently philosophical, the continuous experience of such an environment is to the last degree debilitating and retarding.

Alas for George, sighed Nock, that the limitations of his early environment followed him throughout the rest

[26] Saul K. Padover, *Genius of America*. New York: McGraw-Hill, 1960, p. 231; see also p. 228.
[27] Albert Jay Nock, *Henry George*. New York: William Morrow, 1939, p. 32.

of his life. As an adult he chose self-made, self-educated men as his personal friends almost exclusively and had an innate distaste for the typical academic mind. But from his early childhood environment he gained one inestimable advantage: his early acquaintance with and complete immersion in the King James Version of the Bible and the Book of Common Prayer—George came from a very religious home—exercised a beneficial influence upon his writing style. The intensive reading of these two books, containing "the very best English usage," were responsible for George's persuasive and forceful eloquence, according to Nock.

That George was one of our finest social philosophers, Nock did not doubt. In his pantheon George was the equal of Spencer. Nock accepted the single tax philosophy wholeheartedly but claimed that George's great mistake was that instead of spending his life in philosophical contemplation and writing books on social ethics, he chose the lower life of polemicist, agitator, humanitarian, lecturer. Rather than trying vainly to appeal to the masses and frittering away his energies in various political efforts, he should have concentrated his efforts on the elite of mankind.

It is hard to see how George could have made a living without lecturing or writing magazine articles. Nock himself admitted that it was George's agitation on the Irish land question which catapulted him and *Progress and Poverty* into the public spotlight. Sales of the book had been limping along at a very unsteady pace until that episode. Would anyone have ever heard of George if he had followed the contemplative life? If he had not related his philosophy to the pressing problems of his day, would he and his ideas have been consigned to oblivion as happened to such contemplative precursors as Dove, Ogilvie, Filangieri, Burgess, Spence, even the Physiocrats?

Underlying Nock's whole interpretation was his pessimistic view of the common man and of the institution of government. He did not regard the average man as being very improvable either morally or intellectually. The human race was nine-tenths ineducable, perhaps more. Democracy is failing now, and should be dispensed with; how can perfidious politicians ruled by the fickle whim of the mob ever be expected to produce good government? It was only George's early Philadelphia background "of Murdstone and Quinion" which prevented him from seeing this great truth and which misled him into his unfounded optimism about the perfectibility of mankind through government initiative.

Nock, one of whose earlier books was entitled *Our Enemy the State*, summarized his philosophical anarchy with this quotation from another writer: Nature "condescends now and then to make an ideal tyrant, but she will never make a nation of ideal republicans; you may quite as well ask her to make a nation of Raphaels, Michelangelos, Shakespeares or Molieres."[28]

Should the land value tax yield little revenue, this nothing dismayed Alfred Jay Nock, the Georgist; he did not want much of a government anyway. He professed to believe that George's present-day followers had given up trying to convert the masses but instead were concentrating on acceptance by an undefined elite. Nock was highly gratified by this discovery.[29] His philosophical anarchy— so antithetical, it would seem, to the spirit of his hero, Henry George—served only to lead him down the barren

[28] Albert J. Nock, *Henry George,* p. 133.
[29] Albert Jay Nock, *Henry George,* p. 220. See also pp. 163, 128, 40, for other relevant statements by Nock.

pathway of intellectual snobbery, cynicism and isolation.

In 1955 appeared the first full-length biography of George by a recognized scholar—Charles Albro Barker of Johns Hopkins University—and still the authoritative biography of his subject. The book was the result of many years of thought and work; thoroughness and impartiality were its hallmarks. As Barker explained:[30]

Perhaps I should explain that I determined to do this book in the wake of the depression of the '30s, but that I began without the slightest hostage in the Henry George camp. My family had been Republican since 1856; I had cast my first vote for Norman Thomas; and I believed, as I still do, that at the time the New Deal was essentially what the United States needed. I know now that if I had designed my own background to avoid contact with Georgism, I could have chosen no points of political attachment more indifferent to the ideas of the subject of this biography than these three—traditional Republicanism, Thomas socialism, and the New Deal. Only international communism, or some fascism like Huey Long's, would have been wider of the present subject.

Perhaps this personal detachment, desirable though it may be as a buttress to objectivity, is responsible for the paucity of evaluation of the single tax idea. Is Barker for or against it? What reservations does he have? The answers to these questions are nowhere made clear. His comments on George's proposal are oblique. For instance, George should have advocated public land ownership for conservation purposes—parks, mineral development, grazing, flood control, water use, etc. If he had "admitted the rough-hewn rightness of the 160-acre—or 80-acre—homestead as democratic policy for the well-watered farming regions,"[31] he might have gained the support of the farmers, or at least have avoided their opposition. However, from George's point of view, the government would

[30] Charles A. Barker, *Henry George*, viii.
[31] Charles A. Barker, *Henry George*, p. 298.

not have received a considerable revenue to which it was justly entitled, nor would the "rough-hewn rightness" have remained so for long.

Barker chides George for not citing the support certain fathers of the American Republic gave to the principle that the land belongs to the people. George should also have realized that his ethical views required not merely the nationalization of land but its internationalization by a world organization with power to tax.[32] The fact is that George advocated international acceptance of land value taxation and free trade. But in any case, world government, desirable as it may be, is not a strict prerequisite for the application of George's ethics.

In his evaluation of *Progress and Poverty,* Barker pointed to an alleged confusion, a contradiction, in George's thinking:[33]

> *Progress and Poverty* says, first, that under land-value taxation, Society would thus approach the ideal of Jeffersonian democracy, the promised land of Herbert Spencer, *the abolition of government.* Then, after explaining a bit, appears the equally strong hope that, "Government would change its character, and would become the administration of a great cooperative society. It would become *merely the agency by which the common property was administered for the common benefit.*

The contradiction is removed when we examine George's intervening explanation. After Barker's first-quoted sentence, George wrote, "But of government only as a directing and repressing power."[34] George then explained that by simplifying and even abrogating most of the present government functions, we could safely entrust the management of natural monopolies and certain public welfare functions such as parks, museums, and schools to

[32] *Ibid.,* p. 302.
[33] Charles A. Barker, *Henry George,* p. 298.
[34] Henry George, *Progress and Poverty,* p. 456

the government. With this explanation, the two sentences Barker quoted out of context are more naturally linked.

The chief revision Barker advanced in this biography was that before 1888 George had been known primarily as a castigator of the Spencerian doctrine of inevitable poverty and an advocate of the equal rights of all men to the bounties of Nature, but only secondarily as a tax reformer. After his defeat as a labor candidate in the elections of 1886 and 1887, however, George turned towards the development of organizations whose sole purpose was the propagation of his tax proposal. Before 1888, he was the arouser of millions, the flayer of the public conscience; after that year, he was the *doyen* of a single tax movement. In fact, Barker pointed out, George hardly ever used the term "single tax" before 1888, although he used it consistently thereafter. (The term never fully satisfied George because it did not express his full philosophy, just the means by which one important part of it would be applied.) Barker emphasized that George had always fervently advocated public ownership (or at least regulation) of natural monopolies, the adoption of the Australian secret ballot and other democratic political reforms. Barker realized, however, that there was no essential discontinuity of thought before or after 1888, merely a small difference in emphasis and a large difference in the impression he made upon his contemporaries. The later George, appealing to the middle class, occasioned less hysterical opposition than did the earlier, labor-oriented, more evangelistic George.[35]

As for George's influence, Barker felt that it flowed into three broad streams: the fiscal-reform Georgism of the single tax, of which the present Georgists are the prime exponents; the political Georgism which entered

[35] Charles A. Barker, *Henry George*, chapter 17.

into many varieties of reform activity (cf. Tom Johnson and Newton Baker); and the moral and intellectual Georgism, which influenced the course of American social thought and directed the thinking of men such as Theodore Roosevelt and Woodrow Wilson in ways they were not always fully aware of.[36]

Another biographer, Elwood Lawrence of Michigan State University, attempted to record Henry George's influence in the British Isles, the scene of George's greatest triumphs. For years land value taxation was a vital political issue, echoes of which are still to be heard in England today. In his own time, it was said that next to Gladstone, he was the most talked about person in England. His five visits to that country had implanted an awareness of social problems in the popular mind such as no one else had done. Although an apostle of free enterprise and frontier individualism, he was credited by socialists and non-socialists alike with having been one of the chief popularizers of socialism in England. George Bernard Shaw admitted that his "attention was first drawn to political economy as the science of social salvation by Henry George's eloquence, and by his *Progress and Poverty*, which . . . had more to do with the Socialist revival of that period in England than any other book."[37] It was a mild variation of the single tax that caused the parliamentary crisis of 1909-1911, and George's ideas are still held by some Labor and Liberal party politicians today.

Lawrence quoted lengthy passages from George's speeches in the British Isles (especially in Scotland where his influence was greatest), in order to show how he was able to stir the social conscience of a whole country. For instance, George told a Liverpool audience that if he him-

[36] Charles A. Barker, *Henry George,* chapter 20.
[37] Elwood P. Lawrence, *Henry George in the British Isles,* p. 75.

self "were standing that night on the threshold of another life, and were given the chance to come back into the world as a Tierra del Fuegian, or black fellow of Australia, or any of that class to be found in the London or Liverpool slums, he would choose the lot of the savage in preference to hunger, cold, and starvation. [Applause.]" In the "great and rich city" of Glasgow he found "poverty and destitution that would appal a heathen. Right on these streets of yours the very stranger can see sights that he could not see in any tribe of savages in anything like normal conditions." In the Midlands he asked: "What complaint could agricultural labourers make—men who must live the life of a slave and die the death of a pauper? [Applause, and a Voice: 'None.'] Well might they ask with Herbert Spencer 'at what rate per annum does wrong become right?' [Applause.]"[38]

George castigated the "unholy alliance" between the church and the upper classes. Christianity was being used to perpetuate and justify the sufferings of millions of poor: "The people had not merely been kept in ignorance, but they had been taught by their masters and pastors that this was a natural state of things; and the very name of the Deity—the name of religion itself—had been called on to compel men and induce men to submit quietly to this injustice. The name of God has been called in to show that it was His will that some should be rich and some should be poor—that the man who did nothing should have an income of £100,000 a year, and the man who was working for his living could not get enough to maintain him in his old age."[39]

George was gratified that the discussion of theological questions on the Glasgow green had been supplanted by

[38] Elwood P. Lawrence, *Henry George in the British Isles,* pp. 45-46.
[39] Elwood P. Lawrence, *Henry George in the British Isles,* pp. 47-48.

the land question and the labor question. "What was the use of them, worms of the dust, discussing the attributes of God when there was before them His work to do [Hear, hear.]—when there was with them the poor and the starving and degraded? [Applause.]"[40]

Lawrence—who, incidentally, was not particularly sympathetic to George or the single tax, though he nowhere gave his reasons—performed a real service in documenting why the mistaken charges of land nationalization and socialism were so often aimed at George and his followers. George's public speaking appearances during his earlier trips to the British Isles were almost always sponsored by land nationalization or socialist organizations, and he usually emphasized those aspects of *Progress and Poverty* to which the sponsoring organizations could take least offense. In the early 1880's, he occasionally omitted taxation as the means of returning the land to the people. Usually he went no farther than exhorting his listeners "to make the land free, and they would relieve industry of all taxation, obtain really free trade, and make great progress toward equality and true socialism."[41] When George spoke of "true socialism" he thought of it as a distant goal and he meant socialism of the Owenite voluntary and cooperative type motivated by a religious spirit, and not the Marxist kind of socialism then and now most frequently debated in England—the socialism by which the government owns the means of production. However, this was often a point in semantics too delicate for many people to distinguish.

In his earlier visits, George did not make a strenuous attempt to dissociate his views from those of Alfred Wallace's Land Nationalisation Society; he often endorsed

[40] *Ibid.*, p. 48.
[41] Elwood P. Lawrence, *Henry George in the British Isles*, p. 25.

their program in general philosophical terms and in front of socialist audiences he once referred to the single tax as "the form for the virtual nationalization of land."[42] However, George did not often bow to the pressing expediency of the lecture platform and elsewhere distinguished with great care between his reform and that of Wallace.[43]

Lawrence is worth quoting fully in this context:[44]

The popular view of George's remedy was partly the result of the company he kept. On his first visit, he spoke on Marxist and Land Nationalization platforms; his arrest in 1882 identified him with Irish violence; his books were pushed by Wallace's organization; his campaign was supported by the Socialist magazine *Justice* from 1883 to 1886; his visit in 1884 was backed by the Land Reform Union, an organization of left-wing reformers. Because he did not explicitly dissociate himself from these groups, it was natural for people to think that he represented either successively, or at one and the same time, the measures associated with each group.

By the beginning of 1884, the public identified him with the following doctrines: the land belonged by natural right to the people; people could obtain this right by land nationalization; landlords should receive no compensation for their lands. He was also thought mildly socialistic. George continued to maintain these three doctrines in subsequent visits; these views, and not the tax proposal which he later elaborated, account for most of the British newspapers' attacks on his views. The title

[42] *Ibid.*, p. 78.

[43] For instance, in *Progress and Poverty*, p. 405, George wrote: "I do not propose either to purchase or to confiscate private property in land. The first would be unjust; the second, needless." In his book *A Perplexed Philosopher* (1892), p. 70, he wrote: "I am not even a land nationalizationist, as the English and German and Australian nationalizationists well know. I have never advocated the taking of land by the state or the holding of land by the state, further than needed for public use; still less the working of land by the state." His condemnation of state socialism can be read in *Progress and Poverty*, pp. 319-21 and in other books. Present-day Georgists contend that a high degree of socialism exists when the government can take 52% of a corporation's profits. By making such taxation unnecessary, the land value tax is anti-socialist.

[44] Elwood P. Lawrence, *Henry George in the British Isles*, pp. 54-55.

of one article—"Mr. George and His Crusade of Plunder"—epitomizes the reaction. He was not and never had been a Socialist. But he persisted in viewing with sympathy Socialist efforts to improve the lot of the poor. And he recognized the possibility of the development of some form of Socialism some time in the future. Because Socialism was associated in the public mind with the redistribution of wealth generally, with confiscation, and with nationalization, George continued to carry the name of Socialist.

Not until his second visit did George explicitly link taxation to his land-reform scheme. . . .

Lawrence reached these conclusions as a result of extended research in the British newspapers and magazines of the 1880's.

George in the History Textbooks

It is widely felt that history textbooks contain the most generally accepted facts and interpretations emerging from historical research. If textbook accounts lag behind the findings of the pioneer researcher, it is usually because these findings have not yet received their eventual recognition among scholars, and so have not yet entered that repository of historical knowledge, the textbook.

By the 1930's, scholars had come to believe that Henry George was no enemy of society, no threat to property rights. Although his single tax was rejected as an economic solution, George had given a powerful impetus to the cause of American social reform. This was the interpretation that began to dominate the history textbooks of the 1930's, and became even more prominent thereafter. Wrote Morison and Commager: "George's diagnosis of the causes of poverty and inequality was more profound than his single tax cure."[45]

Hardly ever was any mention made of the land value tax *per se,* but only of the single tax. Seldom was any men-

[45] Samuel Eliot Morison and Henry Steele Commager, *Growth of the American Republic,* v. 2, p. 368 (1937).

tion made of the application of George's ideas in other parts of the world. Somewhat surprisingly, few textbook authors attempted to evaluate the single tax—when they do it is in mild criticism—most being content to state briefly the facts of George's personal life, the bare outlines of his theories, and his influence on reform thinking. In most texts George was accorded a lengthy paragraph or two, plus occasional brief references elsewhere in the volume. He was generally grouped with such dissenters and reformers as Lloyd, Bellamy, Ward, Holmes and Veblen, frequently receiving more mention than any of them. Out of forty-two books surveyed, only seven made no mention of George at all.

As might be expected, high school texts gave George considerably less space than did the college texts, no doubt because their emphasis lay more on politics than thought, on action rather than analysis.

In most cases only a vague description of Henry George's tax proposal appeared. Out of twenty-one recent textbooks making more than cursory reference to George, seven committed what could be considered errors. These are the statements in question:

(1) Henry George's followers supported Populism.[46] (By a great majority they did not; Henry George himself opposed it.)

(2) George wished to "abolish private ownership of land."[47]

(3) The Union Labor Party supported the single tax in 1888.[48]

(4) Henry George believed that capital is a parasite and

---

[46] Foster Rhea Dulles, *The United States Since 1865,* p. 147 (1955).

[47] Roger Butterfield, *The American Past.* New York: Simon & Shuster, 1947, p. 250.

[48] Fremont Wirth, *Development of America.* New York: American Book Co., 1946 (1938), p. 365. See Charles Barker, *Henry George,* p. 495.

that private ownership of land is a remnant of medieval times; also, a land value tax would not help tenants because the tax would be passed on to them in the form of higher rents.[49]

(5) George "would retain private property in everything but land."[50]

(6) "The rate of the single tax would be based not on the existing value of the land, but on its worth if used efficiently."[51]

(7) George conceived of the state as "little more than a tax-collecting agency."[52]

Although they err in their brief sections on Henry George, these same textbooks exhibited a high degree of factual reliability on practically all other subjects.

[49] W. E. Woodward, *New American History*. New York: Farrar & Rinehart, 1936, pp. 650-52.
[50] John B. Rae and Thomas Mahoney, *The United States in World History*. New York: McGraw-Hill, 1955, p. 391.
[51] Henry Bragdon and Samuel McCutchen, *History of a Free People*. New York: Macmillan, 1958, p. 420.
[52] Jeanette P. Nichols, *Twentieth Century United States*. New York: Appleton-Century, 1943, p. 108.

6

HENRY GEORGE'S PLACE IN AMERICAN HISTORY AND ECONOMICS

AN UNAVOIDABLE CONCLUSION OF THIS STUDY IS THAT HENRY George's ideas were not well understood by American historians and economists. To this day, their evaluations of him have often been weakened by vagueness and inaccuracy which in most cases have been so obvious and definite as to be unattributable to mere differences of opinion.

In George's time, the charges of socialism and land nationalization were the ones most frequently levied against him, for reasons that Elwood Lawrence has carefully documented. By now, most historians and economists have come to realize that George was an ardent individualist rather than a socialist, but many still believe that he wanted to transform land into common or state-owned property. The confusion of the single tax with land nationalization still persists strongly, probably because in one place in *Progress and Poverty* George described his remedy as the reduction of land to common property.

However, he emphasized that the best application of this remedy involved not the state ownership of land—this was needless and dangerous—but the taxation of land values, thus leaving the title to land in private hands. Cursory reading can easily miss this vital distinction.

No attempt will be made here to summarize all the various types of misstatements, for the number seems endless. Many have been treated in detail in the foregoing pages. But one question remains unanswered: why do so many distinguished scholars, ordinarily not prone to error, err when they discuss Henry George?

A source of many misconceptions is a mistaken or hazy notion as to how a land value tax would be applied. Many economists and historians felt and still feel that such a tax cannot be administered, forgetting that the single tax has actually had wide application in Australia, New Zealand, the city of Pittsburgh and other parts of the world.

A lack of first-hand acquaintance with George's writings accounts for the misconceptions of many who wrote on the subject. He was not their main concern and it was easy to rely upon often inaccurate secondary treatments, thus perpetuating initial errors. George was an eloquent writer and much of his work reads like prose poetry, but he did not write for the modern reader in a hurry. His eloquence was necessarily interspersed by long discourses on various aspects of economic logic. His thoughts unrolled slowly, one idea building upon the previous ones; the readers of his day were used to this pace and had fewer distractions than we do. Today's reader may find the speculative exposition and slow development of *Progress and Poverty* unsuited to his time schedule and thus fall back upon summaries by others.

George's turbulent and shifting career also misled later generations. Until 1888 he was the agitator, the labor politician, the excoriator of poverty and the arouser of the disinherited; after 1888 he was the single taxer with a comparatively mild approach and a middle class following. He was almost as radical as the socialists on the land issue but more conservative than the Spencerians on the taxation of non-landed property. His followers ranged from anarchists to socialists, as did his opponents. In his day he was considered a leftist; today he is usually classified as a conservative. No wonder many of his evaluators were confused.

Another conclusion made clear by this study was that there has been more support among academicians for land value taxation than most people think. Although the economics textbooks may deprecate George's views, in recent times his academic defenders have been growing in number and have not been afraid to express their support in scholarly articles and books and at conferences. In the past, they have been less vociferous than George's critics, but the trend now seems to be moving in the opposite direction.

George's Economic Analysis

How does George's analysis of the capitalist economy stand up after all these years? Most people would feel that neither statistical facts nor common observation substantiate such an analysis. Land rent has not increased faster than production, as he maintained, nor have wages and interest tended toward the subsistence level. Even many present-day Georgists will concede as much. Who can doubt, for instance, that the hours of labor have been steadily diminishing since 1879?

A theoretical examination of George's economic analysis will reveal certain flaws which corroborate the empirical verdict. For example, in discussing unions, George himself admitted that since they control the supply of labor in a given industry they can advance wages artificially at the expense of rent, although he disliked the methods they had to use—strikes, coercion, restrictions on the freedom of the individual.[1] Even though he predicted otherwise, unions have grown in importance since the appearance of *Progress and Poverty*.

George's economic analysis is based on the assumption of free competition. He was aware of the existence of monopolies and "frictions of the market" (immobility of capital and labor) and he opposed them, but he greatly minimized their economic importance. However, to the extent that these factors do exist they force modification of George's economic analysis. Modern economists place great stress not only on the influence of monopoly and frictions of the market, but also on the influence of oligopoly, or the control of a particular industry by a few producers. These producers levy an "administered price" that is higher than the true competitive price, and meet decreases in demand not by lowering the price, as the classical theory expects, but by decreasing production. That oligopoly exists, few doubt, but its importance is still an open question.

George based his main contention that land rent increases faster than total production on Ricardo's Law of Rent, which states that the rent of land is determined by the excess of its produce over that which the same application of labor and capital can secure from the least productive land in use. George further claimed that increases in productivity would not only enhance the demand for land already having value, but would also bring into use proper grades of land not previously used, until production on the new marginal land would equal what it was

[1] Henry George, *Progress and Poverty*, p. 310.

on the older marginal land. Since, according to George, wages and interest are determined by what can be produced on marginal land, they could never increase, at least not in the long run.

But it is not possible—even probable—that some technological improvements would increase production on marginal land (the least productive land in use)? The Mojave Desert contains the most marginal land in our country; is it not possible that at least some of the marvels of the Industrial Age, especially those in the fields of transportation and communications, have raised the potential productivity of marginal land—and thus, according to George's own reasoning, wages and interest?[2]

There is still another consideration detrimental to George's contentions. It would be hard to refute Professor Francis A. Walker's assertion that improvements in the quality of goods produced would increase the total value of wealth production without increasing the demand for land or the demand for its rent. A better moustrap, since it may command a higher price may increase the total value of wealth production; but it need not increase the demand for marginal land. If it is more compact then previous models, it may in fact lessen that demand. Similarly, a doctor may now use an antihistamine instead of aspirin; this will increase the value of his services but will not increase the demand for land.

On the subject of depressions, George maintained that during periods of prosperity land speculation becomes feverish; as a result, the rent burden on the active producers increases so sharply that further production be-

[2] One of the most astute single taxers, Max Hirsch, recognized that George's marginal land analysis was the most debatable point in *Progress and Poverty;* see his *Democracy Versus Socialism,* p. 432. Note also that in Part V of that book, he completely avoided basing his presentation of the single tax on the Law of Rent.

comes unprofitable and a depression ensues. That land speculation has almost always preceded depression is generally accepted by now. George was probably right in assuming some sort of cause and effect relationship, but was he right in assuming that land speculation was the only or even the principal cause of depressions? To do this, he would have had to show that there were no other causes; this he did not attempt. In his day, depressions went unexplained; according to the accepted classical theory, they could not even exist, and so George felt he had arrived at the one correct answer.

Since George's time, economists have done much thinking about the causes of depressions. Under the influence of John Maynard Keynes, economists today believe that a sudden diminution in the money supply can lessen total demand and bring on a depression. Psychological causes are now thought to be highly important. The public's confidence in the future, a highly volatile factor, affects business activity, and in any case, cycles, long and short, are an inherent feature of life. Why should fickle consumer demand be considered as never varying or always increasing? Although land speculation may be one cause of depressions, it is not the only cause, nor even the principal one.

The Keynesians advocate deficit financing and easy credit as an antidote to depressions. Inflation would not result, they feel, because during a depression, an increase in the money supply would put idle labor and idle capital to work, thus increasing production but not prices. Once full employment is reached, the government should restrict the money supply in order to maintain a constant price level at full employment. Everyone recognizes the political difficulties in this process but, reply the economists, the alternative of depressions is much worse. Georgists should realize that there is nothing in this monetary approach which is in any way antithetical to the single tax. Modern theory emphasizes mass psychology and credit while George emphasized land speculation; there is no conflict except where George felt that he had the *only* answer. There is no reason why one cannot advocate land value taxation, even as a single tax, as well as countercyclical government spending.[3]

Like many other nineteenth-century thinkers, George believed too much in an economic interpretation of history. If poverty existed, then its cause must be economic. While it is obviously true that poverty has its roots in economic maladjustments and injustice, it has sociological roots as well, a fact which George overlooked. If Indians are poor, it is partially because Hinduism puts little emphasis on worldly matters. Ancestor worship can inhibit progress. Racial discrimination severely limits the opportunities of the Southern Negro. Class and caste distinctions do the same for poor people throughout the world. Some cultures look down upon manual labor; others look upon social change as an evil.[4]

[3] George happened to visit Johnstown, Pennsylvania, in 1893, a year in which a severe constriction of the currency had taken place. He was told by the president of a rail manufacturing concern there that although he could get plenty of orders for rails, he could get no money in payment. George suggested that the bonds of the street railroad companies ordering rails should be taken in payment of their orders, and that certificates to be used as money be issued against them. This was done, and the employees and townspeople were prevailed upon to accept these certificates in lieu of money. The company prospered during this period and unemployment was avoided; eventually the certificates were drawn in and redeemed. "Mr. George regarded this as an illustration of what the United States Government could do to clear up the currency difficulties—issue from its own treasury a paper currency, based upon its credit and interchangeable with its bonds." (Henry George, Jr., *Life* . . . , p. 558.)

[4] Thorstein Veblen was one of the first to emphasize that cultural factors play an important part in the distribution of wealth. He

Despite all these qualifications of George's analysis of poverty and depressions, rent remains a not unimportant factor in our modern industrial economy. A glance at recent real estate magazines will show that land prices have been increasing at a geometric pace. When a recent survey shows that vacant lots are the largest single class of property in American cities and when it is a fact of common observation that much land is not being put to its optimum use, then the phenomenon of land speculation requires much more than passing notice. George may have erred in his economic analysis, but this does not necessarily invalidate the usefulness of his tax proposal.

George's Ethical Analysis

George's discussion of ethics was of central importance in *Progress and Poverty*. To him, what is ethical must of necessity be expedient. Should land rent be taxed? Ethics must render the final decision. As a matter of fact, much of George's influence can be ascribed to the eloquent exposition of his ethical philosophy, for eloquence is never so effective as when expounding an ethical viewpoint. It was moral conviction which made his followers so devoted and inspired a whole generation of Progressive reformers. George's ethical system therefore deserves our close consideration.[5]

---

wrote: "A gang of Aleutian Islanders, slushing about in the wrack and surf with rakes and magical incantations for the capture of shellfish, are held . . . to be engaged on a feat of hedonistic equilibration in rent, wages, and interest." (Quoted in Robert Heilbroner, *The Worldly Philosophers*, p. 235.)

[5] "There are those who say that the right of property, as all other rights, is derived from the state. But they do not really think this; for they are as ready as any one else to say of any proposed state action that it is right or it is wrong, in which they assert some standard of action higher than the state." (George, *A Perplexed Philosopher*, p. 211.)

George maintained that because each man is individually organized—because "each particular pair of hands obey a particular brain and are related to a particular stomach; the fact that each man is a definite, coherent, independent whole"—therefore he owns what these faculties can produce. In other words, each person functions as a separate entity; he therefore owns himself and whatever he produces with his own labor. Since no one produces land, no one should own land unless he pays society for that privilege through taxation. And if we are all created equal, then we must have equal rights to the opportunities of nature, namely air, sea and land.[6] This argument rests squarely on the assumptions of individual responsibility and equal rights. Accept the assumptions and George's conclusion becomes difficult to refute.

Some people contend that it is all very well to say "to each the fruits of his own labor," but how is one to know how much he has earned in an industrial economy where few products are produced solely through the efforts of one individual? In a capitalist society, free competition determines the true value of one's own labor. The competitive price measures the true value of your services to others. To the extent that perfectly free competition does not exist, countervailing forces are needed to approach true value. Such forces might be unions to equalize wage bargaining power or such government controls as exercised by the F.T.C., I.C.C., S.E.C., and anti-trust laws.

Other people have objected to George's claim that each man is individually organized and should own himself. This is true only of a Robinson Crusoe, they say; do we

[6] Some people have suggested that the use of the publicly-owned radio and television air waves is a great financial privilege for which the franchised users should pay in the form of a tax based on their value. Presumably, this would be called "air value taxation."

not live and work in a society and are we not integral parts of it? Does not society own at least a part of us? However this may be, our natural individuality is not altered. We still function separately, not like parasites on a tree. What claim can society have on an individual provided he does not violate the equal rights of others?

Although George's labor theory of property merits respect, recent developments regarding taxation force some short-run modification of it. George felt that taxation on things other than land values was unethical so long as land was not fully taxed. Society should not deny a man any part of the fruits of his labor. He assumed that the single tax would be more than ample for the needs of government. What, then, of the ethics of taxation in our day when such an assumption can no longer be made?

The most obvious answer would be that by far the largest part of our tax budget goes to national defense—army, navy, air force, pensions, war research, etc., not to mention police, prisons, and criminal courts. Ethics demands that we defend ourselves against unjust attack—to do otherwise is to condone our own murder and robbery—and if more revenue is needed than land value taxation provides, then the excess taxation is certainly justified.

A democratic government is ethically charged with maintaining that essential condition of true democracy, equality of opportunity. To do this, expenditures are required for anti-trust and fair trade enforcement, free compulsory education, free medical care for the indigent, compulsory unemployment insurance, etc. If such expenditures exceed what a land value tax can provide, then other forms of taxation are required.

All governments perform certain essential services for civilized living which only they can provide, at least with the greatest efficiency. Such services are fire prevention, hospitals, sewers, roads, sanitation, public health, conservation, etc. Generally, local governments perform these services and the taxes to finance them are really charges for benefits received. A gas tax or bridge toll is really a charge for road use. No one expects bus companies to provide their services free of charge; why must we expect otherwise if the bus company is municipally owned? Or if the municipal facility is not a bus company but a garbage disposal plant or a fire department? If the people wish, these services can be provided by the land value tax, but it would be equally equitable if charges were made for these necessary social services in addition to whatever income the land value tax would provide.

Tax money is also spent on subsidies to various special interest groups; expenditures for farm price supports, public housing, tariff protection, post office deficit, etc. may fall into this category. If they do, then such taxation can hardly be ethically justified, for the taxing of one individual to benefit another cannot be condoned. However, many people argue that these expenditures are necessary for the maintenance of equal opportunity.

Life in modern society demands other modifications of the labor theory of property. Thus, we have gun licenses and zoning restrictions, factory inspection laws and narcotics prohibition.

When all these modifications imposed by modern social life and taxation are added to the labor theory of property, does this not amount to a detailed statement of the currently acceptable social utility theory of property? There is no essential contradiction between the two theories. What is best for society is that each man should receive the fruits of his labor. If there is any difference, it is one of emphasis; the social utility theory takes cognizance of temporary concessions that must often be made to current exigencies, whereas George's labor theory has its eyes fixed firmly on the ultimate goal.

Let us move now from the more general realm of ethical theory to some specific considerations concerning the ethics of private land ownership. One argument often advanced by single taxers is that since the community by its presence and activity gives value to land, the income from land values—i.e., the rent of land—rightfully belongs to the community and not to the landowners. This is a facile argument with easy appeal. It has impressed many historians and economists but has convinced few, perhaps because it is not really valid.

As E. R. A. Seligman pointed out, the value of *all* products is set by social demand. Carried to its logical extreme, this argument could justify the social ownership of everything! The truth of the matter is that values are set by the laws of economics (such as supply and demand), whereas ownership is determined by the laws of ethics (such as the labor theory or the social utility theory). Georgists have much sounder arguments than this one for justifying their position.

The question of the confiscation of vested interests in land always arises when the subject of land value taxation is broached. The tax would deprive landowners of their rental income. Is this just? Will landowners suffer? These are vital questions of practical as well as ethical importance.

If the labor theory of property is accepted, then only those things can be privately owned that have been produced by labor. This would exclude land. Since the landowner *per se* has produced nothing, he is living off the efforts of the active producers, labor and capital.

In discussing the issue of confiscation, one must know precisely what the term includes. The landowner is not being denied title to his land. His land value tax will go up but his other taxes, particularly on his improvements, will go down. He will lose the selling price of his land, but if he sells and buys elsewhere he will pay nothing for the land he buys and thus will not be a loser. If he rents, his rent will be lower than it is now because it will not include a building tax. Landowners who make efficient use of their land will benefit by the tax change, while only those who do not will suffer. They can avoid this by improving their land properly.

In the Australian province of South Australia, three-fifths of the landowners in a particular locality must approve any change from the old taxing system to land value taxation; a quirk in the law allows only a bare majority to vote for a reversion to the old system. Each year for a long time more and more localities have been switching to land value taxation, and to date not one reversion poll has been successful. This evidence would indicate that land-owners benefit from George's tax idea more than many historians and economists have thought.

The precipitous increase in taxation in recent years has vitiated "confiscation" arguments somewhat. We have become used to confiscation of earned incomes, purchases, cars and corporation profits by taxation. Whereas the question in George's day was whether we should take land rent from the landowners and redistribute it to other people, now the question is: should the government tax land rent or earned income? The first alternative seems ethically as well as economically preferable.[7]

In any case, not many historians and economists have

[7] Arthur Krock, in his New York Times column of March 17, 1961, pointed out that because local municipalities have refused to tax land values, the only outstanding tax source still available to them, they have not been able to provide the necessary services to their residents. Consequently, they have been forced into a growing reliance upon the federal government.

realized that the gradual imposition of the land value tax amounts to partial or possibly even complete compensation. If the tax is increased by equal annual installments over a period of twenty years, the landowner has been compensated for one-half of his land investment (without interest). If the period is lengthened to forty years, he is fully compensated.

The Case For and Against Land Value Taxation

Henry George's land value tax having been tried in the court of ethics, now the reigning pragmatism demands that we test it according to the immediate results it might achieve.

In George's day, few doubted that land value taxation would produce much more revenue than the government needed; in fact, many claimed dictatorship would result from such a plethora of income. Even as late as 1915, on the eve of our entry into World War I, Wilford I. King, then the leading economic statistician, admitted that the land value tax could be a single tax and yet be able to meet all necessary government expenses. It could probably have been adequate as a single source of government tax income until the 1930's.[8]

Since then, we know well what has happened. Government budgets have soared beyond what a tax on land values could yield, the warfare rather than the welfare state being the chief cause. Should Henry George's single tax be discarded on the grounds that it is not possible in today's world? This is what many historians and economists have done. But are they justified in dubbing the land value tax impractical because it cannot be the single and only

[8] Even in a society of perfectly ethical men, some government would be needed to regulate traffic, business, public health, etc. George's single tax could easily provide enough revenue for such a government. The more we deviate from this ideal society, the less sufficient the land value tax becomes as the sole revenue source.

tax? Must *Progress and Poverty* be accepted or rejected *in toto*, or should we not choose the wiser course of seeing what there is in the book which still has application today? The land value tax should be examined strictly on its own merits, quite apart from whether or not it can be a single tax.

Certainly a good *prima facie* case can be made for it. Many benefits might reasonably be expected from the gradual introduction of land value taxation, in the view of its supporters.

(1) It would force land to be put to the most economic use. The land user must erect improvements that will at least yield an income to pay the rent tax, plus something left over for profit. Rickety buildings on valuable land—slums—would therefore be strongly discouraged. It would also discourage urban sprawl.[9]

(2) It can considerably reduce the burdensome taxation which now falls on labor and industry. The first tax to be abolished should be the real estate tax on buildings.

(3) By reducing the price of land to near zero, it would reduce the total investment capital a builder would need. It would automatically provide builders with the land leaseback advantage now so popular, and it would not be necessary to incur the heavy expense of interest on a land mortgage.

(4) By reducing the price of land to near zero, land acquisition for such eminent domain purposes as highways, playgrounds, parks, public buildings, etc. would become much easier and cheaper.

(5) It would remove one cause of depressions—land

[9] Georgists claim that the present tax system permits vast areas of land to be underused, thus causing superintensive use of the remaining land. The result is skyscrapers, slums and empty lots within the same city boundaries. By making unprofitable the underuse of land, land value taxation also prevents its overuse elsewhere. Continual natural city planning would ensue.

speculation—and by reducing building tax and land costs, it could also help to counter inflation.

In these ways, advocates claim, the causes of urban renewal and proper land use would be well served. America's biggest investment, real estate, would be protected, and construction, our second largest industry, would be spurred to new growth.

The tax offers one unique advantage almost completely overlooked by historians and economists. It is an ideal land reform for underdeveloped areas. Not only would it cost the governments of these impoverished countries nothing, but it would actually bring in additional revenue. It would force the rich people in these countries to divert their savings from sterile land investment to much-needed capital investment. It would end the evil of absentee land-lordism and by forcing land to its most efficient use assure the greatest possible agricultural production. What is more, land value taxation would be a continuing land reform which would constantly act to prevent the reconstitution of large landholdings.

In these troubled and revolutionary times, when 5½ per cent of the landlords own almost 80 per cent of the arable land in Latin America, our national security is involved. So is it also when Iranian tenant farmers can keep only a third of their total produce, and when the Communists give land freely to the peasants in the areas of South Viet Nam which they control, whereas the American-supported regime has required some kind of compensation to dispossessed landlords, to which the peasants are forced to contribute.[10]

Admittedly, the political control that landowners wield in most underdeveloped areas makes any land tenure

[10] *New York Times Magazine,* April 13, 1958 (p. 11), August 6, 1961 (p. 18), August 13, 1961 (p. 89).

reform difficult. Perhaps the gradualness by which the land value tax can be imposed might make it the only alternative to land reform by revolution. Should not America's foreign policy makers examine the ideas of Henry George more closely?[11]

The other side of the coin should also be investigated. What is the most effective argument against the land value tax? Stated succinctly, it is this: the land value tax can bring some benefits but they would not be important enough to outweigh the financial hardship it would cause certain real estate owners. Georgists have been stirring a tempest in a teapot, and although the idea has some merit it does not have enough to justify action. Redistributing the land rent would cause more trouble than it is worth.

Certain criticisms of the historians and economists reveal the advisability of making these minor additions to the land value tax program as George conceived it.

(1) Homeowners may suddenly find that the growth of the city has veered in their direction, causing a sudden increase in their land rent tax which they may not be able to pay. They would have to move, but they could not sell their land for very much if anything, and no one would want their house except to tear it down in order to put up a more profitable improvement, perhaps an apartment or office building. To protect such persons from the loss of their investment in their homes, a land value tax law should also require the new purchaser of a piece of real estate to pay the former owner at least the assessed market value of the improvement thereon.

[11] To be sure, a land tenure reform such as land value taxation must be only one part of a total land reform program in underdeveloped areas. Other aspects of land reform are: government extension of credit at low rates of interest, land reclamation and conservation, consolidation of strip farms, agricultural cooperatives, government research and extension services, industrial development, spread of education and democratic political development.

(2) Local governments should offer low-cost construction loans to those real estate owners who would be paying more taxes under the new system. This would make it easier for them to improve their properties and avoid any excessive hardship which the land value tax might cause.

A method already exists by which any city can immediately introduce a limited amount of land value taxation without causing hardship to any individual. Each year some land becomes tax delinquent under our present system of real estate taxation, and title to it is assumed by the local government. Also, cities buy land for condemnation under urban renewal programs. Instead of reselling the land, would it not make more sense if the land were rented out on a leasehold basis? The city would receive a continuing income and the purchaser would have to make no investment in land. In this painless way, much of the city's land would become taxed on its rental value.[12]

There is still another way by which a city can introduce land rent taxation without direct harm to anyone. Complete tax exemption could be granted to all newly constructed buildings while the land under these buildings would be taxed to the full extent of its annual rental value. This surely is a painless way to encourage new construction.

Theoretical arguments for and against the land value tax have their place, but nothing convinces like a successful application. Such applications exist in Australia, New Zealand and elsewhere, although few economists and historians have shown any awareness of them. Research studies indicate that the results of the land value tax have been very beneficial, and the fact that one community after another has been switching over to it is impressive evidence indeed.

[12] See the official report of Management Services Associates, Inc., New York City, to the city and county commissioners at Dayton, Ohio, March 7, 1962, which supports this proposal.

If the implications of this study are sound, then a discussion of Henry George and his ideas could very well be found in economics textbooks under the following headings:

history of economic thought
housing
land reform—underdeveloped areas
land rent
land use planning
taxation
tax shifting
unearned income
urban renewal

History of Economic Thought

In the history of economic thought, Henry George appears as the last chief exponent of the classical economics school. The year 1880 marks the approximate beginning of dominance by the neo-classical marginal utility economists. Therefore, in the eyes of the younger economists of his day, who stressed data and facts rather than logic and ethics, George's book was out of date as soon as it was published.

Despite their devotion to data and facts, the economists have had to deliver a normative judgment on George, and although he won many adherents among them, the overall evaluation was negative. Perhaps this reaction by T. N. Carver, a conservative economist who reluctantly endorsed the land value tax, is typical:[13]

The inheritance tax has made more headway than the land tax. The arguments for one seem to be about as strong as for the other. The inheritance tax, however, has stood on its merits and has not been championed as an engine of social reform. It has had no body of ardent apostles to set up a fiery

[13] T. N. Carver, *Essays in Social Justice*, p. 304.

cross and preach a crusade against a fortunate class. The land tax has thus been handicapped, which may account for its slow progress. In the ardency of reform, arguments are used which ignite certain inflammable spirits but repel all thinking men. This makes constructive reform impossible and nothing can be done until the inflammable spirits gain control in a sweeping and destructive revolution. This, however, seldom happens. For one such movement which grows to a general conflagration at least ninety-nine flicker out.

Generally, as previous chapters of this study indicate, the histories of economic thought have not been free from serious misconceptions concerning George and his ideas. Also, these histories give George much briefer treatment than one would think he deserves, considering the impact he made on his generation and the one that followed. For example, one of the most commonly used textbooks on the subject (by Erich Roll) is content with briefly rephrasing Karl Marx's evaluation of George, although the source is not mentioned.

Perhaps the reason for this neglect is the feeling that George dealt only with a minor factor in economics—land rent—the importance of which was small and declining. One wonders if our land tenure system—man's basic economic adjustment to nature—can really be unimportant. Only recently, the problems of land usage have been making front page news—urban renewal, urban sprawl, high land prices, housing shortage, road building, land reform. Many authorities feel that George had something worth while to say on these subjects. It would seem that some rewriting of the history of economic thought is needed.

When all is said and done, George wielded a great influence in his time, not only on the general populace but on the young and upcoming economists. It was he who was instrumental in showing that the government had a responsibility in economic reform. He was one of the first to relate economic theory to urgent problems of the day, such as depressions, slums and farm tenancy. He quickened the spirit of Progressive reform. He was one of the first economists to point out the need for the control of natural monopolies. If it is true that he was a vital influence in the development of American social ideas, it is hard to see how he could avoid affecting economic thought. To this day, economists have been affected by his distinction between earned and unearned incomes, and the taxation of land values is still an important issue to many prominent economists.

Most of the historians of economic thought who slight George's contributions nevertheless devote rather extensive sections to the Physiocrats. This is questionable practice when one compares the influence of the earlier and later schools of single taxers on historical events and present-day economic thinking. If soundness of logic is any criterion, then the Physiocrats come out second-best to Henry George. They believed, for example, that only the extractive industries added to the wealth of a nation, that all taxation fell upon landowners, that land value taxes did not reduce the selling price of land—all exploded theories today.

In view of all this, it would seem that Henry George has received less mention than is his due in the histories of economic thought.

Henry George in American History

Although previously, history had been written with a heavy political emphasis, the 1920's and thirties witnessed the advent of intellectual history. As a consequence, there has been a growing historical interest in Henry George. Whereas previously he was mentioned only in connection with his unsuccessful 1886 mayoralty campaign in New

York City, now his pervasive intellectual influence on the Progressive Era that followed him is clearly recognized. Most historians would agree that *Progress and Poverty* made the first major rift in American complacency about such social problems as poverty and depressions, problems magnified by the Industrial Revolution. Few deny that through countless channels, George's ideas filtered out into various areas of American thought. Perhaps Professor Eric Goldman's comment is characteristic:[14]

For some years prior to 1952, I was working on a history of American reform and over and over again my research ran into this fact. An enormous number of men and women, strikingly different people, men and women who were to lead twentieth century America in a dozen fields of humane activity, wrote or told someone that their whole thinking had been redirected by reading *Progress and Poverty* in their formative years. In this respect no other book came anywhere near comparable influence, and I would like to add this word of tribute to a volume which magically catalyzed the best yearnings of our grandfathers and fathers.

Although no one can deny that historians have given due recognition to George's catalytic influence, their treatment of his specific ideas is more open to criticism. These ideas they often have misstated or described in unnecessarily vague terms. The image of Henry George left in the minds of casual readers of their historical accounts is that he favored confiscation of landed property, that he belonged to the "underworld" of economics, that he was a utopian, an old-fashioned crackpot, and has been rejected by all responsible thinkers. Unanswered is the unavoidable question: How could such a person exert so powerful an influence on the course of American history? Edward Bellamy also wrote a best-selling volume, but his influence was ephemeral because his ideas "were like castles in the

[14] Henry George School course announcement.

sky with clouds for their foundation," to use George's words.[15] If Henry George's influence was not ephemeral, then perhaps it was because his ideas contained at least some merit. To understand Henry George's influence fully we must understand his single tax philosophy.

George's unwarranted suspicion, even contempt, for the academic world, an attitude duplicated by many of his followers, undoubtedly created much antagonism for him among the very people whose endorsement he desperately needed. Frequently, this resulted in many of George's critics taking an emotional dislike to him though endorsing his tax proposal in a mild sort of way. However, as his life receded more and more into the dim historical past, many critics recognized his great contribution as an arouser of the social conscience and accepted the man while rejecting the ideas which they only vaguely understood.

One of the reasons why historians have had difficulty in evaluating George's philosophy and career is that he defies easy classification as either a liberal or conservative. He was not a liberal according to the current definition of that term because liberals are not particularly concerned with how government welfare programs are to be financed. George could agree with them that such welfare programs were necessary, but in his case proper financing via the single tax meant a great deal. He could criticize the Social Darwinists for not recognizing the existing inequality of economic opportunity, as when he wrote that "Mr. [Herbert] Spencer is like one who might insist that each should swim for himself in crossing a river, ignoring the fact that some had been artificially provided with corks and others artificially loaded with lead."[16] Yet at the same time, George could oppose the income tax and anti-tenement

[15] Charles A. Barker, *Henry George*, p. 540.
[16] Henry George, *A Perplexed Philosopher*, p. 66.

house legislation as a restriction on individual liberty, believing that the single tax would equalize and expand economic opportunity, making such legislation unnecessary. Many historians and economists were confused by George because he was a reformer without being a liberal. But neither is his basic philosophy that of a conservative. He certainly wasn't on the land question and his sympathies were wholeheartedly with the underprivileged in society. Thus it is ironic, and at the same time another source of misunderstanding, that George contributed to the eventual success of Reform Darwinism and pragmatism although both were antithetical to basic elements in his philosophy.

Many reform movements in American history are related to George's pattern of thinking. From the Jeffersonian tradition in America, he got his belief in natural rights and the primacy of *liberty*. Jefferson was his hero. From the Jacksonian Era he got his belief in *equality,* the enthronement of the common man and his antipathy towards monopoly. He was a Jacksonian by birth. In his own time, he served as the bridge in the transition from Social to Reform Darwinism, gradually converting the Mugwump spirit into full-fledged Progressivism. He helped persuade the Progressive reformers of the following generation that the power of the government should be harnessed to preserve *equal opportunity*. His connection with the New Deal and its desire to protect the economic *security* of its citizens is much less obvious or certain, although he was one of the first to propose that the government pension its elderly citizens, provide hospitals, playgrounds and music halls, etc. (all with single tax revenue, of course).

It is hard to measure the influence of any man, let alone Henry George, influence being such a gossamer substance. Do we measure it by books sold? George did well on that score, for his books were translated into many languages and in the free world *Progress and Poverty* has probably outsold any other book on economics, including *Wealth of Nations* and *Das Kapital*. Do we measure influence by the number of reports about him in the newspapers of his time? George does well here, too, for he had an international reputation during his life. Is it to be measured by the number of references to him in current scholarly literature? Here George fares less well, although we have already noted a renaissance of interest in him. In impact on specific legislation? George exerted little influence of this sort in America, but overseas, particularly in the English-speaking world, his influence continues strong to this moment. If endorsement by many of the thinkers and doers of our country is a good measure of prestige, then George rates well. There is a small but well-established movement still propagating his philosophy, although few laymen know him, and his ideas are not highly regarded or well understood by most economists and historians, if we are to judge by the books (especially textbooks) they write.

In assessing the importance of Henry George, one's evaluation of land value taxation is a vital factor. If one thinks highly of it, then George becomes a key figure in history; if otherwise, then he becomes just one of many agitators of America's social conscience, to be classed with Edward Bellamy and Henry Demarest Lloyd as one of the earliest muckrakers. Because of this, it becomes more than a mere matter of antiquarianism to clear away the misunderstandings and vagaries that permeate the description of George's ideas in most works in American history and economics. In no other way can we properly assess Henry George.

There is still another important reason why the record

should be clarified. Many authorities in the fields of urban renewal, land use planning, public finance and land reform feel that land value taxation can be a highly useful device for social improvement, yet they find their efforts in its behalf to be hampered not only by these vagaries and misstatements, but also by the image of Henry George that has been drawn by the historians and economists. Mention George in connection with land value taxation, they have found, and an unfavorable and unfounded train of thought is set in motion in the minds of many people: Henry George . . . confiscation of landed property . . . socialism . . . nineteenth-century Utopianism . . . single tax . . . exploded theory . . . to be rejected.

As a result, many current proponents of land value taxation have felt it necessary to avoid mention of Henry George altogether or to deny that he had any connection with the idea. Such an example was *House and Home's* special issue on land value taxation which mentioned Henry George only once, and then incidentally. The organizers of the current Pennsylvania campaign for land value taxation studiously avoid employing his name for fear of arousing old antagonisms and misunderstandings.

However expedient this course of action may be, it is incumbent upon us to clear up the historical record of Henry George and to remove the misconceptions and vagaries that surround his ideas. Not only will our concept of history be improved but we will then be better able to determine, without rancor or partisanship, whether land value taxation has merit or not. It is hoped that this study has advanced that purpose.

BIBLIOGRAPHY

ALL LITERATURE CITED IN THIS STUDY IS LISTED IN THIS BIB-
liography. Many other sources, particularly textbooks, have
been reviewed by the author and form part of the basis for
the conclusions reached in this study, although they may
not be referred to in the text.

I. Economic Accounts

A. HISTORY OF ECONOMIC THOUGHT

Abbott, L. D. (ed.), *Masterworks of Economics*. New York:
Doubleday, 1947. Pp. 754.

Bell, John F., *History of Economic Thought*. New York:
Ronald Press, 1953. Pp. 696.

Dorfman, Joseph, *Economic Mind in American Civilization, Volume 3*. New York: Viking, 1959 (first edition
1946). Pp. 494.

Flubacher, Joseph K., *The Concept of Ethics in the History of Economics*. New York: Vantage, 1950. Pp. 460.

Ferguson, J. M., *Landmarks of Economic Thought*. New
York: Longmans-Green, 1950 (2nd ed.). Pp. 295.

Gide, Charles, and Rist, Charles, *History of Economic Doctrines*. New York: D. C. Heath, 1948 (first edition 1909).
Pp. 800.

Haney, Lewis, *History of Economic Thought*. New York: Macmillan, 1949 (first edition 1921). Pp. 896.

Heilbroner, Robert, *The Worldly Philosophers*. New York: Simon & Schuster, 1953. Pp. 342.

Heimann, Edward, *History of Economic Doctrines*. New York: Oxford University Press, 1945. Pp. 263.

Homan, Paul T., *Contemporary Economic Thought*. New York: Harper, 1928. Pp. 475.

Hutchison, T. W., *A Review of Economic Doctrines, 1870-1929*. Oxford: Clarendon Press, 1953. Pp. 456.

Ingram, John K., *A History of Political Economy*. London: Black, 1915. Pp. 315.

Lekachman, Robert, *A History of Economic Ideas*. New York: Harper, 1959. Pp. 427.

Neff, Frank A., *Economic Doctrines*. McGraw-Hill, 1950. Pp. 532.

Newman, Philip, *Development of Economic Thought*. New York: Prentice-Hall, 1952. Pp. 456.

Normano, J. F., *The Spirit of American Economics*. New York: John Day, 1943. Pp. 252.

Patterson, S. H., *Readings in the History of Economic Thought*. New York: McGraw-Hill, 1932. Pp. 745.

Roll, Erich, *History of Economic Thought*. New York: Prentice-Hall, 1956 (first edition 1942). Pp. 540.

Schumpeter, J. A., *History of Economic Analysis*. New York: Oxford University Press, 1955. Pp. 1260.

Scott, W. A., *The Development of Economics*. New York: Appleton-Century-Crofts, 1933. Pp. 540.

Soule, George, *Ideas of the Great Economists*. New York: Viking, 1952. Pp. 218.

Spann, Othmar, *The History of Economics*. New York: W. W. Norton, 1930. Pp. 326.

Spiegel, H. W. (ed.), *Development of Economic Thought*. New York: J. Wiley, 1952. Pp. 811.

Taft, Philip, *Movements for Economic Reform*. New York: Rinehart, 1950. Pp. 614.

Taylor, Overton, *A History of Economic Thought*. New York: McGraw-Hill, 1960. Pp. 524.

Whittaker, Edmund, *A History of Economic Ideas*. New York: Longmans, Green, 1940. Pp. 766.

Wilhite, Virgle G., *Founders of Economic Thought and Policy*. New York: Bookman Associates, 1958. Pp. 442.

Zweig, Ferdynand, *Economic Ideas*. New York: Prentice-Hall, 1950. Pp. 197.

B. PUBLIC FINANCE

Adams, Henry C., *Science of Finance*. New York: Henry Holt, 1892. Pp. 573.

Alyea, Paul E. and Blanche R., *Fairhope, 1894-1954*. Birmingham: University of Alabama Press, 1956. Pp. 351.

Anderson, William H., *Taxation and the American Economy*. New York: Prentice-Hall, 1954. Pp. 410.

Bennett, Orval, and Lippincott, Isaac, *Public Finance*. Cincinnati: Southwestern Publishing Co., 1949. Pp. 728.

Brownlee, C. H., and Allen, Edward, *Economics of Public Finance*. New York: Prentice-Hall, 1954. Pp. 410.

Buehler, Alfred, *Public Finance*. New York: McGraw-Hill, 1948. Pp. 740.

Cauley, Troy Jesse, *Public Finance and the General Welfare*. Columbus, Ohio: P. E. Merrill Books, 1960. Pp. 398.

Committee on Public Finance, *Public Finance*. New York: Pitman, 1959. Pp. 798.

Daniels, Winthrop More, *The Elements of Public Finance*. New York: Henry Holt, 1899. Pp. 383.

Due, John F., *Government Finance, An Economic Analysis*. Homewood, Ill.: R. D. Irwin, 1954. Pp. 562.

Ely, Richard T., *Taxation in American States and Cities*. New York: T. Y. Crowell, 1888. Pp. 544.

Fisher, Ernest M., *Advanced Principles of Real Estate Practice*. New York: Macmillan, 1938. Pp. 522.

Fisher, Ernest M., *Principles of Real Estate Practice*. New York: Macmillan, 1926. Pp. 311.

Fisher, Ernest M. and Robert M., *Urban Real Estate*. New York: Henry Holt, 1954. Pp. 502.

Groves, Harold M., *Financing Government*. New York: Henry Holt, 1958 (first edition 1939). Pp. 630.

Howard, Mayne S., *Principles of Public Finance*. New York: Commerce Clearing House, 1940. Pp. 438.

Hunter, Merlin, *Outlines of Public Finance*. New York: Harper, 1921. Pp. 533.

Hunter, Merlin, and Allen, Kenneth, *Principles of Public Finance*. New York: Harper, 1940 (first edition 1921). Pp. 672.

Jensen, Jens P., *Government Finance*. New York: T. Y. Crowell, 1937. Pp. 595.

Kendrick, M. Slade, *Public Finance*. Boston: Houghton Mifflin, 1951. Pp. 708.

King, Clyde, *Public Finance*. New York: Macmillan, 1935. Pp. 602.

Magill, Roswell (ed.), *Lectures on Taxation*. New York: Commerce Clearing House, 1932. Pp. 254.

Morton, Walter, *Housing Taxation*. Madison: University of Wisconsin Press, 1955. Pp. 262.

Musgrave, Richard Abel, *The Theory of Public Finance*. New York: McGraw-Hill, 1959. Pp. 628.

Paul, Randolph, *Taxation for Prosperity*. Indianapolis: Bobbs-Merrill, 1947. Pp. 448.

Plank, E. H., *Public Finance*. Homewood, Ill.: Richard D. Irwin, 1953. Pp. 772.

Plehn, Carl C., *Government Finance in the United States.* Chicago: A. C. McClurg, 1915. Pp. 166.

Plehn, Carl C., *Introduction to Public Finance.* New York: Macmillan, 1896. Pp. 446.

Sayre, Wallace S., *An Outline of American Government.* New York: Barnes & Noble, 1941. Pp. 219.

Schultz, William J., and Harriss, C. L., *American Public Finance.* New York: Prentice-Hall, 1959. Pp. 631.

Seager, Henry R., *Public Expenditures and Public Revenue.* New York: Henry Holt, 1905. Pp. 55.

Seligman, E. R. A., *Studies in Public Finance.* New York: Macmillan, 1925. Pp. 302.

Shirras, G. Finlay, *Science of Public Finance.* New York: Macmillan, 1936, 2 v.

Strayer, Paul J., *Fiscal Policy and Politics.* New York: Harper, 1958. Pp. 305.

Taylor, Philip E., *Economics of Public Finance.* New York: Macmillan, 1953. Pp. 588.

Tax Policy League Symposium, *Property Taxes.* New York: Tax Policy League, 1939. Pp. 288.

Walker, Mabel, *Business Enterprise and the City.* Princeton: Tax Institute, Inc., 1957. Pp. 120.

Walker, Mabel, *Urban Blight and Slums.* Cambridge: Harvard University Press, 1938. Pp. 442.

Withers, William, *Public Finance.* New York: American Book Co., 1948. Pp. 480.

C. LAND ECONOMICS

Barlowe, Raleigh, *Land Resource Economics.* Englewood Cliffs: Prentice-Hall, 1958. Pp. 585.

Bartholomew, Harland, *Land Values in American Cities.* Cambridge: Harvard University Press, 1955. Pp. 196.

Davies, Pearl Janet, *Real Estate in American History.* Washington: Public Affairs Press, 1958. Pp. 232.

Clawson, Marion, Held, R. Brumell, and Stoddard, Charles H., *Land for the Future*. Baltimore: Johns Hopkins University Press, 1960. Pp. 570.

Culver, Dorothy C., *Land Utilization: A Bibliography*. Berkeley: University of California Press, 1935. Pp. 222. (See also 1937 supplement.)

Doran, Herbert B., and Albert, Herman, *Urban Land Economics*. New York: Macmillan, 1928.

Ely, Richard T., and Wehrwein, George S., *Land Economics*. New York: Macmillan, 1940. Pp. 512.

Ely, Richard T., *Outlines of Land Economics*. Ann Arbor: Edwards Bros., 1922, 3 v.

Fisher, Ernest M., *Advanced Principles of Real Estate Practice*. New York: Macmillan, 1938. Pp. 522.

Fisher, Ernest M. and Robert M., *Urban Real Estate*. New York: Henry Holt, 1954. Pp. 502.

Gray, Lewis Cecil, *Introduction to Agricultural Economics*. New York: Macmillan, 1924. Pp. 556.

Gray, Lewis Cecil, and Baker, O. E., *Land Utilization and the Farm Problem*. Washington: United States Government Printing Office, 1930. Pp. 54.

Hutchinson, A. R., et al., *Public Charges Upon Land Values*. Melbourne: Land Value Research Group, 1961. Pp. 48.

Losch, August, *The Economics of Location*. New Haven: Yale University Press, 1954. Pp. 520.

McMichael, Stanley, *Real Estate Subdivisions*. New York: Prentice-Hall, 1949. Pp. 393.

Nelson, R. L., and Aschman, F. T., *Real Estate and City Planning*. Englewood Cliffs, N.J.: Prentice-Hall, 1957. Pp. 349.

Ratcliff, Richard U., *Urban Economics*. New York: McGraw-Hill, 1949. Pp. 533.

Renne, Roland R., *Land Economics*. New York: Harper, 1947. Pp. 736.

Spiegel, Henry, *Land Tenure Policies.* Chapel Hill: University of North Carolina Press, 1941. Pp. 171.

Taylor, Gerald K., *Relationships Between Land Value and Land Use in a Central Business District.* Washington: Urban Land Institute, 1957. Pp. 77.

Tucker, Gilbert, *The Self-Supporting City.* New York: Robert Schalkenbach Foundation, 1946. Pp. 100.

Turvey, Ralph, *The Economics of Real Property.* London: Geo. Allen and Unwin, 1957. Pp. 150.

Wald, Haskell P., *Taxation of Agricultural Land in Underdeveloped Economies.* Cambridge: Harvard University Press, 1959. Pp. 231.

Wendt, Paul F., *Real Estate Appraisal.* New York: Henry Holt, 1956. Pp. 320.

D. OTHER ECONOMIC LITERATURE

Batson, H. B., *Bibliography of Modern Economic Theory, 1870-1929.* New York: E. P. Dutton, 1930. Pp. 224.

Brown, Harry Gunnison, Buttenheim, Harold S., Cornick, Philip H., and Hoover, Glenn, *Land-Value Taxation Around the World.* New York: Robert Schalkenbach Foundation, 1955. Pp. 216.

Brown, Harry Gunnison (ed.), *Significant Paragraphs from Progress and Poverty.* New York: Robert Schalkenbach Foundation, 1928. Pp. 80.

Brown, Harry Gunnison, *Taxation of Unearned Incomes.* Columbia, Mo.: Lucas Bros., 1925. Pp. 173.

Bullock, Edna, *Selected Articles on the Single Tax.* White Plains: H. W. Wilson, 1915. Pp. 199.

Carver, T. N., *Essays in Social Justice.* Cambridge: Harvard University Press, 1915. Pp. 429.

Clark, J. B., *Distribution of Wealth.* New York: Macmillan, 1899. Pp. 445.

Ellis, Howard (ed.), *Survey of Contemporary Economics.* Philadelphia: Blakiston, 1948. Pp. 490.

George, Henry, *A Perplexed Philosopher*. New York: Robert Schalkenbach Foundation, 1892. Pp. 276.

George, Henry, *Progress and Poverty*. New York: Robert Schalkenbach Foundation, 1879. Pp. 571.

George, Henry, *Science of Political Economy*. New York: Robert Schalkenbach Foundation, 1897. Pp. 545.

Haig, R. M., *The Exemption of Improvements from Taxation in Canada and the U.S.*, a report prepared for the Committee on Taxation of the City of New York, 1915. Pp. 254.

King, Willford I., *The Wealth and Income of the People of the U.S.* New York: Macmillan, 1915. Pp. 278.

Jordan, David Starr, and Stallard, Dr. J. H., *True Basis of Economics*. New York: Doubleday & McClure, 1899. Pp. 130.

Jorgensen, Emil O., *Next Steps Toward Real Democracy*. Chicago: Chicago Single Tax Club, 1920. Pp. 127.

Rosenman, Dorothy, *A Million Homes a Year*. New York: Harcourt, Brace, 1945. Pp. 333.

Scheftel, Yetta, *The Taxation of Land Value*. Boston: Houghton, Mifflin, 1916. Pp. 489.

Seligman, Edwin R. A., *Essays in Taxation*. New York: Macmillan, 8th edition, 1913. Pp. 707.

Speek, Peter A., *The Single Tax and the Labor Movement*. Madison: University of Wisconsin Press, 1915. Pp. 180.

Sumner, William Graham, *The Challenge of Facts and Other Essays*. New Haven: Yale University Press, 1914. Pp. 450.

Taussig, Frank William, *Wages and Capital*. New York: Macmillan, 1896. Pp. 329.

Walker, Francis Amasa, *Land and Its Rent*. Boston: Little, Brown, 1883. Pp. 232.

II. *Historical Accounts*

Beard, Charles, *American City Government*. New York: Century, 1912. Pp. 420.

Beard, Charles and Mary, *The American Spirit*. New York: Macmillan, 1942. Pp. 696.

Beer, Thomas, *Mauve Decade*. New York: Knopf, 1926. Pp. 268.

Curti, Merle, *Growth of American Thought*. New York: Harper, 1943. Pp. 848.

De Witt, B. P., *Progressive Movement*. New York: Macmillan, 1915. Pp. 376.

Dorfman, Joseph, *Thorstein Veblen and His America*. New York: Viking, 1934. Pp. 556.

Einstein, Lewis, *Roosevelt, His Mind in Action*. Boston: Houghton, 1930. Pp. 259.

Ekirch, Arthur, *Decline of American Liberalism*. New York: Longmans, Green, 1955. Pp. 401.

Faulkner, Harold U., *Quest for Social Justice, 1898-1914*. New York: Macmillan, 1931.

Gabriel, Ralph, *Course of American Democratic Thought*. New York: Ronald Press, 1940. Pp. 452.

Goldman, Eric, *Rendezvous with Destiny*. New York: Knopf, 1953. Pp. 503.

Golob, Eugene O., *The "Isms"—A History and an Evaluation*. New York: Harper, 1954. Pp. 681.

Haynes, Fred E., *Social Politics in the U.S.* New York: Houghton Mifflin, 1924. Pp. 414.

Lewis, Edward R., *A History of American Political Thought from the Civil War to the World War*. New York: Macmillan, 1937. Pp. 561.

Merriam, C. E., *American Political Ideas, 1865-1917*. New York: Macmillan, 1920. Pp. 481.

Miller, Perry (ed.), *American Thought, Civil War to World War I*. New York: Rinehart, 1954. Pp. 345.

Parrington, Vernon, *Main Currents in American Thought*. New York: Harcourt Brace, 1927, 3 v.

Rhodes, James Ford, *History of the U.S. from Hayes to McKinley, 1877-1896*. New York: Macmillan, 1928. Pp. 484.

Ross, Edwin A., *Seventy Years of It*. New York: Appleton-Century, 1936. Pp. 338.

Sherwood, Sidney, *Tendencies in American Economic Thought*. Baltimore: Johns Hopkins Studies in History and Political Science, 1897. Pp. 607.

III. *Textbooks*

A. ECONOMICS

Abbott, Lawrence, *Economics and the Modern World*. New York: Harcourt Brace, 1960. Pp. 880.

Baumol, William J., and Chandler, Lester, *Economic Processes and Policies*. New York: Harper, 1954. Pp. 690.

Bullock, Charles J., *The Elements of Economics*. Boston: Silver, Burdette, 1913 (first edition 1905). Pp. 378.

Bullock, Charles J., *Introduction to the Study of Economics*. Boston: Silver, Burdette, 1900 (first edition 1897). Pp. 581.

Bye, Raymond T., and Hewett, William, *Applied Economics*. New York: Appleton-Century-Crofts, 1928 and 1960. Pp. 595.

Calderwood, James, and Quantius, Francis, *Economics*. New York: Prentice-Hall, 1951. Pp. 611.

Carver, T. N., *Elementary Economics*. Boston: Ginn, 1920. Pp. 400.

Carver, T. N., *Principles of National Economy*. Boston: Ginn, 1921. Pp. 773.

Committee on Principles of Economics (numbering 67 economists), *Principles of Economics*. New York: Pitman, 1959, Pp. 873.

Commons, John R., *Distribution of Wealth*. New York: Macmillan, 1893. Pp. 258.

Corbett, James, and Colvin, Minna, *Modern Economics*. New York: Macmillan, 1941. Pp. 591.

Davenport, Herbert J., *Economics of Enterprise*. New York: Macmillan, 1925 (first edition 1913). Pp. 544.

Davenport, Herbert J., *Outlines of Elementary Economics*. New York: Macmillan, 1897. Pp. 280.

Edie, Lionel, *Economic Principles and Problems*. New York: T. Y. Crowell, 1926. Pp. 859.

Ely, Richard T., and Wicker, George, *Elementary Principles of Economics*. New York: Macmillan, 1904. Pp. 388.

Ely, Richard T., *Outlines of Economics*. New York: Macmillan, 1908 (first edition 1893). Pp. 432.

Fairchild, Fred Rogers, *Essentials of Economics*. New York: American Book Co., 1923. Pp. 543.

Fawcett, Henry, *Manual of Political Economy* (edited by Mrs. Fawcett). London: Macmillan, 1887 (first edition 1863). Pp. 639.

Fetter, Frank, *Economics*. New York: Century, 1915, 2 v.

Fisher, Irving, *Elementary Principles of Economics*. New York: Macmillan, 1912. Pp. 531.

Froman, Lewis A., *Principles of Economics*. Chicago: Richard D. Irwin & Co., 1940. Pp. 752.

Gambs, John, and Wertimer, Sidney, Jr., *Economics and Man*. Homewood, Ill.: R. D. Irwin, 1959. Pp. 353.

Garver, Frederick, and Hansen, Alvin, *Principles of Economics*. Boston: Ginn, 1937. Pp. 686.

Grayson, Harry, and Loman, Phillip, *Principles of Economics*. New York: American Book Co., 1958. Pp. 709.

Hadley, Arthur, *Economics*. New York: G. P. Putnam's Sons, 1896. Pp. 496.

Harriss, C. Lowell, *American Economy*. Homewood, Ill.: R. D. Irwin, 1959. Pp. 883.

Homan, Paul T., Hart, Albert Gailord, and Sametz, Arnold, *The Economic Order*. New York: Harcourt, Brace, 1958. Pp. 839.

Ise, John, *Economics*. New York: Harper, 1950. Pp. 872.

Kiekhofer, William, *Economic Principles, Problems and Policies*. New York: Appleton-Century-Crofts, 1951. Pp. 957.

Klein, Jacob, and Woolf, Colvin, *Economic Problems of Today*. Chicago: Lyons & Carnahan, 1942. Pp. 690.

Knight, Bruce, and Hines, Lawrence, *Economics*. New York: Knopf, 1952. Pp. 917.

Laughlin, James L., *Elements of Political Economy*. New York: American Book Co., 1887. Pp. 384.

Laughlin, James L., *Study of Political Economy*. New York: Appleton, 1885. Pp. 153.

Lindholm, Richard W., *Public Finance and Fiscal Policy*. New York: Pitman, 1950. Pp. 732.

Lutz, F. A., and Benham, *Economics, A General Textbook*. New York: Pitman, 1941. Pp. 525.

Lutz, Harley, Foote, Edmund, and Stanton, Benjamin, *Getting A Living*. Evanston: Row Peterson, 1940. Pp. 687.

Marshall, Alfred, *Principles of Economics*. London: Macmillan, 1895. Pp. 823.

Marshall, Leon C., Wright, Chester, and Field, James (eds.), *Materials for the Study of Elementary Economics*. Chicago: University of Chicago Press, 1913. Pp. 927.

Mitchell, Broadus, *General Economics*. New York: Henry Holt, 1937. Pp. 772.

Morgan, Theodore, *Introduction to Economics.* New York: Prentice-Hall, 1956. Pp. 799.

Nicholson, J. S., *Principles of Political Economy.* New York: Macmillan, 1901, 3 v.

Osborn, Grover P., *Principles of Economics.* Cincinnati: Robert Clarke Co., 1893. Pp. 454.

Perry, Arthur Latham, *Principles of Political Economy.* New York: Scribner, 1891. Pp. 599.

Pond, A. Smith, *Essential Economics.* New York: Harcourt, Brace, 1956. Pp. 534.

Refener, L. A., *Principles of Economics.* New York: Houghton, Mifflin, 1927. Pp. 842.

Robinson, Leland, Adams, John, and Dillon, Harry, *Introduction to Modern Economics.* New York: Dryden, 1952. Pp. 942.

Rutledge, R. M., *Everyday Economics.* Boston: Houghton, Mifflin, 1929. Pp. 457.

Samuelson, Paul A., *Economics: An Introductory Analysis.* New York: McGraw-Hill, 1961. Pp. 853.

Seager, Henry Rogers, *Introduction to Economics.* New York: Holt, 1906. Pp. 618.

Seager, Henry Rogers, *Principles of Economics.* New York: Holt, 1913. Pp. 650.

Smith, Augustus H., *Economics for Our Times.* New York: McGraw-Hill, 1959. Pp. 596.

Taussig, Frank William, *Principles of Economics.* New York: Macmillan, 1911, 2 v.

Ulmer, Melville J., *Economics.* Boston: Houghton Mifflin, 1959. Pp. 638.

Walker, Francis A., *First Lessons in Political Economy.* New York: Holt, 1893. Pp. 323.

Wayland, Francis, *Elements of Political Economy.* New York: Sheldon, 1883. Pp. 403.

Wright, David McCord, *A Key to Modern Economics.* New York: Macmillan, 1954. Pp. 520.

B. HISTORY

Abell, Fleming, Levack, McAvoy, and Mannion, *History of the United States of America.* New York: Fordham University Press, 1951. Pp. 683.

Adams, J. T., *March of Democracy,* v. 2. New York: Scribner's, 1933. Pp. 438.

Andrews, E. Benjamin, *History of the U.S. to 1902.* New York: Scribner's, 1903. Pp. 427.

Bailey, Thomas, *The American Pageant.* Boston: Heath, 1956. Pp. 1007.

Baldwin, Leland, *Survey of American History.* New York: American Book Co., 1955. Pp. 786.

Beals, Carleton, *American Earth.* Philadelphia: Lippincott, 1939. Pp. 500.

Billington, Ray, *American History After 1865.* Ames, Iowa: Littlefield, Adams, 1950. Pp. 262.

Billington, Ray, and Loewenberg and Brockunier, *United States, American Democracy in World Perspective.* New York: Rinehart, 1947. Pp. 894.

Blake, Nelson, *A Short History of American Life.* New York: McGraw-Hill, 1952. Pp. 732.

Butler, Nicholas M., *Building the American Nation.* New York: Scribner's, 1923. Pp. 375.

Butterfield, Roger, *The American Past.* New York: Simon & Schuster, 1947. Pp. 476.

Carman, Harry, Kimmel and Walker, *Historic Currents in Changing America.* Philadelphia: J. C. Winston, 1946. Pp. 862.

Carman, Harry, and Syrett, Harold, *A History of the American People.* New York: Knopf, 1952, 2 v.

Craven & Johnson, *The United States.* Boston: Ginn, 1957. Pp. 438.

Curti, Merle, *A History of American Civilization.* New York: Harper, 1953. Pp. 836.

Curti, Merle, Shryock, Richard, Cochran, Tom, and Harrington, Fred, *An American History.* New York: Harper, 1950, 2 v.

Degler, Carl, *Out of Our Past.* New York: Harper, 1959. Pp. 484.

Dulles, Foster Rhea, *The United States Since 1865.* Ann Arbor: University of Michigan Press, 1959. Pp. 531.

Faulkner, Harold U., *American Political and Social History.* New York: F. S. Crofts, 1937. Pp. 772.

Faulkner, Harold U., Kepner and Bartlett, *American Way of Life.* New York: Harper, 1945. Pp. 739.

Forman, S. E., *Our Republic.* New York: Century, 1924. Pp. 852.

Graff, Henry F., and Krout, John A., *The Adventure of the American People.* New York: Rand, McNally, 1960. Pp. 738.

Hamm, William A., *The American People.* Boston: D. C. Heath, 1942. Pp. 1072.

Hartman, Ball and Nevins, *America, Land of Freedom.* Boston: D. C. Heath, 1946. Pp. 644.

Harlow, Ralph, *Growth of the United States, v. 2.* New York: Henry Holt, 1948. Pp. 663.

Hicks, John D., *American Nation.* Cambridge, Mass.: Houghton Mifflin, 1959. Pp. 776.

Hicks, John D., and Mowry, George, *A Short History of American Democracy.* Boston: Houghton Mifflin, 1956. Pp. 864.

Hockett, Homer, and Schlesinger, Arthur M., *Land of the Free.* New York: Macmillan, 1944. Pp. 765.

Hofstadter, Richard, Miller, William, and Aaron, Daniel, *The United States.* Englewood Cliffs, N.J.: Prentice-Hall, 1957. Pp. 812.

Hofstadter, Richard, Miller, William, and Aaron, Daniel,

The American Republic. New York: Prentice-Hall, 1959, 2 v.

Home, Charles, *Story of Our American People.* New York: U.S. History Publishers, 1926. Pp. 540.

Kirkland, Edward, *A History of American Economic Life.* New York: F. S. Crofts & Co., 1933. Pp. 767.

Krout, John A., *The United States Since 1865.* New York: Barnes & Noble, 1960. Pp. 278.

Manis, Jerome, and Clark, Samuel (eds.), *Man and Society.* New York: Macmillan, 1960. Pp. 784.

Martin, Asa, *History of the United States.* Boston: Ginn, 1931, 2 v.

Morison, Samuel Eliot, and Commager, Henry Steele, *Growth of the American Republic.* New York: Oxford University Press, 1951 (4th ed.), 2 v.

Muzzey, David S., *The United States of America.* New York: Ginn, 1924, 2 v.

Nichols, Jeanette P., *Twentieth Century United States.* New York: Appleton-Century, 1943. Pp. 435.

Oberholtzer, Ellis, *A History of the United States Since the Civil War.* New York: Macmillan, 1937, 5 v.

Ogg, Frederick A., *National Progress, 1907-1917.* New York: Harper, 1918. Pp. 430.

Owsley, C. N., *A Short History of the American People.* New York: D. Van Nostrand, 1955, 2 v.

Pease, Theodore, *The United States.* New York: Harcourt, Brace, 1927. Pp. 744.

Rae, John B., and Mahoney, Thomas, *The United States in World History.* New York: McGraw-Hill, 1955. Pp. 832.

Savelle, Max, *A Short History of American Civilization.* New York: Dryden Press, 1957. Pp. 665.

Stephenson, Matthew W., *History of the American People.* New York: Scribner's, 1934. Pp. 1179.

Thorpe, Francis N., *History of the American People.*
Chicago: A. C. McClurg, 1901. Pp. 627.

Wagner, Donald O. (ed.), *Social Reformers.* New York:
Macmillan, 1934. Pp. 749.

West, Willis Mason, *Story of American Democracy.* Boston: Small, Maynard, 1922. Pp. 791.

Williams, T. Harry, Current, Richard N., and Friedel,
Frank, *A History of the United States.* New York:
Knopf, 1959, 2 v.

Wirth, Fremont, *Development of America.* New York:
American Book Co., 1946 (first edition 1936). Pp.
lxviii+808.

Woodward, W. E., *New American History.* New York:
Farrar & Rinehart, 1936. Pp. 900.

IV. Biographies

Aaron, Daniel, *Men of Good Hope.* New York: Oxford
University Press, 1951. Pp. 329.

Barker, Charles A., *Henry George.* New York: Oxford
University Press, 1955. Pp. 696.

Geiger, George, *The Philosophy of Henry George.* New
York: Macmillan, 1933. Pp. 581.

George, Henry, Jr., *Life of Henry George.* New York:
Robert Schalkenbach Foundation, 1900. Pp. 634.

Holbrook, Steward, *Dreamers of the American Dream.*
New York: Doubleday, 1957. Pp. 369.

Johnson, Gerald W., *Lunatic Fringe.* Philadelphia: J. B.
Lippincott, 1957. Pp. 248.

Lawrence, Elwood P., *Henry George in the British Isles.*
East Lansing: Michigan State University Press, 1957.
Pp. 203.

Madison, Charles, *Critics and Crusaders.* New York: Henry
Holt, 1947. Pp. 534.

Nock, Albert Jay, *Henry George*. New York: William Morrow, 1939. Pp. 224.

Padover, Saul K., *The Genius of America*. New York: McGraw-Hill, 1960. Pp. 369.

Young, Arthur, *Single Tax Movement in the United States*. Princeton: Princeton University Press, 1915. Pp. 340.

V. Periodical Literature

American Social Science Association, *Single Tax Discussion*. Held at Saratoga, September 5, 1890. Concord, Mass.: Pp. 127.

Atkinson, Edward, "A Single Tax on Land." *Century Magazine*, v. 18, July 1890.

Brown, Elizabeth Read, "How College Textbooks Treat Land Value Taxation." *The American Journal of Economics and Sociology*, January 1961, v. 20, pp. 148-167.

Commons, John R., "A Progressive Tax on Bare Land Values." *Political Science Quarterly*, v. 37, March 1922, pp. 41-68.

Davenport, Herbert J., "Theoretical Issues in the Single Tax." *American Economic Review*, v. 7, March 1917, pp. 1-30.

Davenport, Herbert J., "The Single Tax and the English Budget." *Quarterly Journal of Economics*, v. 24, February 1910, pp. 279-92.

Field, David Dudley vs. Henry George, "Land and Taxation." *North American Review*, v. 141, July 1885, pp. 1-14.

Friedenberg, Daniel, "Coming Bust in the Real Estate Boom." *Harper's Magazine*, v. 222, pp. 29-40.

Gaffney, Mason, "Urban Expansion—Will It Ever Stop?" *Land: The Yearbook of Agriculture*, 1958, Washington, D.C., USDA, pp. 503-22.

Henry George News, New York, January 1961, January 1964.

House & Home, August 1960 issue. New York: Time, Inc.

Johnson, Alvin S., "The Case Against the Single Tax." *Atlantic Monthly,* v. 113, January 1914, pp. 27-37.

Krock, Arthur, *New York Times,* March 17, 1961, editorial page.

Land & Liberty. London: International Committee for Land Value Taxation and Free Trade, August 1958.

Laughlin, John L., "The Study of Political Economy in the United States." *Journal of Political Economy,* December 1892, v. 1, pp. 11ff.

Miller, Joseph Dana, "Is the Single Tax Making Progress?" *Independent Magazine,* 1902, v. 54, pp. 212-94.

Nearing, Scott, "Single Tax Section." *Annals of the American Academy of Political and Social Science,* March 1915, v. 58, pp. 149-157.

New York Times Magazine, April 13, 1958 and August 6, 1961.

The People (New York), June 5, 1892.

Seligman, Edwin R. A., "Halving the Tax Rate on Buildings: Pro and Con." (Seligman taking the "con" side.) *Survey,* March 7, 1914, 31:697-702.

Seligman, Edwin R. A., "Newer Tendencies in American Taxation." *Annals of the American Academy of Political and Social Science,* March 1915, v. 58, pp. 1-17.

Silverman, Leon, "Municipal Real Estate Taxation as an Instrument for Community Planning." *Yale Law Journal,* v. 58, December 1957, pp. 219ff.

Spahr, Charles B., "Single Tax." *Political Science Quarterly,* v. 6, December 1891, pp. 625-34.

Sumner, William Graham, "Henry George." *Scribner's Monthly,* v. 22, June 1881, pp. 312-13.

Walker, Francis Amasa, "The Tide of American Economic Thought." *Reports of the Proceedings of the American*

Economic Association, Fourth Annual Meeting, 1891, pp. 15-38.

VI. Pamphlets, Reports and Other Materials

Becker, Arthur, Program Chairman, "An Institute on Land Value Taxation and Contemporary Economic Problems," held at Boulder, Colorado, August 24-26, 1961. New York: Robert Schalkenbach Foundation, mimeographed report.

Brown, Harry Gunnison, "The Challenge of Australian Tax Policy." New York: Robert Schalkenbach Foundation, pamphlet, 1949, 12pp.

Brown, Harry Gunnison, and Brown, Elizabeth R., "The Effective Answer to Communism and Why You Don't Get It in College." New York: Robert Schalkenbach Foundation, 1958, 100pp.

Clancy, Robert, Faculty Letter of the Henry George School, June 1952, February 1960, May 1961, March 1962, mimeographed.

Fillebrown, Charles B., "Henry George and the Economists." Boston: Charles Fillebrown, 1914, 16pp. pamphlet.

Fillebrown, Charles B., "The Farmer and the Single Tax." Boston: Charles Fillebrown, 16pp. pamphlet.

Haig, Robert M., "The 'Single Tax Limited' in War Time," an address delivered before the National Tax Association at Atlanta, Georgia, November 15, 1917, reprinted in pamphlet form, 7pp.

Neilson, Francis, "Henry George the Scholar." New York: Henry George School, 1940, 20pp. pamphlet.

Patten, Simon Nelson, "The Educational Value of Political Economy." *American Economic Association*, 1890, 36pp. pamphlet.

Pleydell, Albert, "Report to the City and County Commissioners of Dayton, Ohio." New York: Management Services Associates.

Rawson, Mary, "Property Taxation and Urban Development." Washington: Urban Land Institute, 1961, 54pp. pamphlet.

Rothbard, Murray N., "The Single Tax: Economic and Moral Implications." Irvington-on-Hudson: Foundation for Economic Education, Inc., no date (but probably early 1950's), 10pp. pamphlet.

Schwartz, Eli, and Wert, James E., "An Analysis of the Potential Effects of a Movement Toward a Land Value Based Property Tax." Albany: Economic Education League, 1958, 95pp. pamphlet.

Thomas, Norman, "Democratic Socialism—A New Appraisal." New York: League for Industrial Democracy, 1953, 39pp. pamphlet.

Thompson, Joseph, S., "An Analysis of 'The Single Tax,'" commenting upon a memorandum by Dr. Harley Lutz, 8pp. pamphlet, no date (but probably early 1950's).

NAME INDEX

Aaron, Daniel, 206-7
Abbott, Lawrence, 172
Adams, H. C., 32, 93-4
Allen, Kenneth, 152-3
Alyea, Paul & Blanche, 162
American City magazine, 8
Anderson, William H., 156-7
Andrews, E. Benjamin, 29, 32, 51, 72
Atkinson, Edward, 49

Barker, Charles Albro, 9, 211-4
Baumol, William, 177
Beard, Charles Austin & Mary, 111-112, 199-200
Beer, Thomas, 135
Bellamy, Edward, George's opinion of, 242-3
Bragdon, Henry, 220
Brown, Elizabeth Read, 171-2, 179
Brown, Harry Gunnison, 10, 131-2, 148, 163-5, 171, 175-6
Buehler, Alfred G., 153
Bullock, Charles, 93
Buttenheim, Harold, 8, 161
Butterfield, Roger, 219
Bye, Raymond, 128-9, 171, 172-3

Carver, T. N., 130-1, 239-40
Chandler, Lester, 177
Chapin, Rev. A. L., 38
Churchill, Winston, 168-9

Clancy, Robert, 191-5
Clark, John Bates, 57-60, 76
Colean, Miles, 168
Commager, Henry Steele, 218
Committee on Principles of Economics, 179
Commons, John R., 36, 72, 120
Curti, Merle, 200-1

Daniels, Winthrop, 94
Davenport, Herbert, 32, 100-3, 122
De Mille, Anna George, 203
Dewey, John, 133, 147
DeWitt, Benjamin P., 113-4
Dulles, Foster Rhea, 219

Edie, Leon, 128
Einstein, Lewis, 136
Ekirch, Arthur, 201
Ellis, Howard S., 188n.
Ely, Richard T., 66-9, 186

Fairchild, Fred Rogers, 123
Faulkner, Harold U., 137-8
Fawcett, Henry, 47-8
Fels, Joseph, 148
Fetter, Frank, 98
Field, David Dudley, 38
Fillebrown, Charles, 79-80
Fisher, Ernest M., 168, 186

268

SUBJECT INDEX

(The abbreviation *lvt* stands for land value taxation.)

271